能源与环境的经济研究简集

Essays of Economic Issues on Energy and Environment

吴小芳　吴姗姗　著

武汉大学出版社
WUHAN UNIVERSITY PRESS

图书在版编目（CIP）数据

能源与环境的经济研究简集:英文/吴小芳,吴姗姗著.—武汉:武汉大学出版社,2021.4

　ISBN 978-7-307-22110-9

　Ⅰ.能…　Ⅱ.①吴…　②吴…　Ⅲ.①能源经济—文集—英文　②环境经济—文集—英文　Ⅳ.①F407.2-53　②X196-53

中国版本图书馆 CIP 数据核字(2020)第 272869 号

责任编辑:谢群英　　　责任校对:李孟潇　　　版式设计:韩闻锦

出版发行: **武汉大学出版社** 　(430072　武昌　珞珈山)

(电子邮箱: cbs22@whu.edu.cn　网址: www.wdp.com.cn)

印刷:武汉邮科印务有限公司

开本:787×1092　1/16　　印张:14.75　　字数:329 千字　　插页:1

版次:2021 年 4 月第 1 版　　2021 年 4 月第 1 次印刷

ISBN 978-7-307-22110-9　　定价:43.00 元

This work is supported by the National Natural Science Foundation of China (Grant No. 71803193 and 71804194) and the Fundamental Research Funds for the Central Universities, Zhongnan University of Economics and Law (Grant No. 2722019JCT006).

内容提要

　　本书收录了作者已发表的 9 篇能源与环境经济学领域论文。全书分为前言、第一、二、三章和附录。前言概述了本书研究领域的学术背景，并对书中章节安排进行了说明。第一章共三小节，分别讨论了全球需求侧、全球供给侧以及中国供需相关经济活动中的能源使用情况，并通过追踪供应链，建立了能源使用的源–汇清单。第二章共三小节，以中国和波多黎各为研究案例，讨论了地区经济活动引起的环境污染问题，并采用泰尔指数和基尼系数对污染物的空间分布进行了评估。第三章共三小节，介绍了基于经济、能源和环境多指标的可持续性量化核算模型。附录中，对书中研究方法和结果数据进行了补充说明。在当今能源短缺和环境污染的背景下，本书旨在从多个角度探究经济、能源与环境之间的关系，以期加深人们对可持续发展的认识。

Preface

Economic growth in a region provides insights into the economic well-being of the residents. This is perhaps what we all familiar with. Owing to two centuries of economic expansion in the large-scale industrialization, we now have the chance to enjoy a more comfortable life with easier access to a wide and diverse variety of goods and services. According to World Bank, between 1990 and 2015 the world Gross Domestic Product (GDP) was tripled, and meanwhile the number of people worldwide living below the international extreme poverty line was more than halved. However, this is only one side of the story. The irreversible ecological degradation that is happening everywhere is the other side. The Earth has provided the society and economy with necessary support, like land, water, air and various mineral resources. But unfortunately, we just take it for granted. The immoderate human activities for economic profits over the past centuries have greatly diminished these natural resources, and caused a sharp decrease in public ecological welfare. For example, the increasing scarcity of energy resources and the continuous deterioration of environment are already affecting every country and every person in the world.

In fact, quantitative development in economic aspect and qualitative development related to the environment together constitute human development. The latter, however, is often overlooked. This is why we would exchange ecological benefits for economic ones in the story above. But it is proved to be unsustainable as natural resources on the Earth are limited, and there will be few resources that can be left for future generations to exchange. The development that can meet both the present and the future needs is defined as sustainable development. How to switch to a sustainable development path has become the biggest challenge for today's world. In 2015, the United Nations proposed 17 Sustainable Development Goals to call for action worldwide to protect the planet. All the goals are designed to support the three pillars of sustainability, i. e., environmental, economic and social sustainability. This is to say, for the sustainability problem to be solved, the environment, economy and society must all be sustainable. But how to identify if they are sustainable? It requires a scientific evaluation system, of which the key is to link the environmental issues to economic and social development process. To deal with the linkage problem, many scholars in various academic fields have made much effort. The extensive researches have paved the way for a better understanding of sustainability. In this book, a series of essays focusing on the relationship between the environment and the economy, are collected. Two questions are mainly discussed in these articles, including how the energy use and environmental pollution are driven by economic activities at both aspects of production and consumption, and how to build a science-based evaluation system for sustainability with environmental and economic values on a common measure. Nowadays, the Belt and Road Initiative has entered adulthood, and brought new opportunities and challenges for global sustainability. In this context, we hope the book can provide insight into current economic, energy and environmental issues, and give reference for future sustainability research.

The collected essays are divided into three groups and presented in three separate chapters, where economic analysis on energy use, economic analysis on environmental pollution and sustainability measures based on economic, energy and environmental factors are introduced, respectively. In Chapter One, there are two articles simulating the energy use in global economy, and one article about the energy use in Chinese economy. As is well-known, energy resources, especially fossil energy fuel the economic growth. Although the market has labeled a price for coal, oil, gas and others, these limited natural resources actually have a far higher value than the currency price because the free environmental inputs fail to be taken into account by money. The solar radiation, wind and other inputs from the environmental system together produce the energy resources required in economic system. Energy resources, indeed act as the bridge between the environment and the economy. In these regards, the physical or thermodynamic units are adopted to evaluate the resource footprint of economic activities related to production, consumption, and trade. How energy resources flow from the ecological environment and along with intermediate and final goods and services within global economic network is comprehensively revealed, via the economic analysis tool of the input-output analysis (Sections 1.1 and 1.2). Moreover, given the economic miracle of China with roaring economic growth over the past decades, In Section 1.3, a systems investigation on its energy use is conducted, in order to explore a low-energy development path.

Chapter Two views the pollution issues from an economic perspective. Since pollution is "bad", society may wish to distribute the cost of pollution evenly across regions just as it may wish to distribute the benefit of income equally. Therefore, the application of inequality or concentration measures in quantifying the geographic distribution of pollution has become an important research topic. Sections 2.1 and 2.2 use the Theil index and the environmental Gini coefficient to measure the distribution of pollution, respectively. One advantage of the Theil index over the Gini coefficient is that Theil index can be decomposed (Section 2.1). Equal distribution of environmental issues will also achieve environmental justice, and in Section 2.2 the study examines possible determinants that may have caused environmental injustice. In Section 2.3 the study provides a detailed understanding of the linkages through which industrial activity affects the environment in China. Both formal and informal regulations are also investigated.

In Chapter Three, the term of sustainability is evaluated with the help of various indicators. A main problem in sustainability measure is quantitative understanding of the relationship between human and natural systems, which necessitates expressing the economic and environmental effects in common terms. The first two articles introduce the thermodynamic concepts. As all matters in the world contain energy, the thermodynamic theory is expected to provide a powerful tool to integrate the values of free environmental resources, economic goods and services in a common unit. Here, we resort to energy and exergy, which are the major concepts in the first and second law of thermodynamics, respectively. Therefore, solar emergy as embodied energy (Section 3.1) and cosmic exergy (Section 3.2) are separately adopted to measure the sustainability for an integrated biogas engineering that is used for renewable energy production and waste treatment in China. In Section 3.3, the study provides a methodology to measure regional sustainability from an economic point of view. Building up a metric of Green Net National Product, and then examining the time trend of this metric, if it moves downwards in certain time periods, the region may walk on a path away from an economic sustainability.

Wu Xiaofang

Wu Shanshan

Contents

Chapter One
Economic Analysis on Energy Use

1. 1　Energy Overview for Globalized World Economy: Source, Supply Chain and Sink[①]

1. 1. 1　Introduction

The development of social economy requires massive inputs of natural resources, especially energy, which is regarded as the main driver of economic growth. In 2014 alone, the world primary energy consumption ascended to approximately 13 billion tons oil equivalent, increasing by 22% and 54% respectively compared to that in 2004 and 1994 (BP, 2015). The rapidly rising demand has accelerated the exploitation of energy resources from the natural environment, and ultimately brought severe challenges of energy scarcity and climate change. According to BP, the world's proved reserves of oil, natural gas and coal at end-2014 were expected to meet 53, 54 and 110 years of global production at most, separately. Energy resources conservation has therefore become an urgent concern in today's world. Meanwhile, as energy-related greenhouse gases (GHG) emissions account for over 80% of global anthropogenic emissions, energy saving is also essential for the mitigation of global warming.

In this context, extensive policies for sustainable energy use have been formulated in different countries, such as the Energy Independence and Security Act in the United States. However, the strategies were made merely for the energy consumed within its corresponding sovereign territory, and didn't account for the energy used outside the country to meet the domestic demand. In fact, the world economy has developed into an integrated network at this age of globalization dominated by international trades. All countries in the world are connected by this network and have become increasingly interdependent. It is common that a product is produced in one country using energy by either local exploitation or foreign trade

---

① Published on *Renewable and Sustainable Energy Reviews*, Volume 69, pp. 735-749, with a few modifications due to space constraints. Reuse permission has been obtained from Elsevier.

and is then exported to another country for reprocessing or consumption. As a result, the actual energy requirement of a country is always overestimated or underestimated. In order to justly identify the responsibility of countries and sectors in international cooperation for energy conservation and carbon reduction, it is imperative to perform a comprehensive review for inter-regional energy use flows and connections for the globalized village.

To reveal the systems energetics, one can resort to the well-known concept of embodied energy in systems ecology (Odum, 1996). For an economic system, energy use can be concretely quantified by embodied energy, which is defined as the total (direct plus indirect) primary energy inputs to generate and sustain a product or service, considered as if the energy was embedded in the product or service itself. In contrast to the direct energy accounting which merely considers the on-site immediate energy use, embodied energy analysis also incorporates historical and off-site information and facilitates the accounting for actual energy consumption from a systems perspective.

Hence, in the pursuit of effective policy to maintain energy sustainability, the embodied energy method has gained wide applications in various economic systems of different scales. At the city scale, Li et al. (2014) performed an assessment of energy embodied in Macao's external trade from 2000 to 2011, and pointed out that Macao's indirect energy consumption surpassed the direct energy consumption. At the national scale, Bordigoni et al. (2012) examined the role and consequences of embodied energy in the European industry, and found that about one quarter of the energy embodied in the European industry output came from outside the European Union. At the global scale, Chen and Chen (2011) employed a systems embodiment model to investigate the energy use of the world economy. Moreover, the embodied energy method has also induced attention as a valid tool to appraise the performance of production systems at the industrial scale. Those aforementioned studies on embodied energy have contributed significantly to deepening people's understanding of direct and indirect energy use, in addition to providing precious information for energy conservation.

In the present study, energy use flows within the 2010 world economy are depicted by means of the embodied energy method. Different from most existing researches based on the environmentally extended input-output analysis associated with technical consumption of primary or secondary energies within technical apparatus belonging to various production sectors, this work presents an embodied energy study in terms of systems input-output analysis based on primary energy exploitation from the environment for the economy. Associated with technical processes, primary energy resources like crude oil and coal are burned to provide heat, wind kinetic energy and hydro-potential are converted to provide power, and secondary energy resources like petroleum is burned to propel an engine and electricity is utilized in different ways. There are so many different ways of technical consumption of energy resources. But from the perspective of system ecology, primary energy resources are natural resources that originally belong to the environmental system outside the economic system. Once being exploited, energy resources are removed from the environmental system and enter the economic system. From the economic point of view, the genuine primary energy resources are used at the point of energy exploitation, and all the non-primary energy resources, no matter conventionally referred to as primary or secondary energies, are only energy products, out of the economic use of primary energy and other primary natural resources such as water. In this regard, primary energy is used in the interaction boundary between the environment and the economy through the exploitation by quarrying, mining and recipient processes, then the energy use is embodied in the product flows within the economy to the final demand by the society. In short, primary energy is an environmental input for the economy, and there are only embodied energy flows in the socio-economy. Costanza (1984) evaluated both the technical consumption and the economic use of energy resources in the United States economy in 1963, 1967 and 1972. Wiedmann et al. (2013) presented a time series analysis of various natural resources flows from the point of resources exploitation in the global economy. Grounded in the existing studies, this work takes the exploitation process as the source of energy use flows to explore an all-inclusive world energy budget. Energy flows embodied in inter-regional trades are tracked from the source of energy exploitation to the sink of final use connected by the global energy supply chains.

1. 1. 2 Methodology and Data Sources

1. 1. 2. 1 The Input-output Analysis (IOA)

The input-output analysis (IOA) was originally proposed in the 1930s as a technique to describe interactions between industries within an economic system (Miller and Blair, 2009). Then to explore the relationship between the environment and the economy, numerous efforts were made to apply the method of IOA to environmental researches. Leontief (1970) firstly extended the IOA to measure the carbon monoxide released by economic activities, which has been widely used for environmental studies and referred to as environmentally extended IOA. Then based on the conservation law, Bullard Iii and Herendeen (1975) proposed a modified IOA scheme to study the flows of energy embodied in goods flows, as generalized by Chen and his collaborators for embodiment analysis for various ecological elements as natural resources and environmental resources, in terms of the systems IOA model (Chen and Chen, 2011).

In the two IOA models, the economic input-output table is extended to include two types of energy data, one for internal, technical energy consumption and another for external, environmental energy supply. In the environmentally extended IOA, for each economic sector the direct technical consumption of energy (the internal technical consumption of secondary energy as product of primary energy as environmental supply) is assigned to be the virtual energy consumption of the final demand satisfied by the sector. In this way, one tries to promptly predict the energy requirement when there is a change in the final demand for a certain commodity. As intermediate products are considered as internal feedback within the economy for finally providing the society with the final use, energy use flows caused by intermediate production are not depicted. That is, the concept of virtual energy is only applied to the final demand, explicitly exclusive to the intermediate product. In contrast, by the systems IOA model as a conservational scheme, for each sector the embodied energy, defined as the total primary energy use induced by the total output, is equal to the exogenous primary energy input by the sector plus embodied energy of intermediate input from the economy into the sector. Not only energy utilization for final demand but also energy communication among intermediate production activities are delineated.

Let's consider the energy use flows associated with a typical sector. Illustrated in Figure 1.1.1 are the physical input-output flows of the sector. From an economic perspective, this sector receives intermediate inputs from other sectors or itself (Z_{in}) to produce total outputs (X), which is composed by the outputs for sectors' intermediate production (Z_{in}) in the economic system, and the outputs for final use (F) in the social system. With regard to energy resources, $E_{exploitation}$ records the sector's exploitation of primary energy resources from the environmental system as the exogenous, external supply for the economic system, and is denoted by a blue line. Given the fact that all primary energy resources exploited by a sector is usually not technically consumed by this sector, on-site technical energy consumption is denoted as $E_{consumption}$ for comparison. For example, raw coal exploited by the mining sector may be traded and is then combusted in the electricity production sector. There are many different ways of technical consumption of energy resources as discussed above, and all these ways essentially try to convert the energy contained in natural resources to available heat and work, both of which will finally disperse to the environment in the form of heat. The red earth symbol is therefore drawn to represent such heat dispersal and identified as $E_{consumption}$. According to the environmentally extended IOA, the direct energy consumption related to the on-site technical consumption of all investigated sectors are attributed to the final use with the aid of the Leontief inverse or the total requirements matrix, corresponding to a total-impact coefficient (virtual energy intensity) ε^* defined to stand for the total amount of energy consumed per unit of the sector's final demand presented to the society. Under an assignment mapping, the so-called production-based responsibility for $E_{consumption}$ of the sector is assigned to the sector's the final users as consumption-based responsibility.

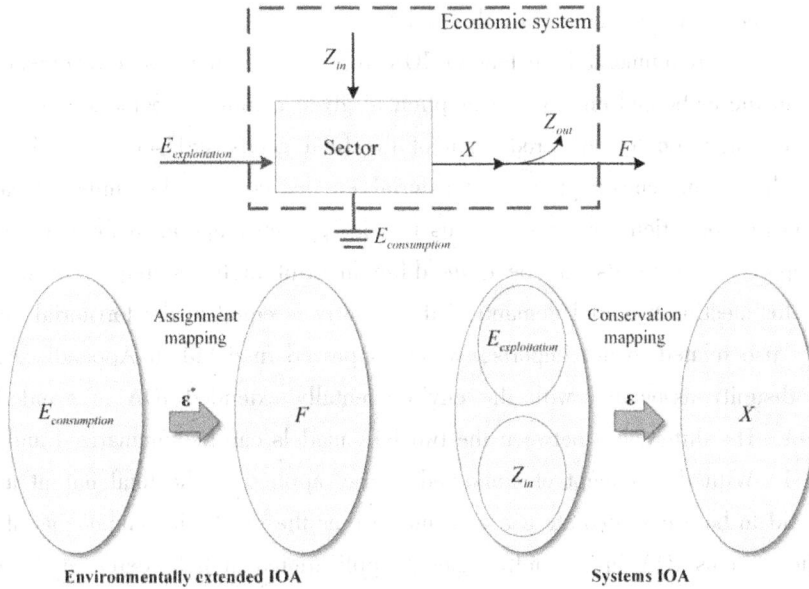

Figure 1. 1. 1   The Mapping Relationships for Environmentally Extended IOA Model and
Systems IOA Model

However, in the systems IOA model, all commodity flows, no matter if they are for intermediate or final use purposes, are considered with energy use hidden or embodied in them. As a consequence, the systems IOA begins with the sector's direct energy exploitation ($E_{exploitation}$) in terms of the external energy inputs to the economic system from the environment. Guided by a conservation mapping, the systems IOA model adds the direct energy use to the indirect use (εZ_{in}) in terms of embodied energy of intermediate inputs in the economic system, to finally obtain the total energy use (εX) embodied in the total outputs, including the intermediate outputs as the feedback to the economic system and final use outputs to the social system, where the embodied energy intensity ε is defined as the total amount of energy required to produce per unit of the corresponding sector's output for either immediate or final use. Different from the traditional concept of energy in thermodynamics as a condition variable, embodied energy is a process variable of which the value depends on the production process of the goods or service.

What's more, regarding the energy use embodied in the sector's trades, the environmentally extended IOA only accounts for the goods or services for final use in trades, while the systems IOA takes account of total trades including trades for intermediate use and for final use, which is consistent with monetary trade accounting. For widespread environmental accounting, obviously the virtual intensity is only for goods or service as final use, but the embodied intensity is for all products, no matter they are taken as intermediate inputs for the economy or final use by the society.

In previous environmentally extended IOA researches, there is a divergence in the accounting of the embodied energy consumption of given countries. Some studies accounted the energy consumption for the production of the final goods and service of the country, while the others took consumption as territorial energy consumption minus local energy consumption in production for exports, plus the energy consumption in foreign countries to produce imports. The results can be quite different. But in the systems IOA model, the energy use for meeting the final demand of the country is equal to the territorial energy use plus energy use related to net imports, which is proved in detail in Appendix A. In this way, this disunity associated with the environmentally extended IOA is avoided by the systems IOA. The differences between the two IOA models can be summarized and listed in Table 1.1.1. With the concept of embodied energy applied to the total output and equal attention paid to both intermediate use and final use as the two basic components of the total output, the systems IOA in its multi-regional application can help perceive the complete picture of how energy flows between both economic sectors and regions in the world. Therefore, in the present study, we adopt the systems IOA for a systematic analysis of energy use by the globalized economy, with focus from sources to sinks via supply chains in inter-regional trades. Also, it should be noted that the systems IOA model introduced here can also be applied to other ecological elements in addition to energy resources.

Table 1.1.1　Comparison Between Environmentally Extended IOA and Systems IOA Models

	Environmentally extended IOA	Systems IOA
Direct energy input	$E_{consumption}$, the on-site technical consumption of primary or secondary energies.	$E_{exploitation}$, the primary energy exploitation from the environment as the exogenous, external supply for the economy.
Model formula	$E_{consumption} = \varepsilon^* F$	$E_{exploitation} + \varepsilon Z_{in} = \varepsilon X$
Intensity	ε^*, virtual intensity that is only applied to the goods or service as final use. It is therefore not applicable to environmental accounting for production activities.	ε, embodied intensity that is for all products, no matter they are taken as intermediate inputs or final use. It is essential for environmental accounting for both production and consumption activities.
Economic flows under consideration	Sector's outputs for final use; Trades related to final use.	Sector's inputs for intermediate production; Sector's outputs for intermediate production; Sector's outputs for final use; Trades related to intermediate production; Trades related to final use.

Continued

	Environmentally extended IOA	Systems IOA
Regional application	Virtual energy assigned to the region's final use ≠ Territorial energy consumption + Virtual energy related to final net imports.	Embodied energy in the region's final use = Territorial energy exploitation + Embodied energy related to total (intermediate and final) net imports.
Global application	Total energy consumption = Virtual energy assigned to the final use.	Total energy exploitation = Embodied energy in the final use. This is because the international trades offset each other when all regions in the world are taken into account.
Objective	Assign producers' responsibilities to consumers.	Understand the energy use flows in the economic system.

1. 1. 2. 2　Energy Input-output Table and Data Sources

The first step in the systems IOA is to compile an energy input-output table. For the world economy, the systems table is presented as Table 1. 1. 2, which integrates monetary flows (denoted as z and f in Table 1. 1. 2) in economic input-output table with data on energy (denoted as e in Table 1. 1. 2). Although economic input-output tables for national economies are regularly constructed by statistics departments in many countries, the table for the whole world economy has never been officially released. Fortunately, some databases that are contributed by researchers and organizations (e. g., the Eora multi-region input-output database at http://worldmrio. com/, and the Global Trade Analysis Program, or GTAP database at https://www. gtap. agecon. purdue. edu/default. asp) have built a time series of global economic input-output tables. In the present work, the Eora Database Version 199. 74 is adopted to construct the global economic input-output table, in which the world economy is simulated as a 186-region, 26-sector coupled system. Related data for the regions and sectors are listed in Appendix B and Appendix C, separately. In an attempt to combine the most recent statistics, the year of 2010 is chosen for analysis. Therefore, in Table 1. 1. 2, z_{ij}^{rs} is the monetary value of intermediate inputs from Sector i in Region r to Sector j in Region s, and f_i^{rs} is the monetary value of goods from Sector i, Region r that are used for final use in Region s. Based on the classification of economic statistics, the final use of Region s includes household use, non-profit institution use, government use, fixed capital formation, inventory increase and acquisitions of valuables. Final use represents the end of the production cycle and goods used for final use no longer appear in the economic system. Hence, final use is regarded as the sink of embodied energy flows in this study. Both z_{ij}^{rs} and f_i^{rs} are expressed in basic price with a unit of one thousand dollars (1, 000 USD hereafter).

Table 1.1.2   Scheme of the Energy Input-output Table for the World Economy

Sale \ Purchase			Intermediate use					Final use		
			Region 1		...	Region 186		Region 1	...	Region 186
			Sector 1	...	Sector 26	Sector 1	...	Sector 26			
Intermediate input	Region 1	Sector 1	z_{ij}^{rs}					f_i^{rs}		
		...								
		Sector 26								
	...									
	Region 1	Sector 1								
		...								
		Sector 26								
Direct energy input	Crude oil		e_{kj}^{s}							
	Coal									
	Natural gas									
	Biomass									
	Hydroenergy									
	Nuclear energy									
	Other renewables									

Similarly, e_{kj}^{s} represents the amount of kth energy resource directly extracted by Sector j in Region s from the natural environment, in unit of terajoule (TJ). Seven sources for external energy are included, namely crude oil, coal, natural gas, biomass, hydroenergy, nuclear energy and other renewable energy, which sum up to 5.32E+08 TJ, corresponding to about 95% of the global primary energy consumption in 2010. The statistics of energy exploitation are collected from the International Energy Agency (IEA) database (http://www.iea.org/) and BP Statistical Review of World Energy. Both IEA and BP provide the energy production data for the region, but for each sector in the region, the data are not available. In recognition of the fact that in statistics crude oil, coal and natural gas are generally mined by corresponding mining sectors, for each region, the data of the three kinds of energy taken from IEA or BP are all allocated into Sector 3 (*Mining and quarrying*). Likewise, the production data of biomass, hydroenergy, nuclear energy and other renewables are allocated into Sectors 1 (*Agriculture*), 13 (*Electricity, gas and* water), 3 and 13, respectively. In addition, it could be witnessed that part of the fossil sources as crude oil, coal and natural gas are used as raw materials for industrial production instead of energy sources. According to the IEA database, the global non-energy use portions of crude oil, coal and natural gas in 2010 are calculated as 8.00%, 0.89% and 4.77%, respectively. But in the economic input-output table, energy resources that are traded for energy use and for non-energy use are recorded together without identifying the difference between the two parts. It is not viable to take the data related to non-energy use out from the economic table. Therefore, the energy resources used for non-energy purpose are neglected in the energy inventory in the present study to be consistent with the economic data.

1. 1. 2. 3 Algorithm

After the systems input-output table is complied, the second step is to build a balance model of embodied energy flows, and to obtain the embodied energy intensity for each sector in each region. Embodied energy flows for Sector i in Region r are described in Figure 1. 1. 2. e_i^r ($= \sum_{k=1}^{7} e_{ki}^r$) adds up the total of the seven kinds of energy extracted by Sector i in Region r. ε_j^s is defined as the embodied energy intensity of products from Sector j in Region s, that is, the amount of primary energy exploited that is embodied in per unit of the outputs of Sector j, Region s. Its unit is TJ/1,000USD. For Sector i in Region r, it receives direct energy inputs (e_i^r) and indirect energy inputs embodied in intermediate goods from other sectors or itself ($\sum_{s=1}^{186} \sum_{j=1}^{26} (\varepsilon_j^s z_{ji}^{sr})$). Meanwhile, the sector provides energy support to sustain other sectors' production and its own production ($\sum_{s=1}^{186} \sum_{j=1}^{26} (\varepsilon_i^r z_{ij}^{rs})$, and to meet the final demand (($\sum_{s=1}^{186} (\varepsilon_i^r f_i^{rs})$). So a physical balance of embodied energy flows can be induced as

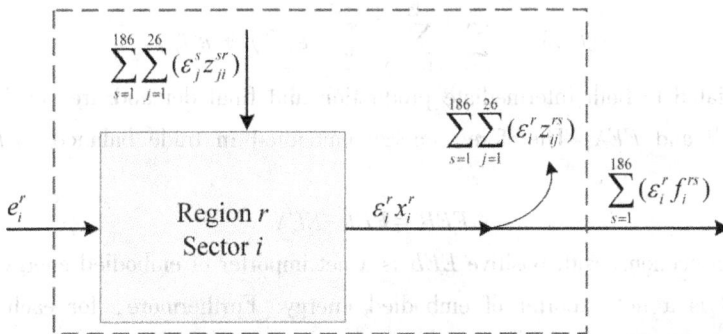

Figure 1. 1. 2 Embodied Energy Flows for a Typical Sector in the World Economy

$$e_i^r + \sum_{s=1}^{186} \sum_{j=1}^{26} (\varepsilon_j^s z_{ji}^{sr}) = \varepsilon_i^r x_i^r \qquad (1.1.1)$$

where $x_i^r = \sum_{s=1}^{186} \sum_{j=1}^{26} z_{ij}^{rs} + \sum_{s=1}^{186} f_i^{rs}$ is the monetary value of total outputs of Sector i in Region r.

Subsequently, for the whole world economy with 4,836 (186×26) sectors concerned, a matrix form of Equation (1.1.1) is readily deduced as

$$\mathbf{E} + \varepsilon \mathbf{Z} = \varepsilon \hat{\mathbf{X}} \qquad (1.1.2)$$

in which $\mathbf{E} = [e_i^r]_{1 \times 4,836}$, $\varepsilon = [\varepsilon_i^r]_{1 \times 4,836}$, $\mathbf{Z} = [z_{ij}^{rs}]_{4,836 \times 4,836}$, and $\mathbf{X} = [x_i^r]_{4,836 \times 1}$ ($\hat{\mathbf{X}}_{4,836 \times 4,836}$ is the corresponding diagonal matrix). Therefore, with properly given direct energy inputs matrix $\mathbf{E}$, intermediate inputs matrix $\mathbf{Z}$ and total outputs matrix $\mathbf{X}$, the embodied energy intensity matrix ε can be obtained as

$$\varepsilon = \mathbf{E}(\hat{\mathbf{X}} - \mathbf{Z})^{-1} \qquad (1.1.3)$$

With the embodied energy intensities of the 4,836 sectors obtained, it is prompt to figure out the amount of energy embodied in concerned economic flows. In particular, the amount of embodied energy of a commodity can be obtained via multiplying its economic value by the embodied energy intensity of the corresponding sector. Evidently, the energy embodied in Region r's final use (EEF^r) can be calculated as

$$EEF^r = \sum_{s=1}^{186} \sum_{j=1}^{26} (\varepsilon_j^s f_j^{sr}) \qquad (1.1.4)$$

In contrast to EED^r ($= \sum_{i=1}^{26} e_i^r$), which is defined as the total energy exploited directly in Region r to enunciate the direct energy requirements of Region r as a source in energy supply chain, EEF^r records the actual energy requirements of Region r as a sink.

For Region r, energy embodied in its imports (EEI) and energy embodied in its exports (EEX), as two basic indicators to reflect its trading pattern, can be acquired by.

$$EEI^r = \sum_{s=1(s \neq r)}^{186} \sum_{j=1}^{26} (\sum_{i=1}^{26} (\varepsilon_j^s z_{ji}^{sr}) + \varepsilon_j^s f_j^{sr}) \qquad (1.1.5)$$

$$EEX^r = \sum_{i=1}^{26} \sum_{s=1(s \neq r)}^{186} (\sum_{j=1}^{26} (\varepsilon_i^r z_{ij}^{rs}) + \varepsilon_i^r f_i^{rs}) \qquad (1.1.6)$$

The trades related to both intermediate production and final demand are considered by the indices of EEI and EEX. Therefore, energy embodied in trade balance (EEB) can be determined as

$$EEB^r = EEI^r - EEX^r \qquad (1.1.7)$$

Obviously, an economy with positive EEB is a net importer of embodied energy, while with negative EEB is a net exporter of embodied energy. Furthermore, for each region, the following identity holds with related proof that can be found in Appendix A.

$$EEF^r = EED^r + EEB^r \qquad (1.1.8)$$

1. 1. 3 Results and Discussion

1. 1. 3. 1 Embodied Energy Intensity

Illustrated in Figure 1. 1. 3 are average embodied energy intensities of the world's 26 industry sectors, which are obtained as the average of the intensities in 186 regions weighted by sectoral total outputs. It can be seen that the intensities vary greatly between the 26 sectors. The sector with a larger intensity requires more energy resources from the environmental system to support one unit of its product in the economic system, and hence imposes bigger pressure on the environment. According to the results, Sector 3 (*Mining and quarrying*) has the largest intensity of 2. 14E-01 TJ/1,000USD, nearly 3 times larger than the second largest intensity of 5. 22E-02 TJ/1,000USD owned by Sector 13 (*Electricity, gas and water*), and 108 times larger than the least intensity of 1. 97E-03 TJ/1,000USD of Sector 21 (*Financial intermediation and business activities*). In fact, Sector 3 plays the role as a porter or bridge between the systems of environment and economy. It exploits energy resources from the environmental system and then delivers them to other sectors in the economic system, so these energy resources enter the economic system through this sector. There are mainly four kinds of energy resources that are mined by Sector 3, namely crude oil, coal, natural gas and nuclear energy, which altogether account for 87. 46% of world total energy demand. As a result, 87. 46% of world energy resources flow through Sector 3, making this sector with the largest energy inputs from and the biggest pressure on the environment.

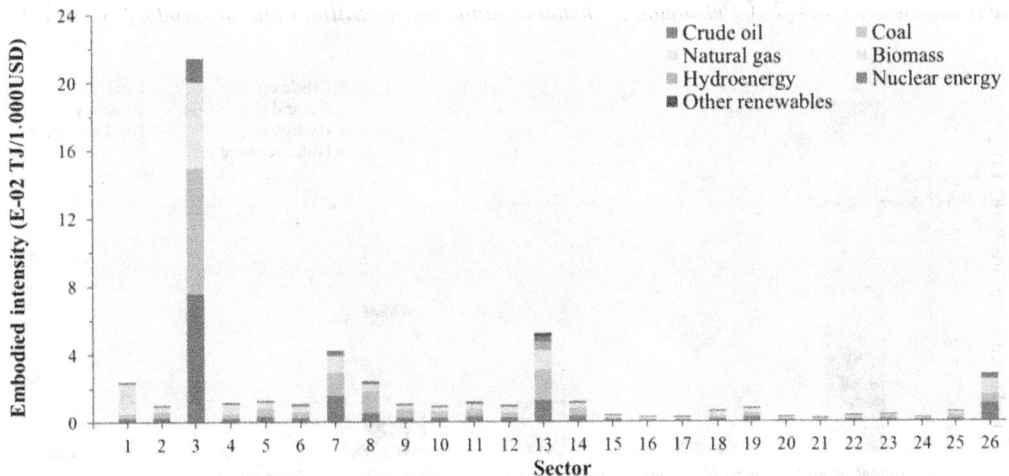

Figure 1. 1. 3 Sectoral Embodied Energy Intensity for the World Economy (Sectoral information corresponding to the sector code is provided in Appendix C.)

Besides, the contributions of different sources of energy to sectoral intensities are identified by the colors in this figure. In Sector 3, 93.53% of energy embodied in its outputs are attributed to fossil energy resources (i. e. crude oil, coal and natural gas), larger than those in the other twenty-five sectors. By contrast, non-fossil energy resources (including biomass, hydroenergy, nuclear energy and other renewables) take up the biggest share of 69.69% in Sector 1 (*Agriculture*), indicating Sector 1 is the least dependent on fossil energy. Since developing alternative and renewable energy can also help relieve the pressure from the increasing energy demand, the government should take some actions to encourage its utilization in sectoral productive activities.

1.1.3.2   Embodied Energy in Final Use

For the whole world, the total energy embodied in final use (EEF) is equal to the total energy resources exploited (EED), amounting to 5.32E+08 TJ. Regarding the six final use categories (see Figure 1.1.4), energy embodied in household use has the largest value of 3.23E+08 TJ, accounting for 60.71% of total. In light of the intensive investment worldwide, energy embodied in fixed capital formation (1.38E+08 TJ) ranks the second in the list, followed by energy embodied in government use (5.02E+07 TJ) and non-profit institution use (1.72E+07 TJ). For inventory increase, negative values are noticed in the use of coal, natural gas and nuclear energy, representing the amount of coal, natural gas and nuclear energy offered by previous years' inventory to help reduce the mining quantity in this year. According to Equation (1.1.4), goods in final use are provided by the 26 sectors in 186 regions. Figure 1.1.5 illustrates sectoral contribution to final use. Sector 14 (*Construction*) provides the largest fraction of 16.05% due to the considerable capital investment. Sectors 7 (*Petroleum, chemical and non-metallic mineral products*) and 13

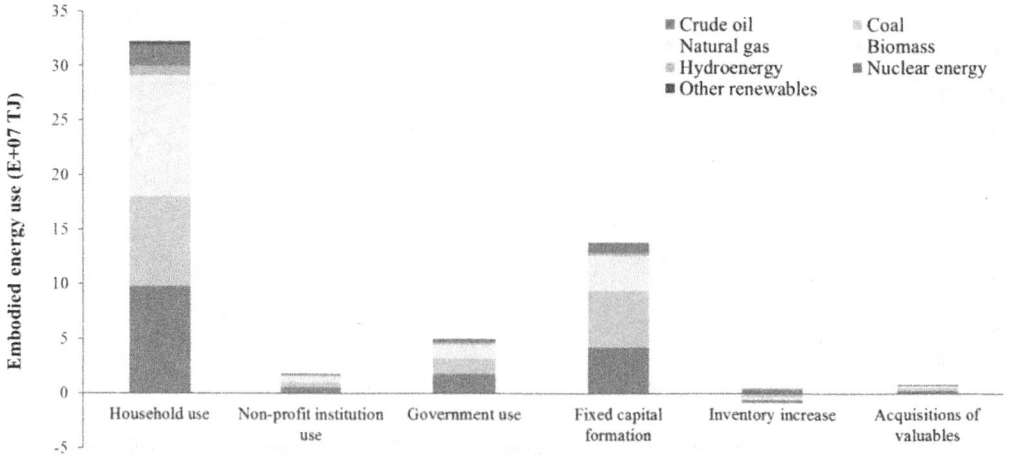

Figure 1.1.4   Composition of Energy Embodied in Final Use for the World Economy

(*Electricity*, *gas and water*) provide the second and third largest fractions of 14. 34% and 10. 54%, mainly attributed to their important roles in energy supply. Embodied energy in Sector 23 (*Education*, *health and other services*) exceeds that in Sector 4 (*Food and beverages*), declaring the increasing attention to education and health on the globe.

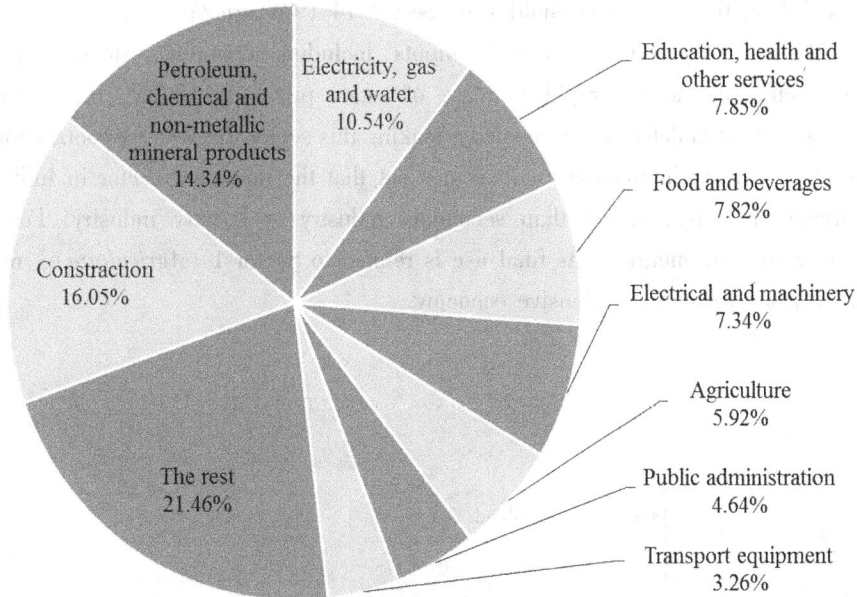

Figure 1. 1. 5 Sectoral Contribution to Final Use of the World Economy

EEFs of the 186 regions are calculated respectively and presented in Figure 1. 1. 6 (numerical results are provided in Appendix B). The United States is the largest user in terms of embodied energy with an *EEF* of 1. 01E+08 TJ. It represents that 1. 01E+08 TJ of energy are extracted from the environmental system to sustain the consumption activities of households and governments, and the investment activities of enterprises in the United States. China is the second largest user with 8. 46E + 07 TJ of energy resources that are required from the environment, followed by Japan with a requirement of 3. 56E + 07 TJ, India with a requirement of 2. 00E+07 TJ, and Germany with a requirement of 1. 68E+07 TJ. The top 5 users respectively contribute 19. 01%, 15. 89%, 6. 70%, 3. 76% and 3. 16% of the global energy use. For the United States as the largest user, the structure of embodied energy in its six final use purposes (see Figure 1. 1. 7) are similar to that for the world economy as a whole (household use and fixed capital formation occupying dominant proportions). Embodied energy in the inventory increase of the United States is found to be negative, indicating that the inventories of the United States dwindle in the year of 2010.

Among the 26 sectors, Sector 13 (*Electricity, gas and water*), Sector 7 (*Petroleum, chemical and non-metallic mineral products*), Sector 22 (*Public administration*), Sector 23 (*Education, health and other services*) and Sector 4 (*Food and beverages*) account for the five largest shares of 29.45%, 23.71%, 13.26%, 9.52% and 6.98% of the United States' final use, separately. Different from the United States, China invests more energy in fixed capital formation than household use. Sector 14 (*Construction*) is a heavy user of energy with lots of building materials inputs including concrete, steel, engineering equipment, etc. Due to the rapid increase of estate prices in China, the construction industry is greatly stimulated and promoted, making this sector the leading contributor to the final use of China. An interesting result comes out that the dominant sector in India's final use is primary industry, rather than secondary industry or tertiary industry. For India, 31.38% of embodied energy in its final use is related to Sector 1 (*Agriculture*), revealing its status as a big agriculture-intensive economy.

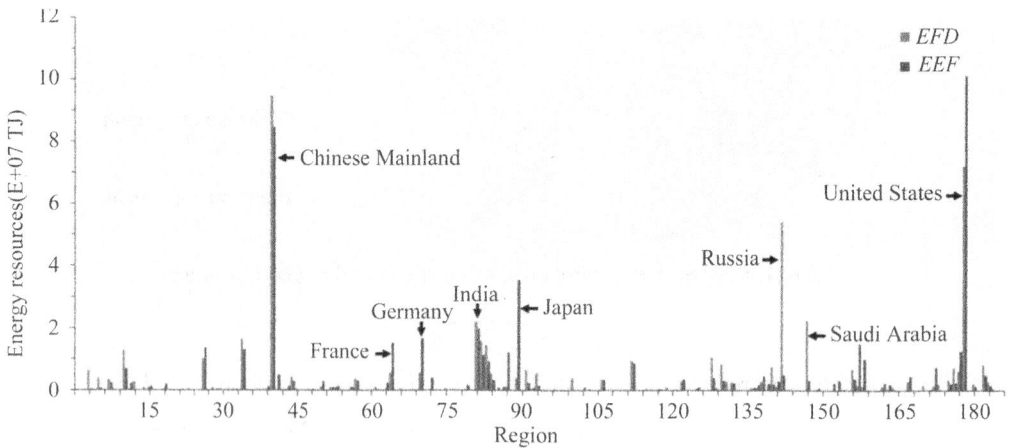

Figure 1.1.6   *EED* (Energy Resources Exploited Directly) and *EEF* (Energy Resources Embodied in Final Use) of the 186 Regions (The names of the 186 regions are shown in Appendix B.)

Besides, the two indices of *EED* and *EEF* of the 186 regions are compared in Figure 1.1.6. In essence, energy resources are natural assets, and the utility of energy resources can be regarded as the welfare gained by human beings from the natural environment. Accordingly, *EED* of a region measures the energy welfare offered by local environment, while *EEF* evaluates the energy welfare acquired by the region from both local and non-local environments. In terms of *EED*, the United States drops to second, and China takes the first place. It is worth noting that Japan which ranks third in *EEF* around the world, has a much lower value of *EED*. The amount of energy required in its final use is 7.55 times larger than that exploited in this region. Massive energy requirement of Japan for its developed economy and insufficient energy resources in local area is behind this phenomenon. In addition to Japan, other regions like Germany, France, South Korea, the United Kingdom, Italy, Spain and Hong Kong, China are also found to be in a similar condition. On the contrary, Russia, Saudi Arabia, Iran and Nigeria turn out with a different pattern with more energy resources exploited than that embodied in final use. 5.41E + 07 TJ of energy resources are exploited directly in Russia, in magnitude up to 10.83 times that embodied in its final use.

   This result confirms that energy resources are greatly redistributed by inter-regional trades. A region with few energy resources taken from local environment may grab a considerable quantity of the usefulness of energy resources from other regions. Hence, it is possible for the region to increase the imports from other regions, and thus to gain a decline in local energy use to meet the regional goal of energy conservation. But in that case, the total amount of world energy use may increase. That is, an absurd situation of "regional decrease, global increase" may happen if the conservation work of energy resources is conducted at the region level, rather than at the global level. Given the above considerations, the index of *EEF*, which takes all inter-regional trades into consideration, can be regarded as a promising criterion for allocating regional responsibility for energy saving. (see Figure 1.1.7)

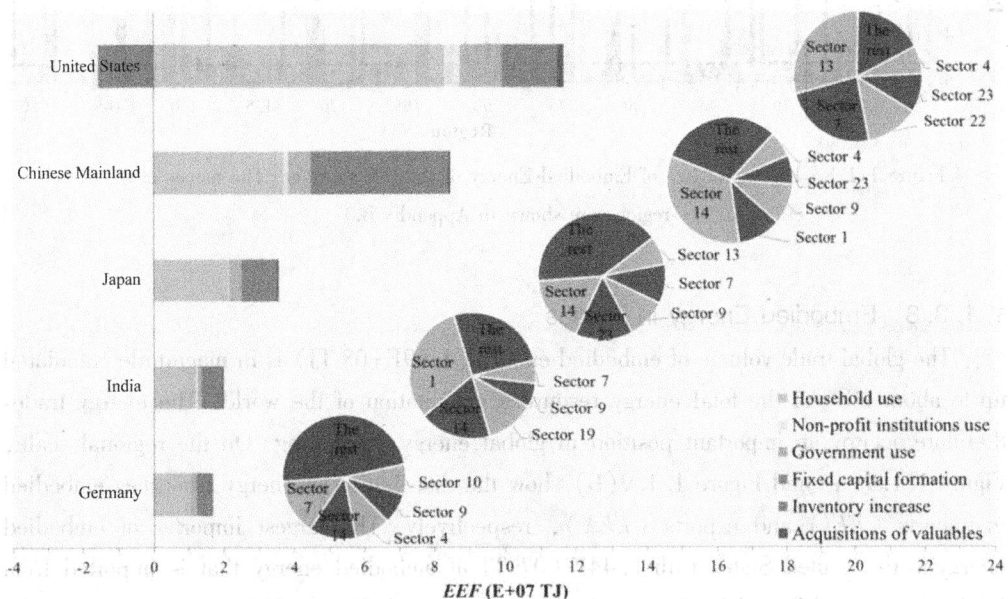

Figure 1. 1. 7   Composition of *EEF* (Energy Resources Embodied in Final Use) for the Top 5 Users of Embodied Energy (Sectoral information corresponding to the sector code is provided in Appendix C.)

In Figure 1.1.8, the per-capita *EEF* for each region is shown (numerical results are provided in Appendix B). And an extremely unbalanced distribution can be seen in this figure. Energy embodied in the final use of per capita varies from 1.60E-03 TJ (Somalia) to 1.57 TJ (Bermuda). That is, one person in the most energy-consuming region has nearly 1,000 times of energy use to that in the least energy-consuming region. The world average *EEF* (shown by the dashed line) is calculated as 7.81E-02 TJ per capita. But only one fifth of the population (1.39 of 6.82 billion) from 78 regions own a higher standard of energy welfare than the average. The other 108 regions fail to reach the global average level, which are mostly developing or underdeveloped countries and are mainly distributed in Asia, Africa and South America.

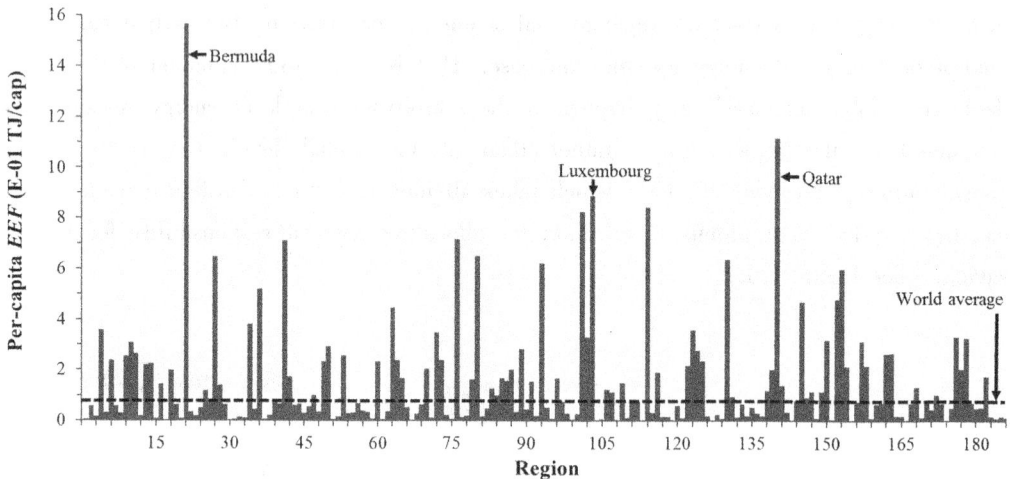

Figure 1.1.8   Per-capita Use of Embodied Energy of the 186 Regions (The names of the 186 regions are shown in Appendix B.)

1.1.3.3 Embodied Energy in Trades

The global trade volume of embodied energy (4.69E+08 TJ) is in magnitude calculated up to about 90% of the total energy resources exploitation of the world. The energy trades therefore occupy an important position in global energy accounting. On the regional scale, Figure 1.1.9(a) and Figure 1.1.9(b) show the distribution of energy resources embodied in imports (*EEI*) and exports (*EEX*), respectively. The largest importer of embodied energy is the United States with 6.44E+07 TJ of embodied energy that is imported from foreign regions, followed by Japan, Germany and South Korea. This is in contrast to the ordering of energy embodied in the exports by region. Russia and China are the leading embodied energy exporters, with 5.37E+07 TJ and 3.57E+07 TJ of embodied energy that are exported to other regions, respectively, followed by the United States and Germany.

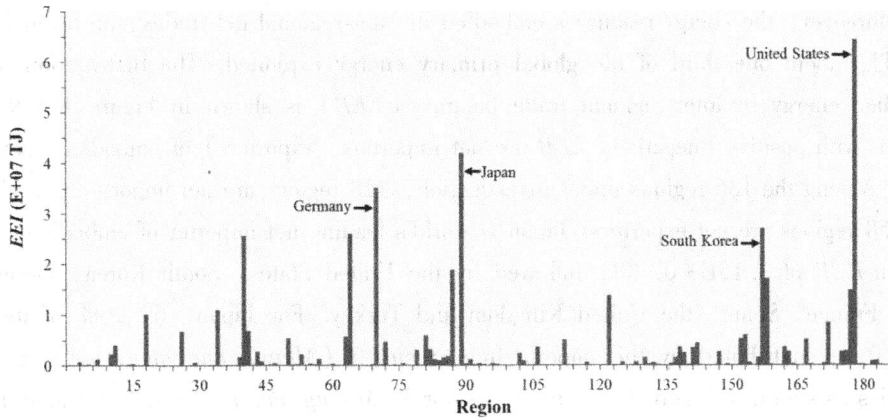

(a)

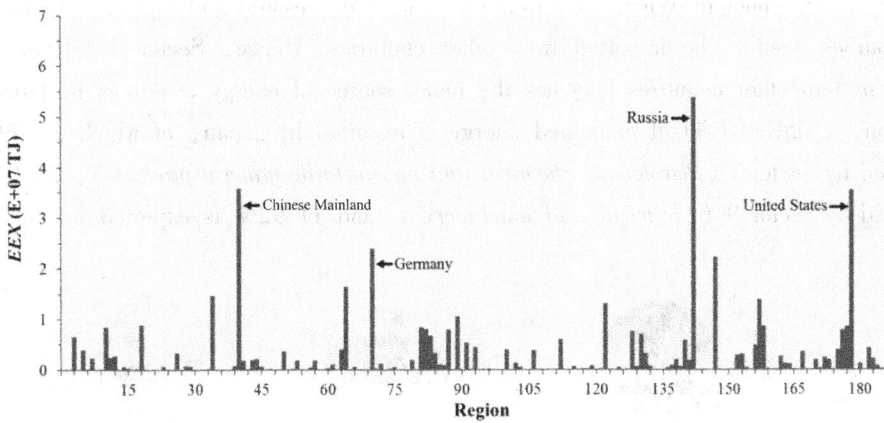

(b)

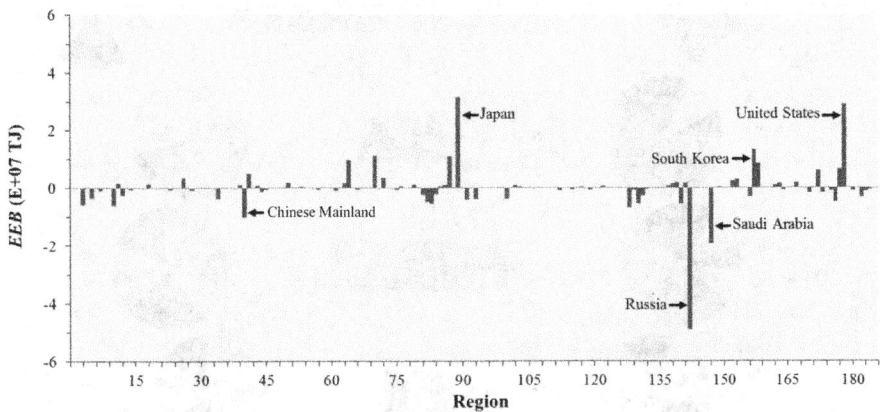

(c)

Figure 1. 1. 9 (a) *EEI* (Energy Resources Embodied in Imports), (b) *EEX* (Energy Resources Embodied in Exports) and (c) *EEB* (Energy Resources Embodied in Trade Balance) of the 186 Regions(The names of the 186 regions are shown in Appendix B.)

Moreover, the energy resources embodied in inter-regional net trades sum up to 1. 78E +08 TJ, about one third of the global primary energy exploited. The distribution of the embodied energy in inter-regional trade balance (*EEB*) is shown in Figure 1. 1. 9 (c). Regions with positive (negative) *EEB* are net importers (exporters) of embodied energy in trade. Among the 186 regions under investigation, 128 regions are net importers, while the other 58 regions are net exporters. Japan is world's leading net importer of embodied energy with an *EEB* of 3. 15E + 07 TJ, followed by the United States, South Korea, Germany, Italy, France, Spain, the United Kingdom and Turkey. For Japan, 69. 26% of its total imports are contributed by the imports from Sector 3 (*Mining and quarrying*) in other countries as shown in Figure 1. 1. 10(a). Sector 3 (*Mining and quarrying*) is a main miner of energy resources from the environmental system, and plays an important role in energy supply for the economic system. Due to the lack of energy resources in Japan, large amounts of resources need to be imported from other countries. Hence, Sector 3 (*Mining and quarrying*) in other countries becomes the major source of energy resources in Japan. In addition, 1. 05E + 07 TJ of embodied energy is exported by Japan, of which 34. 99% is exported by Sector 7 (*Petroleum, chemical and non-metallic mineral products*), 29. 04% is exported by Sector 9 (*Electrical and machinery*), and 11. 92% is exported by Sector 10

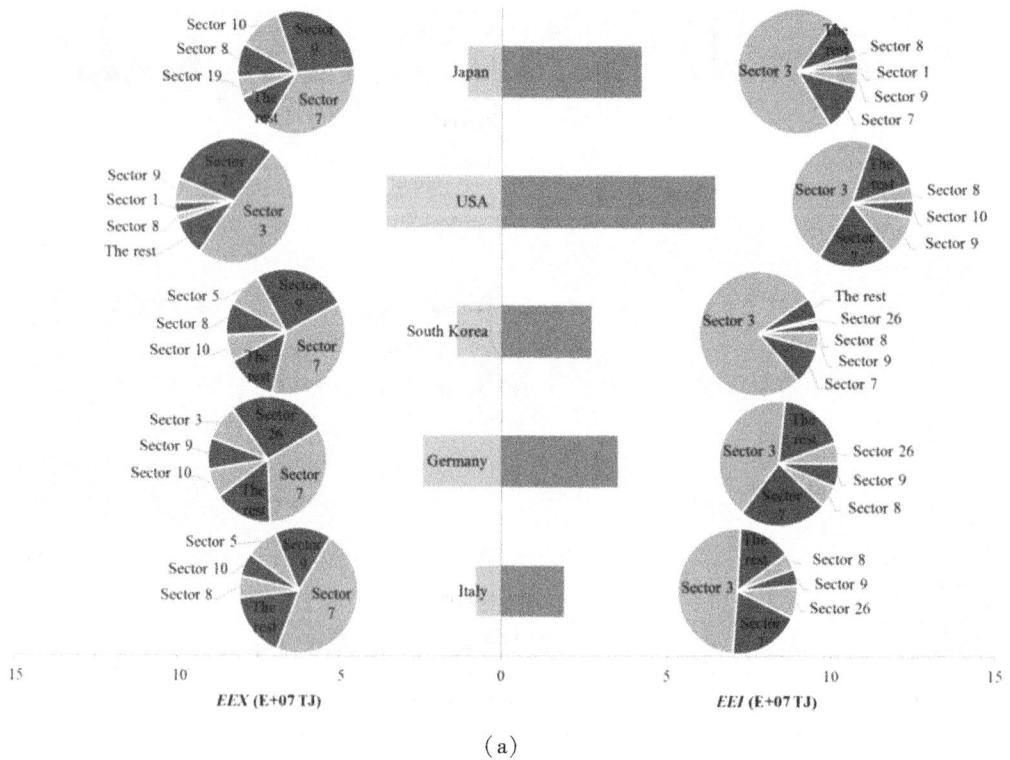

(a)

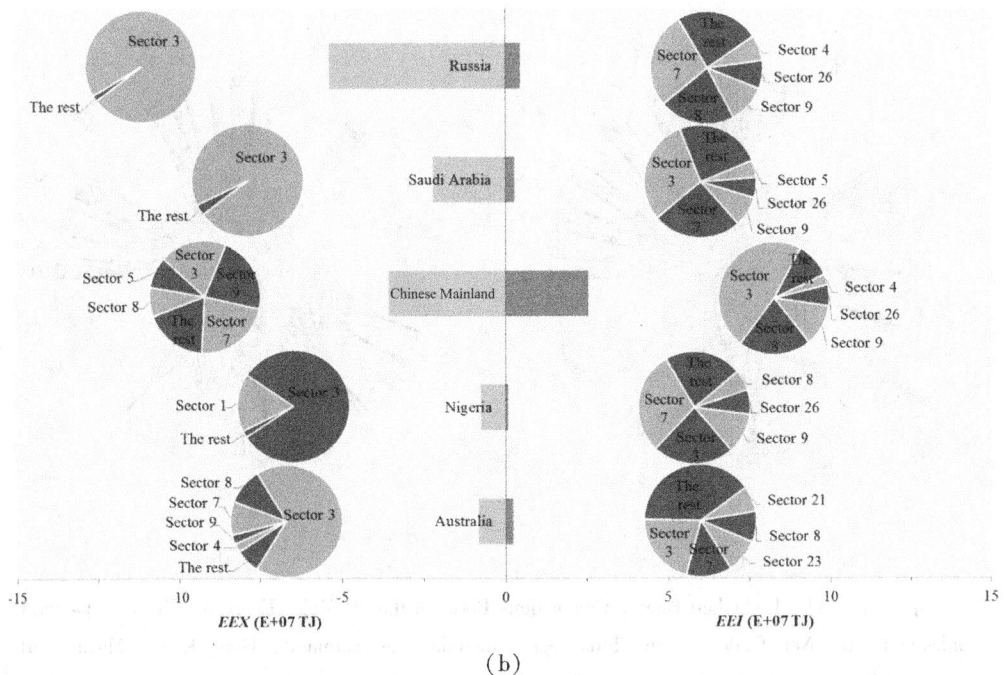

(b)

Figure 1. 1. 10   Composition of *EEI* (Energy Resources Embodied in Imports) and *EEX* (Energy Resources Embodied in Exports) for (a) the Top 5 Net Importers and (b) the Top 5 Net Exporters (Sectoral information corresponding to the sector code is provided in Appendix C.)

(*Transport equipment*). Electronic products manufacturing industry and motor industry are pillar industries for the Japanese economy, thus contributing the most to the country's exports. Similarly, the United States imports the most energy from Sector 3 (*Mining and quarrying*). But it also exports the most energy from its own Sector 3 (*Mining and quarrying*). Because of the discovery of shale gas, the United States has gradually transformed into a big oil producer. In this regard, Sector 3 as the major shale gas miner, dominates the export market of the United States.

On the other hand, the top 10 largest net exporters are Russia, Saudi Arabia, China, Nigeria, Australia, Algeria, Qatar, Iran, Norway and UAE, most of which are developing and energy-abundant regions in the world. For Russia and Saudi Arabia (see Figure 1. 1. 10(b)), embodied energy exports are only concentrated in Sector 3 (*Mining and quarrying*). 98. 23% of exports in Russia are caused by Sector 3 (*Mining and quarrying*), while the ratio is 96. 84% in Saudi Arabia. It reflects the fact that energy resources extracted locally are the main export commodities of the two nations.

Presented in Figure 1. 1. 11 (a) are major inter-regional trade flows in terms of embodied energy. The whole world is divided into 20 regions in this figure, i. e., China (including the mainland, Hong Kong, Macao and Taiwan), the European Union (EU27,

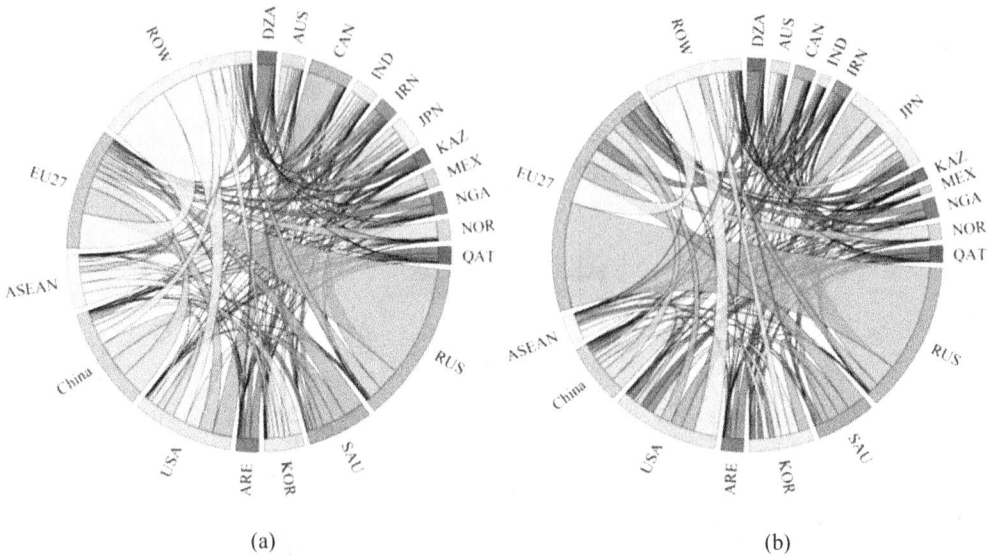

Figure 1. 1. 11 Embodied Energy Connections Between the 20 Major Economies by (a) General Trades and (b) Net Trades (The China region includes the mainland, Hong Kong, Macao and Taiwan; ASEAN stands for Association of Southeast Asian Nations; 27 member states, excluding Croatia, of the European Union are aggregated into one economy indicated as EU27; ROW refers to the rest of the world. The abbreviations of the other regions' names can be found in Appendix B. (a) The general trade relations between every two economies are portrayed by the chords. The different thicknesses at the two ends of the chord respectively respect the two connected economies' export volumes of embodied energy to each other. The chord's color corresponds to the larger exporter of the two. (b) The net trade relations between every two economies are portrayed by the chords. The thickness at both ends of the chord respects the net trade volume of embodied energy between the two connected economies. The chord's color corresponds to the net exporter.)

including 27 member states, excluding Croatia, of the European Union), Association of Southeast Asian Nations (ASEAN, including 10 member states), the top 16 largest export regions of embodied energy among the other 145 regions, and the one that integrates the rest regions (ROW) together. Since every pair of regions have two connections, there are totally 380 flows of embodied energy described here. Among these flows, the largest flow is related to the exports of Russia to EU27. 3. 92E+07 TJ of embodied energy is exported from Russia, of which 72. 95% is to EU27. The second largest flow is from ROW to EU27. As the largest economic entity in the world, EU27 requires large amounts of energy imported from other countries. EU27 imports 1. 13E+08 TJ of embodied energy in total, making it the biggest importer of embodied energy among the 20 regions. Regarding the United States, the largest energy flow associated with its exports occurs in its trades with Canada, 7. 14E+06 TJ, accounting for 20. 16% of its total exports. Meanwhile, the United States also imports from

Canada a considerable quantity of embodied energy (1.17E+07 J). It shows that Canada is one of the most important trade partners of the United States towards embodied energy. For China as a "world factory", it consumes lots of energy resources to meet local demand of manufacture, and serves the international market with the commodities "made in China". According to the results, the ROW is the leading foreign receiver of the commodities "made in China", followed by EU27, Japan and the United States.

In addition, the net trade relationships between the 20 regions are portrayed in Figure 1.1.11(b). It can be seen that EU27 occupies the biggest part of the circle, which is attributed to its extremely imbalanced status in energy trades with other regions. To be specific, the energy embodied in the imports of EU27 is 2.77 times that in the exports. Especially, in the bilateral trade of EU27 with Russia, the incoming energy is 22.19 times larger than the leaving one. EU27 acts as a typical receiver in inter-regional trade of embodied energy. In addition to EU27, the United States and Japan are also two notable receivers. However, Russia, Saudi Arabia and China show a different pattern as suppliers of embodied energy. EU27 is the biggest contributor to both Russia's and Saudi Arabia's trade imbalance, while for China, the biggest contributor is Japan. China exports 7.15E+06 TJ of embodied energy to Japan, but only imports 2.51E+06 TJ from Japan.

Although EU27 is a net importer of embodied energy in the bilateral trade with Russia, it is noted that EU27 actually gains a trade surplus of 4.03 billion USD, as presented in Figure 1.1.12. The net energy flow between EU27 and Russia is in the same direction as the net currency flow. Similarly, China exports 4.65E+06 TJ of embodied energy in its net trade with Japan, but obtains a deficit of 3.46E+01 billion USD in the economic trade. Products made in different countries have different embodied energy intensities, which is determined by local technological level and energy conservation measures. This is one of the major reasons for the disparity between economic trade imbalance and energy trade imbalance.

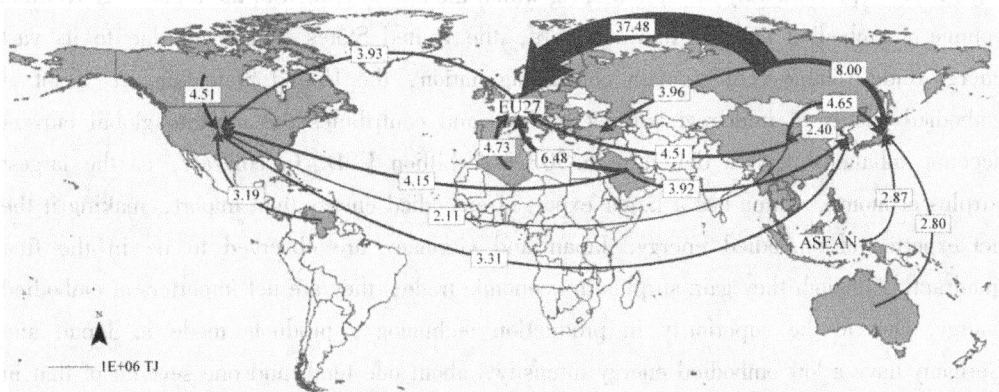

(a)

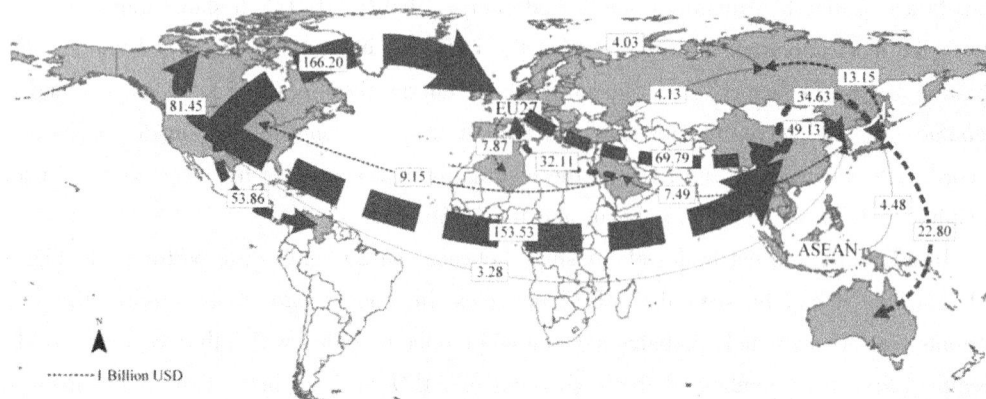

(b)

Figure 1.1.12   Major Flows in Inter-regional Net Trades in Terms of (a) Embodied Energy and (b) Currency (27 countries in the European Union (EU) are aggregated into one region; the China region includes the mainland, Hong Kong, Macao and Taiwan; ASEAN stands for Association of Southeast Asian Nations. (a) The energy flows are represented by solid lines. Number in the box indicates the trade volume from the exporting region to the importing one in unit of E+06 TJ. (b) The currency flows are displayed by dotted lines. Number in the box is in unit of billion USD.)

For the 186 regions, economic trade imbalance and energy trade imbalance are compared in Figure 1.1.13. The four quadrants in the rectangular coordinate represent four different trade patterns. Regions in the first quadrant are net importers in terms of both embodied energy and currency; regions in the second quadrant are net importers in terms of embodied energy but net exporters in terms of currency; regions in the third quadrant are net exporters in terms of both embodied energy and currency; regions in the fourth quadrant are net exporters in terms of embodied energy but net importers in terms of currency. The 186 regions are represented by the spheres, of which the size is related to the region's gross trade volume of embodied energy. In this figure, the United States stands out due to its vast energy trade volumes. As a main consuming nation, the United States imports a lot of embodied energy in inter-regional net trades, and contributes the most to global current account imbalance with a deficit of 5.90E+02 billion USD. In contrast, as the largest surplus economy, China has a larger export of embodied energy than import, making it the net exporter of embodied energy. Japan and Germany are observed to be in the first quadrant. Although they gain surplus in economic trade, they are net importers of embodied energy. Due to the superiority in production technology, products made in Japan and Germany have a low embodied energy intensity, about one tenth and one seventh of that in China, respectively. As a result, less energy is required in Japan and Germany than in their trade partners to manufacture one unit of product, and less energy is embodied in their exports than the imports.

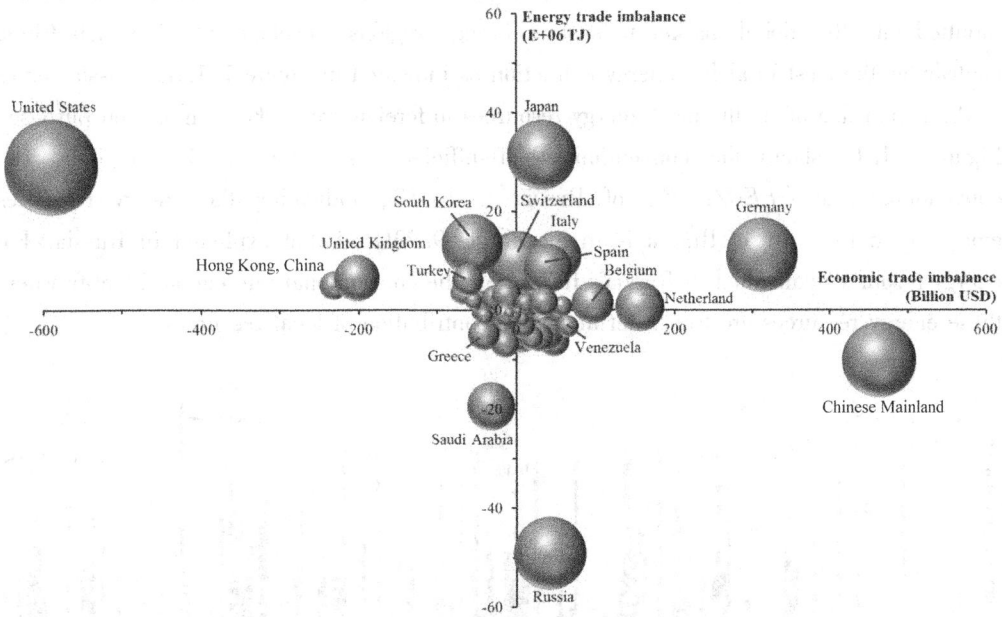

Figure 1. 1. 13   Trade Imbalance in Terms of Embodied Energy and Currency of the 186 Regions
(The size of the sphere respects the corresponding economy's gross
trade volume of embodied energy.)

1. 1. 3. 4   Source-to-sink Energy Budget

As discussed above, energy resources extracted in Region A, can be used in Region B to produce export goods for Region C's final use. To explore the relations between the source (Region A) and sink (Region C) in global energy supply chain, energy resources are tracked from exploitation to final use, and a source-to-sink energy budget is explored in the present study. For the 186 regions as primary energy sources, they extract energy resources from local environment, and provide these resources for its own or foreign regions' final use. A self-sufficiency rate of the source region can therefore be defined as the ratio of energy exploited locally for its own final use over total energy exploited locally. For each region, this rate assesses the contribution of local energy resources to its final use, which is different from the conventional self-sufficiency rate as the ratio of total energy exploited (EED) over total energy embodied in final use (EEF), to simply reveal the mathematical relationship between exploitation and consumption. As shown in Figure 1. 1. 14 (a), Serbia has the maximum self-sufficiency rate among the 186 source regions. For China and the United States as the two largest sources (see Figure 1. 1. 6), their rates are respectively 70. 16% and 69. 42%, indicating that most of the energy resources extracted in the two regions are

23

consumed by themselves. However, Russia as the third largest source has an extremely low rate of 3.73%. The vast majority (5.21E+07 TJ) of energy resources mined in Russia are inputted into the global market to sustain foreign regions' development. Although China contributes the most in global energy extraction as indicated in Figure 1.1.6, Russia serves as the region that offers the most energy resources to foreign areas. For comparison purpose, Figure 1.1.15 shows the conventional self-sufficiency rate for the 186 regions. The conventional rate (*EED/EEF*) of Russia is 10.83, indicating the energy resources embodied in final use of Russia is in magnitude 9.23% of that exploited in Russia. For energy resources embodied in Russia's final use, the conventional rate cannot identify where these energy resources are from, let alone the contribution of local resources.

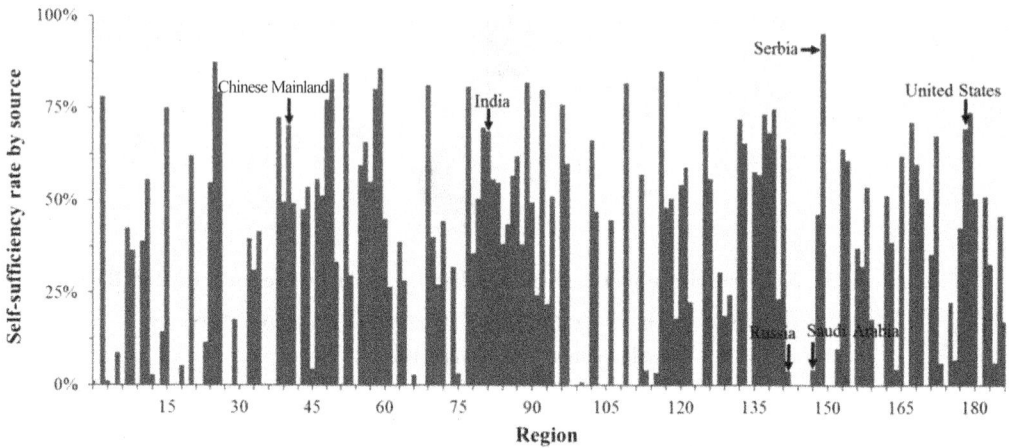

(a)

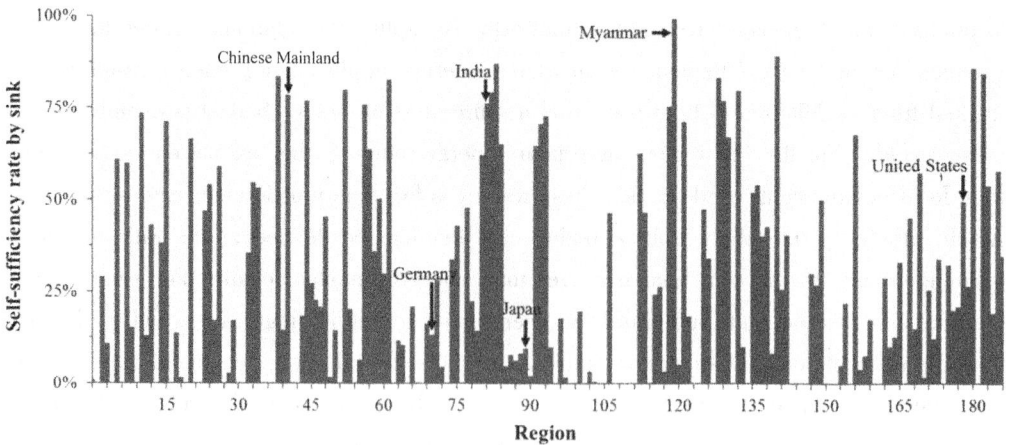

(b)

Figure 1.1.14   Self-sufficiency Rate of the 186 Regions by (a) Source and (b) Sink
(The names of the 186 regions are shown in Appendix B.)

Analogously, for the sink region in the energy supply chain, many energy resources are required to meet its final demands. These energy resources can also be classified into two parts. One is provided by the local environment, and the other is imported from foreign regions. Hence, the share occupied by the former part is regarded as the self-sufficiency rate of the sink region and is presented for the 186 regions in Figure 1. 1. 14(b). For the United States as the largest sink, its self-sufficiency rate is 49. 50%, manifesting half (5. 11E+07 TJ) of its embodied energy use is required from foreign regions. The rate of China is revealed much higher, with 78. 56% of embodied energy in China's final use is provided by itself. In contrast, the ratio for Japan as the third largest sink, is much smaller, which is 9. 55%. Most energy resources (3. 22E+07 TJ) embodied in Japan's final use are imported from foreign regions, due to the shortage of energy resources in Japan.

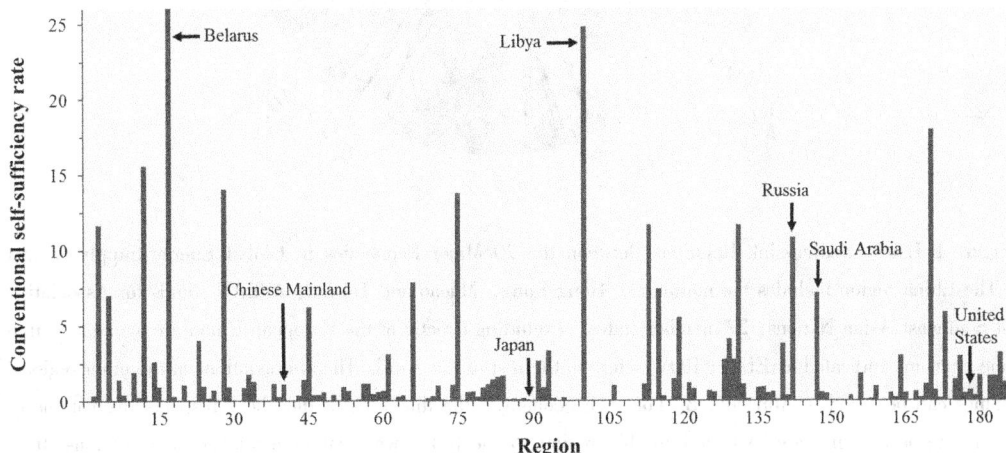

Figure 1. 1. 15 Conventional Self-sufficiency Rate of the 186 Regions
(The names of the 186 regions are shown in Appendix B.)

A source-to-sink energy budget for the global supply chain is presented in Figure 1. 1. 16. In this figure, the whole world is also divided into 20 regions, i. e., China (including the mainland, Hong Kong, Macao and Taiwan), the European Union (EU27, including 27 member states, excluding Croatia, of the European Union), Association of Southeast Asian Nations (ASEAN, including 10 member states), the top 16 biggest extractors of energy resources among the other 145 regions, and the one that integrates the rest regions (ROW) together. The largest flow between two different regions in global energy supply chain is from Russia to EU27. 5. 41E+07 TJ of energy resources are extracted in Russia, of which 54. 53% are for EU27's final use. Consequently, as the biggest beneficiary of Russian energy resources, EU27 would suffer the biggest impact if Russia ran into supply problems.

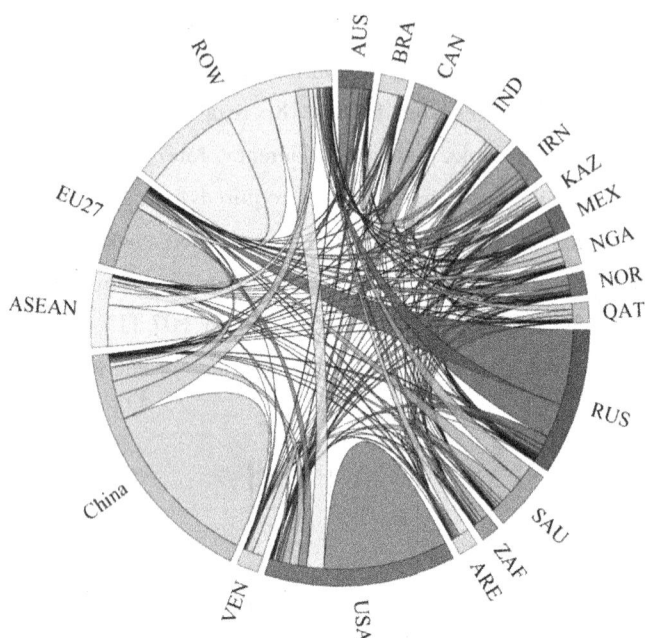

Figure 1.1.16   Source-sink Relations Between the 20 Major Economies in Global Energy Supply Chains (The China region includes the mainland, Hong Kong, Macao and Taiwan; ASEAN stands for Association of Southeast Asian Nations; 27 member states, excluding Croatia of the European Union are aggregated into one economy indicated as EU27; ROW refers to the rest of the world. The abbreviations of the other regions' names can be found in Appendix B. For each economy, the thickness of the chord respects the volume of energy resources that are extracted in this region to meet its own final demands or other regions' final demands. For the chord connecting two regions, its color corresponds to the region with more energy resources extracted to meet the other one's final demands.)

From the perspective of energy sources, China produces the most energy resources among the 20 regions, followed by ROW, the United States, Russia and EU27. For China, 9.53E+07 TJ of energy resources are extracted in its territory, of which 72.64% are consumed for its own final use, 9.67% for ROW's final use, 6.37% for EU27, 5.83% for the United States and 5.49% for other foreign regions. From the perspective of energy sinks, EU27 is the largest user of embodied energy among the 20 regions, followed by ROW, the United States and China. 1.07E+08 TJ of energy resources are embodied in EU27's final use, of which 27.59% are from Russia, 23.73% are extracted in local environment, 16.61% are from ROW, 5.68% are from China, 5.58% are from Saudi Arabia, and 20.81% are from the other 15 foreign regions.

1. 1. 4 Concluding Remarks

In the times of globalization, the energy connections between regional economies become more complex due to the increasing volume of international trades. In view of the necessity to allocate regional responsibility in international cooperation for energy conservation and carbon reduction, this study presents an overview of the global energy profile based on an integration of statistics for 2010, by means of a systems embodied energy analysis. The world economy is portrayed as a 186-region, 26-sector coupled network and a systems multi-regional input-output simulation is applied to comprehensively illustrate the connections from the source of primary energy exploitation to the sink of final use through inter-regional trade.

For the world economy as a whole, over 60% of energy exploited is embodied in household final use, with less than 30% in investment and more than 10% in government and non-profit institution final use. For each region, the actual amount of energy requirement is substantially different from that of energy exploited in the local area. The United States, China, Japan, India and Germany are found to be the five largest final users of embodied energy, in contrast to China, the United States, Russia, Saudi Arabia and India as the top five energy exploiters. This result indicates that a region with few energy resources exploited from local environment may grab a considerable quantity of the usefulness of energy resources from other foreign regions. This phenomenon of "energy grabbing" is similar to the "water grabbing" inherent in the globalized economy.

In total, about one third of global energy exploited is embodied in net trades, and the global trade volume by embodied energy amounts up to nearly 90% of the global energy exploited. Japan turns out to be the leading net importer of energy use, compared with Russia as the leading net exporter of energy use. Sectoral contributions to their imports and exports are discussed in detail, which can help guide regional regulation of trade structure. Besides, two new indicators of self-sufficiency are developed to explore the relations between energy exploiters and energy users in global energy supply chain. For China as the largest energy exploiter, about 30% of its exploited energy is for foreign regions' final use, and 70% for its own final use. The European Union is illustrated to be the main beneficiary of energy exploited in China. For the European Union as the largest energy user, nearly 80% of the energy required in its final use is from foreign regions, among which approximately one third is from Russia. The indicators can be considered as a reference for policy-makers to enhance energy security.

Owing to the huge trade volume, the energy resources are essentially redistributed among regions. Through increasing the imports from foreign regions, a region can gain a decline in local energy use to meet the regional goal of energy conservation. But the total amount of world energy use may keep constant or even increase. The substitution of local energy exploitation through imports indeed extends the environmental burden from the regional to the global level. Hence, regional energy regulation in isolation can make little sense to energy conservation in this context of globalization, and it is necessary to take the whole world into consideration. In addition, countries' economic development tends to be associated with a high degree of specialization following the law of comparative advantage, and this is particularly true for WTO (World Trade Organization) members. Lots of energy-intensive and pollution-intensive industries are witnessed to transfer from developed countries to developing countries. The efficient and clean technologies in the developing countries are therefore of essential importance for the realization of the global common goal of energy conservation and emissions reduction. Compared with the regional energy regulation with the production-based accounting, the regulation at the global scale in accordance with the consumption-based accounting principle can greatly encourage developed countries to export the energy-saving and cleaner production technologies to developing countries. Therefore, this global overview from the energy user perspective can serve as a supplement to the prevailing view focused on the energy producer.

Results in this study can also provide significant implications for energy-related GHG mitigation policy. As the issue of carbon leakage introduced by the separation of production and consumption has been discussed extensively, the present systems embodiment model is expected to become a promising quantitative approach to support related policy making at both regional and global scales.

References

Bordigoni, M., Hita, A., Le Blanc, G., 2012. Role of Embodied Energy in the European Manufacturing Industry: Application to Short-term Impacts of a Carbon Tax. *Energy Policy*, 43, 335-350.

Bullard Iii, C. W., Herendeen, R. A., 1975. The Energy Cost of Goods and Services. *Energy Policy*, 3, 268-278.

Chen, Z. M., Chen, G. Q., 2011. An Overview of Energy Consumption of the Globalized World Economy. *Energy Policy*, 39, 5920-5928.

Costanza, R., 1984. Embodied Energy and Economic Value in the United States Economy: 1963, 1967 and 1972. *Resources and Energy*, 6, 129-163.

Lenzen, M., Kanemoto, K., Moran, D., Geschke, A., 2012. Mapping the Structure of the World Economy. *Environmental Science & Technology*, 46, 8374-8381.

Leontief, W., 1970. Environmental Repercussions and the Economic Structure: An Input-output Approach. *The Review of Economics and Statistics*, 52, 262-271.

Li, J. S., Chen, G. Q., Wu, X. F., Hayat, T., Alsaedi, A., Ahmad, B., 2014. Embodied Energy Assessment for Macao's External Trade. *Renewable and Sustainable Energy Reviews*, 34, 642-653.

Miller, R. E., Blair, P. D., 2009. Input-output Analysis: Foundations and Extensions. Cambridge University Press, UK.

Odum, H. T., 1996. Environmental Accounting: Emergy and Environmental Decision Making. John Wiley and Sons, New York.

Wiedmann, T. O., Schandl, H., Lenzen, M., Moran, D., Suh, S., West, J., Kanemoto, K., 2013. The Material Footprint of Nations. *Proceedings of the National Academy of Sciences*, 112, 6271-6276.

1. 2　Global Primary Energy Use Associated with Production, Consumption and International Trade[①]

1. 2. 1　Introduction

Energy is fundamental to the economic progress and social development. Over the last 35 years, worldwide energy use has doubled, contributing significantly to the unprecedented economic growth and living standards improvement. The global Gross Domestic Product (GDP) increased 6-fold and the average income per capita in the world quadrupled during that period (WB, 2015). In addition to the great benefits, the implications of such widespread energy consumption extend across a range of environmental problems. The majority of energy currently used globally is derived from fossil fuels, such as crude oil, natural gas and coal, which are also regarded as the dominant contributors to the air pollutants emissions and the greenhouse gases emissions. As the key link among the three pillars of economy, society and environment in sustainable development, energy use has become the most critical challenge of the world today.

In this context, extensive researches have been carried out to explore sustainable energy use. In these studies, indirect energy use has received great attention. Different from direct energy use recording a region's energy consumption on its territory, indirect energy use measures the energy consumed in other regions to produce the goods and services that are demanded by this region. With economic globalization, countries in the world are closely connected by international trade, making indirect energy use an increasingly prominent phenomenon. For Italy, about 70% of the total household final demand is met by the

---

① Published on *Energy Policy*, Volume 111, pp. 85-94, with a few modifications due to space constraints. Reuse permission has been obtained from Elsevier.

indirect energy use (Cellura et al. , 2011).

In order to combine the indirect energy use with the direct one, the embodied energy was conceptualized in the 1970s as a significant indicator for estimating the total energy requirements. For a product or service, embodied energy is defined as the total (direct plus indirect) primary energy inputs to generate and sustain it (Costanza, 1980). So far, the embodied energy method has gained wide application in various economic systems at different scales. Most of these previous researches applied the embodied energy concept to final consumption activities in economic systems, aiming at identifying the amount of energy embodied in the commodities and services that are used to meet the consumers' final demand. The consumers' demand is the driving force of economic production and energy consumption. A clear understanding of each consumer's contribution can help track the final destination of energy resources in global supply chains. What's more, numerous studies have pointed out that high-income countries tend to play the consumer role in global market, and other countries, especially emerging countries, become the producers and produce goods to serve the high-income countries through international trade. As a result, the consumption-based energy accounting can greatly encourage the high-income countries to export the energy-saving and cleaner production technologies to emerging countries, which is conductive to achieving a reduction in global total energy use.

However, regarding the intermediate production, which holds an equally important position as the final consumption activity in the economic system, few investigations have been performed on the related embodied energy use. In general, the conventional production-based energy accounting merely considers the energy resources that are directly used by local production processes, in line with the territorial-based principle under the Kyoto Protocol. But presently, countries' economic development is with a high degree of specialization following the law of comparative advantage. It becomes necessary for the producers to trade and cooperate with each other. For example, to sustain the manufacture of motor vehicles in Europe, local motor vehicles producers import steel as intermediate inputs from steel producers in China. To produce these steel products, substantial energy resources are consumed in China. In fact, such trade induced by intermediate production activities accounts for about two-thirds of global total trade volume, in magnitude twice the trade for final consumption (Chen and Han, 2015). It is therefore imperative to discuss the indirect energy use accompanied with the trade of intermediate products to probe into the producer's indirect effect on energy depletion.

Several organizations and scholars have tried to explore the producers' indirect responsibility for resource utilization and pollutant discharge. As early as 1994, the Organization for Economic Co-operation and Development (OECD) introduced the idea of extended producer responsibility for the purpose of waste minimization. According to OECD, producers should bear the responsibility not only for the direct or on-site environmental impacts during the production process of their products, but also for the indirect or off-site impacts associated with upstream activities, such as materials selection and products design, and downstream activities of treatment or disposal of the products. Afterwards, Peters (2008) illustrated a detailed calculation for the production-based greenhouse gas emissions inventory, and the production-based emissions of a region were defined as the emissions embodied in its final production, i. e., the production of goods and services for both local and exported final consumption. On the basis of Peters' analysis, Kanemoto et al. (2012) clearly explained the term of production-based inventory, and redefined it as the total factor used to produce the products for final consumption. Recently, Liang et al. (2015) presented a downstream-production-based framework, to trace both direct and indirect mercury emissions caused by the production activities of a nation. In the work of Chen and Han (2015) regarding arable land use, the indirect land use associated with intermediate trade is integrated with local direct land use to compute the production-based land use for each producer. Yet the indirect energy use of the producers in global supply chains is still unclear.

Given the increasingly serious energy crisis worldwide, the present study places emphasis on primary energy resources, and aims to provide a systematic analysis of embodied energy use for the world economy. The direct and indirect energy use of various economic entities in global market, including the exploiter, producer, consumer, intermediate goods trader and final goods trader, are investigated from the embodiment perspective, in order to provide additional insights for energy conservation and carbon reduction.

1. 2. 2　Methodology and Data

1. 2. 2. 1　Input-output Analysis

Originally proposed as an economic tool to represent the financial interactions between industries of a nation, the input-output analysis (IOA) has now developed into a main technique for embodiment accounting in the environmental field. As this technique gives a panorama of embodied physical flows for the entire system, it performs well in studies on the complicated economic system, especially global economic system. Leontief firstly extended the economic IOA table to include the environmental data, which has been widely used and referred to as the environmentally extended IOA model. In this model, the direct energy consumption of each economic sector is assigned to be the virtual energy consumption of the goods and services delivered by the sector to meet final demand. In this way, one can predict the energy requirement when there is a change in the final demand for a certain goods or service. It is noted that the concept of virtual energy in environmentally extended IOA is only applied to the goods and services for final consumption, explicitly exclusive to those for intermediate production.

31

However, as discussed above, intermediate production and its associated trade occupy a considerable share in economic activities, and it is of great importance to uncover the related energy use to help shed light on how energy resources flow between both sectors and regions before being used for final consumption. Hence, based on the idea of "conservation of embodied energy", Bullard Iii and Herendeen (1975) proposed a modified IOA scheme and applied the concept of embodied energy to both intermediate production and final consumption as two basic components of total outputs. Then Chen and his co-workers generalized the modified IOA for embodiment analysis for various ecological endowments, like energy resources, water resources, land resources, greenhouse gases, mercury and so on, and termed it as the systems IOA model (Shao et al., 2017; Chen and Han, 2015). In the systems IOA model, all goods and services, no matter if they are for intermediate or final use purposes, are considered with energy use hidden or embodied in them. Therefore, we adopt the systems IOA method in the present study, for a systematic analysis of primary energy use by the globalized economy, with focus on production, consumption and international trade.

1.2.2.2 Algorithm

For the world economy as a m-region, n-sector coupled network, there are totally $m \cdot n$ entities in the table, as shown in Figure 1.2.1. z_{ij}^{rs} (r, $s \in \{1, 2,\ldots, m\}$, i, $j \in \{1, 2,\ldots, n\}$) is the monetary value of goods and services sold by Sector i in Region r for intermediate production in Sector j of Region s, and f_i^{rs} is the monetary value of goods and services from Sector i, Region r to Region s for final consumption. The gray segment in Figure 1.2.1 represents the trades of Region 1 with other foreign regions for both

Sale \ Purchase			Intermediate production							Final consumption		
			Region 1			…	Region m					
			Sector 1	…	Sector n	…	Sector 1	…	Sector n	Region 1	…	Region m
Inter-mediate input	Region 1	Sector 1	z_{11}^{11}	…	z_{1n}^{11}	…	z_{11}^{1m}	…	z_{1n}^{1m}	f_1^{11}	…	f_1^{1m}
		⋮	⋮		⋮		⋮		⋮	⋮		⋮
		Sector n	z_{n1}^{11}	…	z_{nn}^{11}	…	z_{n1}^{1m}	…	z_{nn}^{1m}	f_n^{11}	…	f_n^{1m}
	⋮		⋮		⋮		⋮		⋮	⋮		⋮
	Region n	Sector 1	z_{11}^{m1}	…	z_{1n}^{m1}	…	z_{11}^{mm}	…	z_{1n}^{mm}	f_1^{m1}	…	f_1^{mm}
		⋮	⋮		⋮		⋮		⋮	⋮		⋮
		Sector n	z_{n1}^{m1}	…	z_{nn}^{m1}	…	z_{n1}^{mm}	…	z_{nn}^{mm}	f_n^{m1}	…	f_n^{mm}
Direct energy input			e_1^1	…	e_n^1	…	e_1^m	…	e_n^m			

Exports for intermediate production and final consumption

Imports for intermediate production and final consumption

Figure 1.2.1 The Structure of the Input-output Table for the World Economy

intermediate production and final consumption. The intermediate goods are defined as the goods that need further processing, including raw materials, while the final goods do not need further processing. The energy resources originally exist in the environmental system, and then are exploited and inputted into the economic system (Odum, 1996). Hence, e_i^r records the amount of primary energy resources directly exploited by Sector i in Region r from the natural environment as the exogenous supply to the economic system.

Embodied energy intensity (ε) is an important indicator. For a sector, it implies the average amount of direct plus indirect energy required in the supply chain to produce one unit of goods or service based on the current technology. In the systems IOA, the embodied intensity is calculated based on the biophysical input-output balance that the total energy inputs equal the total energy outputs.

$$e_i^r + \sum_{s=1}^{m} \sum_{j=1}^{n} (\varepsilon_j^s z_{ji}^{sr}) = \varepsilon_i^r \left(\sum_{s=1}^{m} \sum_{j=1}^{n} z_{ij}^{rs} + \sum_{s=1}^{m} f_i^{rs} \right) \qquad (1.2.1)$$

where ε_i^r denotes the embodied energy intensity of Sector i in Region r.

With the sectoral embodied energy intensities obtained, the energy use embodied in intermediate trade (import of EEI_p and export of EEX_p), final trade (import of EEI_c and export of EEX_c) and total trade as a combination of intermediate and final trade (import of EEI and export of EEX) can be calculated via multiplying its economic value by the embodied energy intensity of the corresponding sector.

The energy use embodied in production (EEP) and consumption (EEC) are therefore presented as

$$EEP^r = EED^r + EEI_p^r - EEX_p^r = \sum_{i=1}^{n} \sum_{s=1}^{m} (\varepsilon_i^r f_i^{rs}) \qquad (1.2.2)$$

$$EEC^r = EED^r + EEI^r - EEX^r = \sum_{s=1}^{m} \sum_{j=1}^{n} (\varepsilon_j^s f_j^{sr}) \qquad (1.2.3)$$

where $EED^r (= \sum_{i=1}^{n} e_i^r)$ is defined as the total energy exploited directly in Region r. EED, EEP and EEC represent three different accounting methods for regional energy use. The responsibilities of energy use are ascribed to energy exploitation, final production and final consumption, respectively, in the three methods. As the primary energy resources are used by the economic system once they are exploited, EED enunciates the direct energy use or the direct energy requirements of the region. EEP describes the direct and indirect energy requirements to sustain the final productive activities within the region, and thus attributes the energy use to the producers who produce goods and services for final consumption. In contrast, EEC determines the total amount of energy required to maintain the region's final consumptive activities, because all energy use is assumed to occur with the ultimate goal to deliver the goods or services for final consumption.

33

1. 2. 2. 3   Data Sources

In the present study, the economic input-output table for the world is adopted from the Eora Database Version 199. 82, in which 26 sectors from 188 regions are included. Detailed information of the sectors and regions are listed in Appendix C and Appendix E, respectively. In an attempt to combine the most recent statistics, the year of 2013 is chosen for the analysis. The statistics of direct energy inputs are collected from the International Energy Agency (IEA) World Energy Statistics and Balances and BP Statistical Review of World Energy. Seven energy sources are included, namely crude oil, coal, natural gas, biomass, hydroenergy, nuclear energy and other renewable energy.

1. 2. 3   Results

1. 2. 3. 1   Energy Use Associated with Production and Consumption

The world economy consumes 5. 63E + 08 TJ of primary energy resources. In order to identify which region is responsible for the energy use, three different accounting principles as recorded by the indicators of *EED* (energy resources exploited directly), *EEP* (energy resources embodied in production) and *EEC* (energy resources embodied in final consumption), respectively, are adopted in Figure 1. 2. 2. According to *EED*, China, the United States, Russia, Saudi Arabia and India are the 5 largest exploiters, and together they are responsible for 51% of global total energy use. In addition, China is also the largest producer with 1. 22E+08 TJ of energy resources embodied in its production, based on the

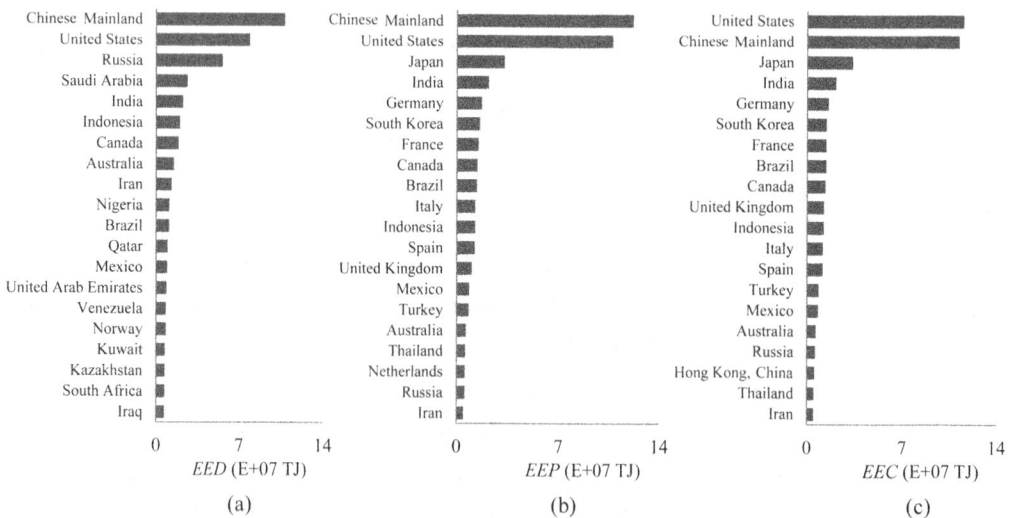

Figure 1. 2. 2   Top 20 Largest Regions Regarding (a) *EED* (Energy Resources Exploited Directly), (b) *EEP* (Energy Resources Embodied in Production) and (c) *EEC* (Energy Resources Embodied in Final Consumption)

results of *EEP*. It indicates that 1.22E + 08 TJ of energy resources are used globally to sustain the final production activities in China. The United States is the second largest producer, followed by Japan, India and Germany. When it comes to *EEC*, the United States surpasses China as the largest consumer of embodied energy. The world total energy use is the same under different accounting principles, however, the three methods differ by which region is allocated the energy use.

The difference between *EEP* and *EEC* is small at the regional level, because the goods and services used for final consumption in one region are mainly produced in the same region. For China, the energy resources embodied in its final production are 9% larger than those embodied in its final consumption. Due to the price advantage, a number of commodities "made in China" have poured into the international market. Therefore, industrial production has become the dominant force to promote economic development in China. In contrast, the United States has gradually transferred its energy-intensive industries to the emerging countries, and domestic consumers' demand cannot be fully satisfied by local production. Therefore, the energy use associated with the production activities in the United States is 7% less than that associated with its consumption activities. When taking the index of *EED* into consideration, an obvious distinction appears. In particular, the amount of energy exploited in Japan is 1.17E + 06 TJ, only 4% and 3% of those embodied in its production and consumption, respectively. But for Russia, local energy exploitation is 10.04 and 9.08 times those embodied in the production and consumption, respectively. It can be seen that the size of a region's economy is decoupled from its energy exploitation, which depends on the available energy resource locally.

1.2.3.2　Energy Use Associated with Trade

The global energy use embodied in trade is calculated as 5.19E+08 TJ, of which 85% is traded for intermediate production, while 15% is attributed to final consumption. The energy use embodied in the trade for intermediate production is more than 5 times that in the trade for final consumption. Evidently, a partial accounting of energy use associated with final trade cannot give a complete picture of global energy trade. For the 188 regions, energy trade embodied in intermediate production and final consumption are quantified and presented in Appendix E.

In the intermediate trade, Japan, the United States, China, South Korea and Germany are the largest net importers. For these 5 regions, the sectoral contributions to their imports and exports in intermediate trade are analyzed respectively in Figure 1.2.3 to help understand the trade structure in these regions. The 26 sectors are aggregated for illustration purpose, with details shown in Appendix C. 74% of the intermediate import in Japan is contributed by the import from mining industries in other regions. Due to the critical shortage of local energy resources, Japan imports large quantities of energy resources from foreign regions. As the mining industry plays a key role in energy resources supply for the economic system, it becomes the major source of imported energy in Japan. In addition, 9.70E+06 TJ of embodied energy use is exported by Japan, of which 87% is concentrated on the industry of heavy manufacturing, including the electronic products manufacturing industry and the motor industry, which are two pillar industries in Japanese economy. For the United States, 5.83E+07 TJ of energy use is imported as intermediate inputs for local production, while 2.95E+07 TJ is exported as intermediate inputs for production in foreign regions. The mining industry is the second largest contributor to its intermediate export. The shale revolution in the United States has greatly improved the relation between energy supply and demand, and energy resources mined by the United States are gradually entering the international market.

The 5 largest net exporters in intermediate energy trade are Russia, Saudi Arabia, Qatar, Australia and Iran, which are also the 5 largest net exporters in total energy trade, revealing the great influence of intermediate trade on total trade. The 5 regions feature a similar export structure as their intermediate exports are dominated by the mining industry in Figure 1.2.3.

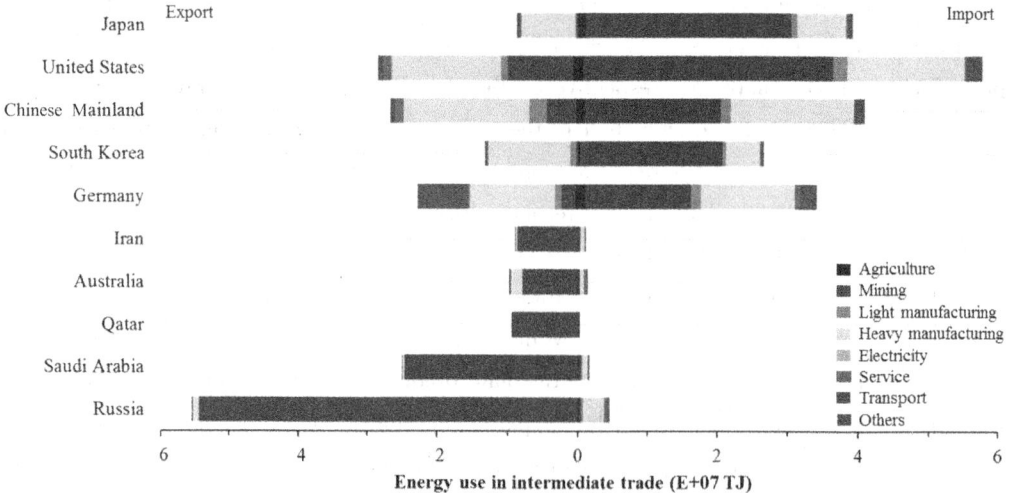

Figure 1.2.3   Balance of Energy Use Embodied in Imports and Exports of the Largest Net Importers/
Exporters in Intermediate Trade (Sectoral information is provided in Appendix C.)

With respect to the trade of goods for final consumption, a different scene emerges. Figure 1.2.4 depicts the balance of final trade in embodied energy use for the top 5 largest net importers and exporters. Different from the major net importers in intermediate trade, whose imports are mainly from the mining industry for intermediate production, the net importers in final trade primarily import goods from the manufacturing industry in foreign regions. The United States is the largest net importer in final trade, with 65% of its import from the industry of heavy manufacturing, and 26% from the industry of light manufacturing.

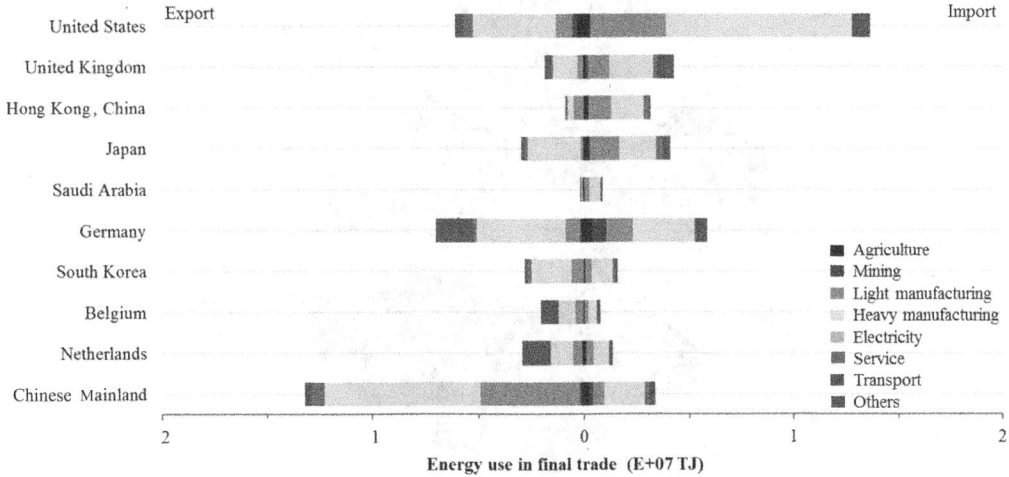

Figure 1. 2. 4　Balance of Energy Use Embodied in Imports and Exports of the Largest Net Importers/
Exporters in Final Trade (Sectoral information is provided in Appendix C.)

The top 5 largest net exporters in final energy trade are China, Netherlands, Belgium, South Korea and Germany. In contrast to the unified export structure for the leading net exporters in intermediate trade, the export markets of the net exporters in final trade show a structural diversity. In Netherlands, the tertiary industry, including the industries of service, transport and others considered in Figure 1. 2. 4, makes up the largest component of its energy export. The tertiary industry is usually regarded as a low-energy consumption industry, and this is true when only the on-site energy consumption is considered. The off-site energy consumption of the tertiary industry, however, can be surprisingly intensive because the industries in today's economy are highly interconnected.

1. 2. 3. 3　Trade Connections

Inter-regional trade causes the transfers of embodied energy use, which are important for balancing regional energy budget and for understanding the drivers of energy use. Shown in Figure 1. 2. 5 are the major inter-regional embodied energy fluxes in terms of intermediate trade and final trade. The world economy is divided into 13 regions. In Figure 1. 2. 5, China includes the mainland, Hong Kong, Macao and Taiwan; Association of Southeast Asian Nations (ASEAN) includes 10 member states; the European Union (EU) includes 28 member states; the information of the other 10 regions can be found in Appendix D. In intermediate trade, Russia stands out because of its huge export volume of intermediate materials. The largest export flow from Russia goes to EU, which is the biggest intermediate importer of embodied energy among the 13 regions.

(a)

(b)

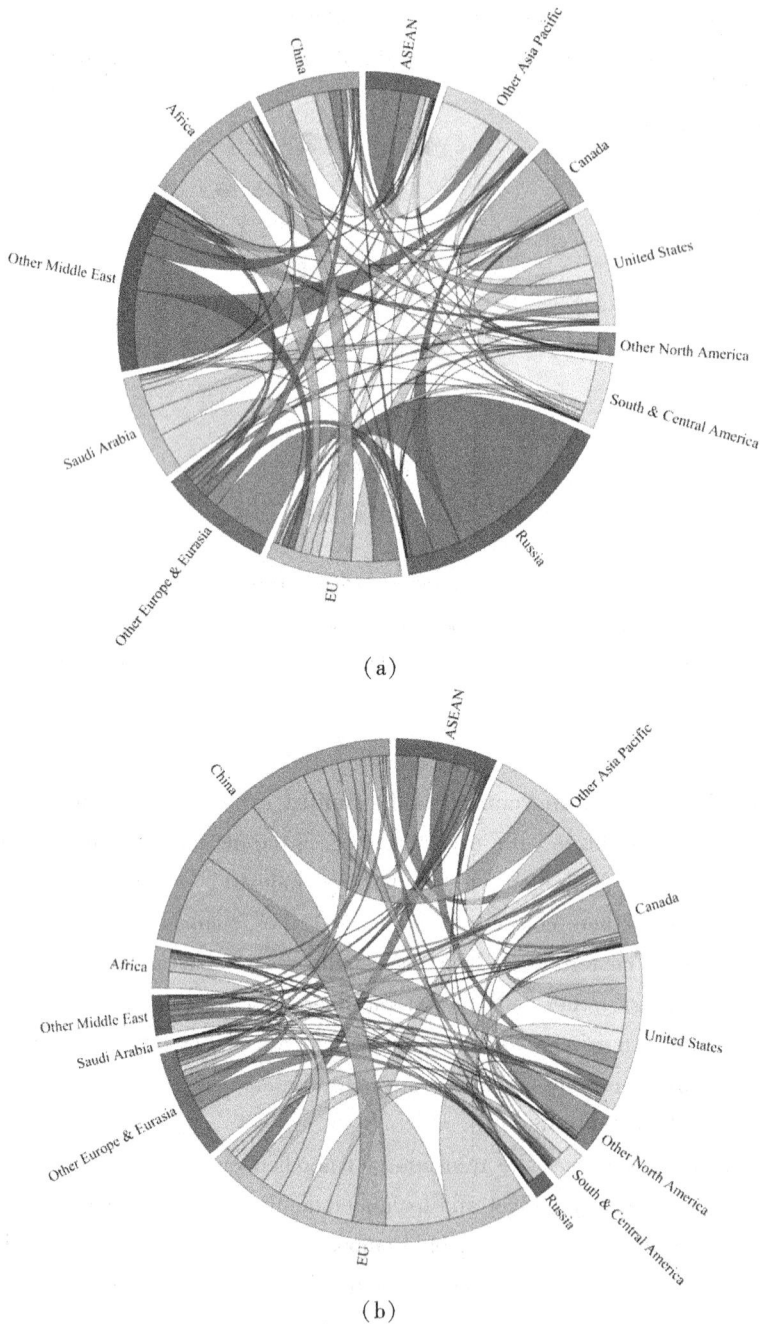

Figure 1. 2. 5　Embodied Energy Connections Between Major Economies by (a) Intermediate Trade and (b) Final Trade (The China region includes the mainland, Hong Kong, Macao and Taiwan; ASEAN stands for Association of Southeast Asian Nations; EU represents the European Union. Other regions are aggregated and detailed information can be found in Appendix D. The trade relations between every two economies are portrayed by the chords. The different thicknesses at the two ends of the chord respectively represent the two connected economies' export volumes of embodied energy to each other. The chord is colored by the larger exporter of the two.)

By contrast, EU and China hold the dominant positions as the leading exporters in final trade, while the United States is the largest final importer. Among all these final trade flows, the largest flow is related to the export from China to the United States. 1. 24E+07 TJ of embodied energy is exported from China, of which 29% is to the United States and 22% to EU. As for the United States, both its biggest import and export market is Canada in the intermediate trade. But in the final trade, China becomes the leading supplier of imported embodied energy use for the United States, and EU is the leading receiver of the United States' export. Russia occupies a smaller part of the circle in final trade (Figure 1. 2. 5(b)) than that in intermediate trade (Figure 1. 2. 5 (a)), because the export of Russia is dominated by energy products, like oil and oil products, which are mostly used for intermediate production instead of final consumption.

In Figure 1. 2. 6, the net trade relationships between the major regions are portrayed for

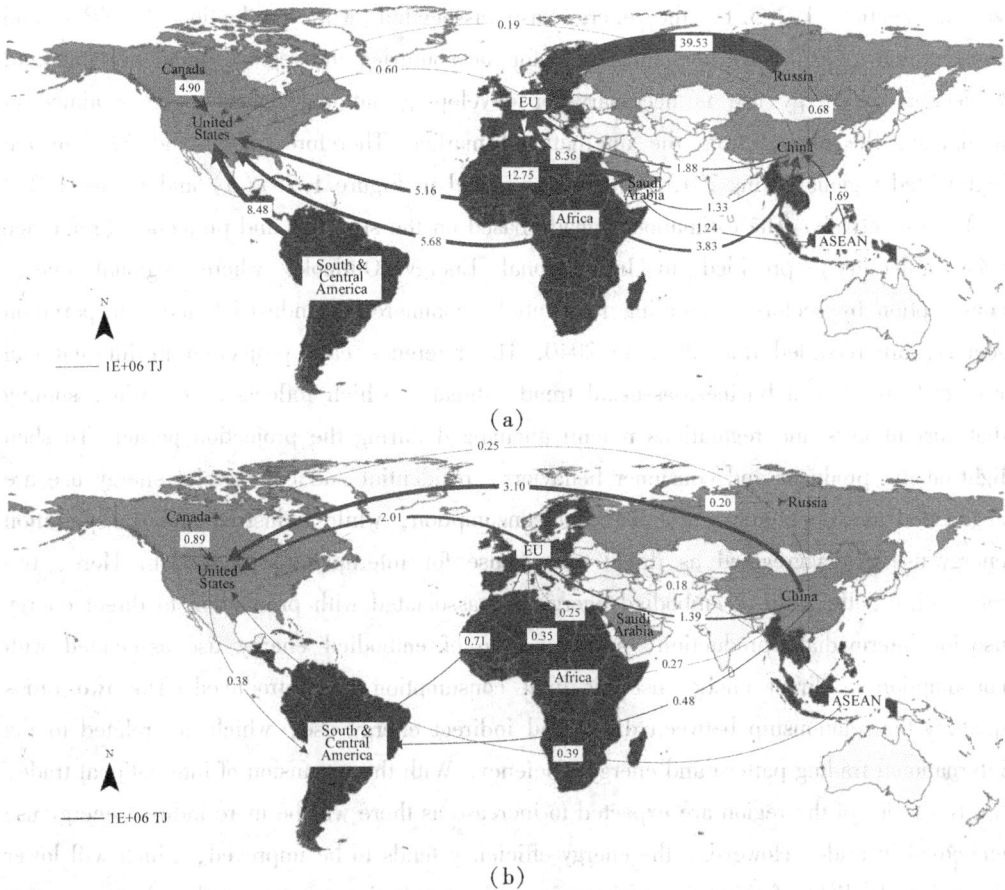

(a)

(b)

Figure 1. 2. 6   Major Net Inter-regional Transfers of Embodied Energy Use in (a) Intermediate Trade and
(b) Final Trade (The numbers expressed by arrows, whose unit is million terajoule energy
use, indicate the amounts of net flows of embodied energy use.)

both intermediate and final trade. In intermediate trade, the United States, EU and Russia are shown as the world's dominant trading centers. Russia acts as a supplier of embodied energy because the energy embodied in its intermediate import is larger than that in its intermediate export, while the United States and EU are two receivers of embodied energy.

In final net trade, the United States is still a typical receiver, but EU turns into a net exporter and Russia becomes a net importer. It is noticed that the arrow between Russia and EU in final trade is in a different direction with that in intermediate trade. Russia exports intermediate materials to EU, but imports finished products from EU. This phenomenon can also be found in the trade between Saudi Arabia and EU and the trade between the African regions and China.

1.2.4 Discussions

1.2.4.1 Energy Use Projection

In Section 1.2.3.1, the energy use associated with production (EEP) and consumption (EEC) have been illustrated for the countries and regions under investigation. Projection of energy use is necessary for developing national energy policies aimed at minimizing the impact from the international market. Therefore, EEP and EEC of ten highlighted regions during 2013-2040 are estimated in Figure 1.2.7(a) and Figure 1.2.7 (b), respectively. The estimation is made based on the statistics and projection (reference case projection) provided in International Energy Outlook, where regional energy consumption by sectors, including residential, commercial, industrial and transportation sectors, are recorded from 2012 to 2040. The reference case projection in International Energy Outlook is a business-as-usual trend estimate, which reflects a scenario assuming that current laws and regulations remain unchanged during the projection period. To shed light on the producer and consumer behaviors, residential and commercial energy use are aggregated as direct energy use for final consumption, while industrial and transportation energy use are aggregated as direct energy use for intermediate production. Here, two ratios, i.e., the ratio of embodied energy use associated with production to direct energy use for intermediate production, and the ratio of embodied energy use associated with consumption to direct energy use for final consumption are introduced. The two ratios quantify the relationship between direct and indirect energy use, which are related to the international trading pattern and energy efficiency. With the expansion of international trade, the two ratios of the region are expected to increase as there will be more indirect energy use embodied in trade. However, the energy efficiency tends to be improved, which will lower the ratios. In light of this, for each region, the two ratios are assumed to keep constant during the focused period as in previous studies.

In 2013 China's EEP is 13% larger than that of the United States and is projected to be

57% larger by 2040. Production activities play a dominant role in China's economy of 2013, but the situation will change in 2028 when for the first time the energy use related to the consumption activities in China is expected to exceed that related to the production activities there. Nowadays, China is committed to expanding domestic consumption demand, in order to create a consumption-led economy for stable economic development in the long term. Therefore, a consumption boom is predicted to come to China in the near future. Energy use in India is the world's fastest growing (Figure 1. 2. 7), with India projected to replace Japan as both the world's third largest producer (*EEP*) by 2028 and third largest consumer (*EEC*) by 2031. Helped by the decline in global oil prices, India's economy has experienced a fast development in recent years, making "made in India" increasingly popular in international markets, further increasing India's energy use (Figure 1. 2. 7).

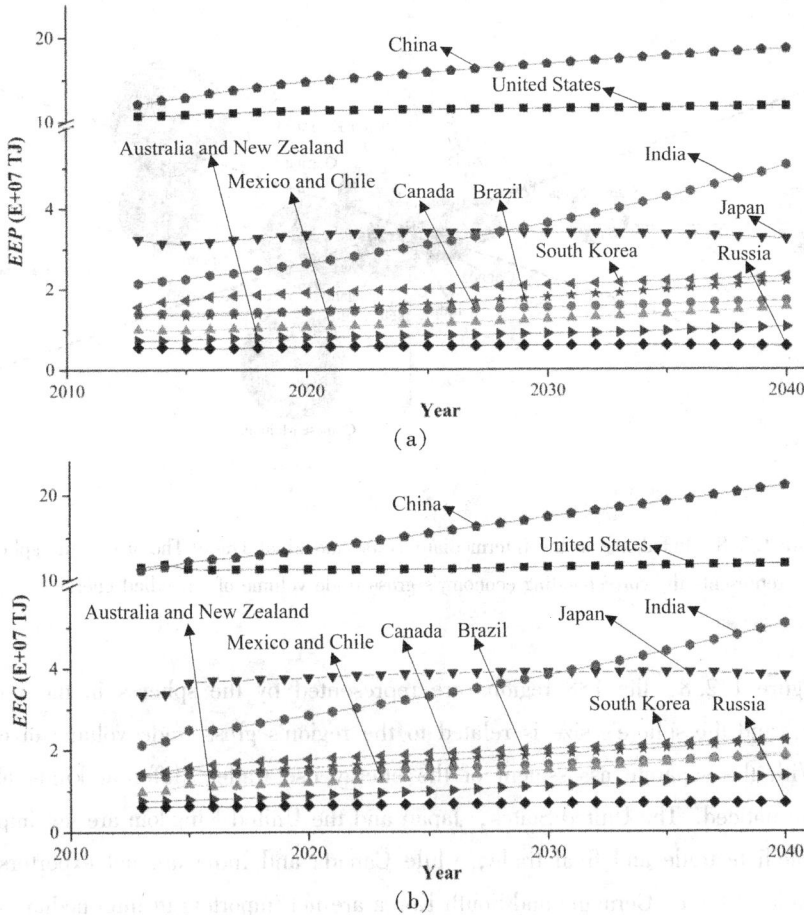

Figure 1. 2. 7　Energy Resources Embodied in (a) Production (*EEP*) and (b) Consumption (*EEC*) for the Ten Regions During 2013-2040 (Australia and New Zealand represents the combined results of Australia and New Zealand, while Mexico and Chile refers to the combined results of Mexico and Chile, in line with the U. S. Energy Information Administration (EIA) statistics.)

1. 2. 4. 2   Energy Trade Imbalance

An increasing scale of global trade imbalance has been witnessed over the years, which is recognized as a source of tensions between nations and a threat to globalization. According to the comparative advantage theory, regions striving for a competitive advantage in the production or delivery of energy-intensive goods or services are more likely to be net exporters of embodied energy. Such energy imbalance occurs in trade for both intermediate production and final consumption, and a comparison between the two energy trade imbalances is made in Figure 1. 2. 8. The net import volume of embodied energy is used to indicate the region's trade imbalance.

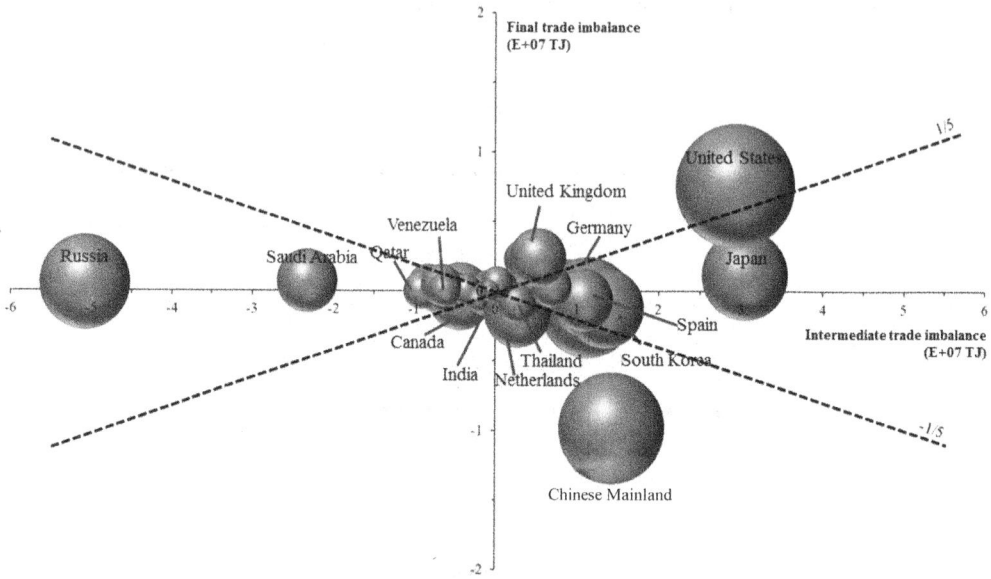

Figure 1. 2. 8   Imbalance in the Intermediate Trade and Final Trade(The size of the sphere represents the corresponding economy's gross trade volume of embodied energy.)

In Figure 1. 2. 8, the 188 regions are represented by the spheres in the rectangular coordinate, and the sphere's size is related to the region's gross trade volume of embodied energy. With the separate assessment of the energy use trade, different kinds of trading patterns are noticed. The United States, Japan and the United Kingdom are net importers in both intermediate trade and final trade, while Canada and India are net exporters in both kinds of trade. China, Germany and South Korea are net importers in intermediate trade but net exporters in final trade, in contrast to Russia and Saudi Arabia as net exporters in intermediate trade but net importers in final trade. For the world as a whole, energy use embodied in intermediate trade is about 5 times that embodied in final trade. Hence, two dotted lines with respective slopes of 1/5 and −1/5 are drawn to represent the global general trading pattern. For the economies that lie between the two lines and are close to the horizontal axis, like Russia, Saudi Arabia, Canada and Germany, they are in a production-oriented trading pattern. In international trade, these nations tend to sell or buy the basic materials and the semi-manufactured goods, which are mainly used for intermediate production instead of directly entering final consumption. On the other hand, the United States, the United Kingdom, India and China are found in a consumption-oriented trading pattern. Their trades mainly focus on the finished products that are directly used for final consumption. The traditional analyses on international energy trade merely confine to the trade of energy commodities themselves, and fail to take account of the indirect energy trade related to non-energy goods. The embodiment research discussed here supplements direct trade theory and clarifies energy trade imbalances.

1.2.4.3 Distinctive Trading Economies

The United States and China are the two biggest economies in international trade of embodied energy, which occupy 10% and 9% of the world's total trade, respectively. For the two countries, the geographic and sectoral patterns of their embodied energy trades are analyzed in further detail in Figure 1.2.9. For the United States, 26% of its total import is from North America, followed by the Asia Pacific (19%) and South and Central America (16%). The mining industry and the heavy manufacturing industry in the foreign regions serve as the two biggest sources of imported goods for the United States. About half of the imported goods are products produced by foreign mining industry, and these goods are mostly required by local heavy manufacturing industry for intermediate production. The import for its final consumption is dominated by the products produced in the heavy and light industry.

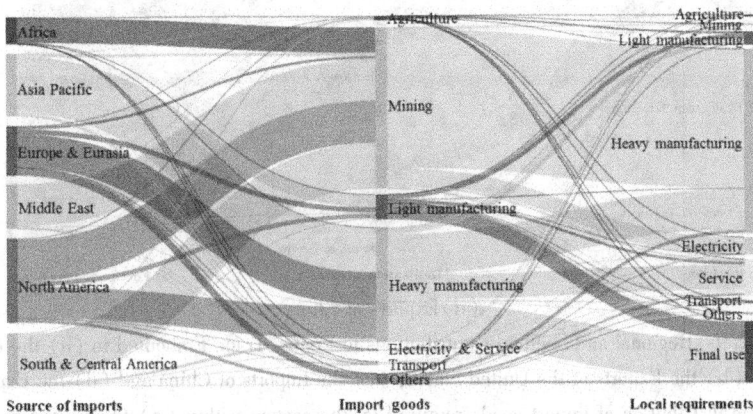

(a) Imports of the United States

43

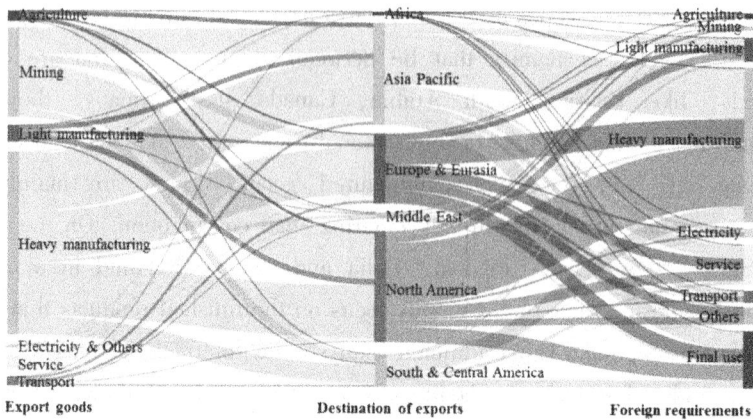

(b)Exports of the United States

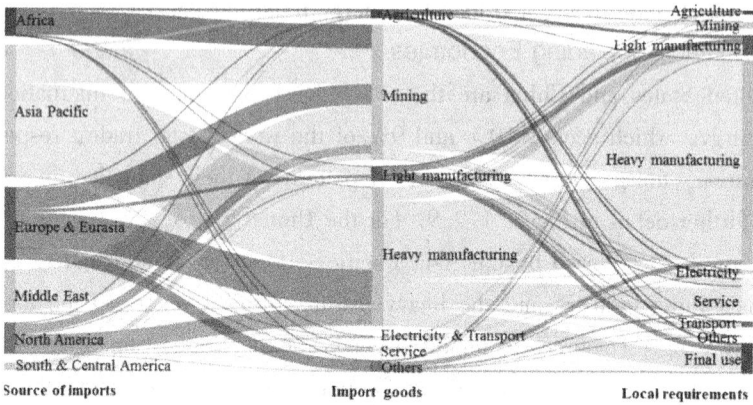

(c)Imports of China

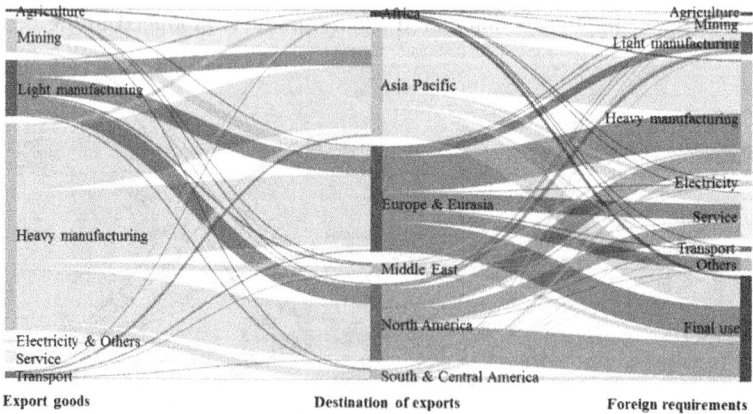

(d)Exports of China

Figure 1. 2. 9   Regional and Sectoral Contributions to Energy Trade Embodied in (a) the Imports of the United States; (b) the Exports of the United States; (c) the Imports of China and (d) the Exports of China (The geographic distribution of import goods required by the sectors within (a) the United States and (c) China are described by the Sankey diagrams. The sectoral structure of export goods from (b) the United States and (d) China driven by foreign regions' demand are analyzed by the Sankey diagrams.)

The embodied energy import of the United States reaches 7. 13E+07 TJ, nearly 3 times of its direct energy import (2. 60E+07 TJ). In recent years, the shale gas revolution has greatly improved the security of energy supplies in the United States. Its direct import of primary energy has continued to decline since 2007 (EIA, 2016b). However, as the United States also needs to import a number of non-energy goods, such as energy-intensive industry products from foreign markets, whether a decline can also be witnessed in its embodied energy import remains to be explored.

In China, the heavy manufacturing industry is the biggest receiver of the imported goods, especially the goods imported from the mining industry in foreign regions, led by the Middle East. Among the United States' export to North America, only 14% is used for final consumption, and the remaining 86% is for intermediate production. But for China, most of its export to North America is to sustain the final consumption there.

1. 2. 5 Conclusions and Policy Implications

Sustainable energy use has become a key issue in sustainable development. In the times of globalization dominated by international trade, regional energy use should not only be confined to the direct use in terms of the on-site consumption of energy products, but also include the indirect use related to the use of non-energy products that require energy inputs during the products' production processes. In both intermediate production and final consumption activities of the economic system, this indirect effect can be witnessed. Based on the embodiment concept, this study provides additional insights into the energy use associated with intermediate production, final consumption, intermediate trade and final trade via the systems input-output method.

For China as the biggest producer, the energy use embodied in its intermediate and final goods exports accounts for approximately one-third of its total exploitation. In contrast, the United States is shown to be the leading consumer, and more than three-fifths of its total (direct and indirect) energy requirements are attributed to the import of intermediate and final goods. Based upon the traditional direct energy accounting, the producers and consumers tend to focus on the reduction of local energy use. The embodiment accounting, however, takes account of the transfer of energy use from the downstream regions to the upstream regions in global supply chains. The producers' and consumers' responsibilities of energy saving and carbon reduction are therefore extended to include those of the upstream regions. This leads the high-income countries to improve the production technologies in the middle- and low-income countries, by sharing their advanced science and technology. The unified and systematic accounting framework for embodied energy described here is of essential importance to implement such extended responsibility at the global scale.

Overall, the energy use embodied in international trade has reached ninety percent of global energy use, in which the energy use trade induced by intermediate production is about five times that for final consumption. Different trading patterns are noticed when the energy trades embodied in intermediate production and final consumption are discussed separately. Russia and Saudi Arabia are the two biggest net exporters of embodied energy in intermediate trade, but in final trade they become net importers with significant dependence on foreign energy. There are few discussions on the issue of energy security for Russia and Saudi Arabia as they are energy-abundant countries. However, their remarkable indirect energy imports in final trade make this issue noteworthy, because any obstacle to the final imports can impact the daily life of local resident immediately. Therefore, the scale of non-energy goods import and the structure of final goods import should arouse the attention of local governments. In addition, China is a net importer in intermediate trade but a net exporter in final trade, acting just as a factory absorbing intermediate goods and producing final goods. Japan's energy trade imbalance is mainly caused by intermediate trade while final trade contributes the most to the United States' trade imbalance. Therefore, intermediate and final trade should be regarded as the focus, respectively, in the trade structure adjustment for Japan and for the United States, in order to address the trade imbalance issue.

As the size of a region's economy has been greatly decoupled from its direct energy use for production or consumption, this embodiment analysis adds to the growing literature showing the importance of considering indirect effects in the pursuit of global energy conservation and carbon reduction.

References

Bullard Iii, C. W., Herendeen, R. A., 1975. The Energy Cost of Goods and Services. *Energy Policy*, 3, 268-278.

Cellura, M., Longo, S., Mistretta, M., 2011. The Energy and Environmental Impacts of Italian Households Consumptions: An Input-output Approach. *Renewable and Sustainable Energy Reviews*, 15, 3897-3908.

Chen, G. Q., Han, M. Y., 2015. Global Supply Chain of Arable Land Use: Production-based and Consumption-based Trade Imbalance. *Land Use Policy*, 49, 118-130.

Costanza, R., 1980. Embodied Energy and Economic Valuation. *Science*, 210, 1219-1224.

Kanemoto, K., Lenzen, M., Peters, G. P., Moran, D. D., Geschke, A., 2012. Frameworks for Comparing Emissions Associated with Production, Consumption, and International Trade. *Environmental Science & Technology*, 46, 172-179.

Liang, S., Wang, Y., Cinnirella, S., Pirrone, N., 2015. Atmospheric Mercury

Footprints of Nations. *Environmental Science & Technology*, 49, 3566-3574.

Odum, H. T., 1996. Environmental Accounting: Emergy and Environmental Decision Making. John Wiley and Sons, New York.

Peters, G. P., 2008. From Production-based to Consumption-based National Emission Inventories. *Ecological Economics*, 65, 13-23.

Shao, L., Guan, D., Wu, Z., Wang, P., Chen, G. Q., 2017. Multi-scale Input-output Analysis of Consumption-based Water Resources: Method and Application. *Journal of Cleaner Production*, 164, 338-346.

WB (Work Bank), 2015. http://data.worldbank.org/indicator/NY.GDP.MKTP.CD.

1. 3　Energy Use by Chinese Economy: A Systems Cross-scale Input-output Analysis[①]

1. 3. 1　Introduction

China has achieved impressive economic growth over the past three decades of reform and opening-up. According to World Bank statistics, China's GDP (Gross Domestic Product) has risen from a mere 6% of the United States levels in 1978 to over 60% in 2015, and its per capita income has increased by 40 times during that period. However, such rapid development is associated with a high cost of natural resources and the environment. In 2015, China's primary energy consumption ascended to 3 billion tons oil equivalent, accounting for 23% of the global total. The proved reserves of fossil fuels in China at the end of 2015 are supposed to be merely able to sustain local production for 31 years. As China keeps up its fast pace of industrialization, the growing demand for the limited energy resources is becoming a major challenge. Meanwhile, energy use is the largest source of anthropogenic emissions of carbon dioxide, which, along with other greenhouse gases, is believed to be the major cause of global climate change. On November 4, 2016, the world's first comprehensive climate agreement of the *Paris Agreement* entered into force. In order to achieve the long-term temperature goal set out in Paris, it is urgent for China, as a leading player among the contracting parties, to explore sustainable development patterns of low energy consumption and low carbon emission.

For the increasingly globalized economy, various researches have pointed out that not only goods and services, but also energy use and pollution emissions can be transferred along the supply chains in inter-regional trade. With the assistance of trade activities, a region or

---

①　Published on *Energy Policy*, Volume 108, pp. 81-90, with a few modifications due to space constraints. Reuse permission has been obtained from Elsevier.

an industry sector could import energy-intensive commodities from other regions or sectors, to avoid its direct energy use. In a previous study on the energy consumption of economic sectors in China, the total amount of indirect energy consumption hidden in the domestic trade was reported in magnitude up to four times of that of direct energy consumption (Liu et al., 2012). Ignorance of the indirect energy use can therefore undermine the efforts for energy conservation and emission reduction.

In this context, embodied energy as a combination of direct and indirect energy, has aroused numerous attention in the academic field towards energy assessment for China. Tang et al. (2016) carried out an evaluation of energy embodied in China's external trade, and found that the embodied energy exports of China approximately tripled between 2002 and 2007. Zhang et al. (2016) turned their attention to China's domestic trade, and provided detailed analyses on regional embodied energy transfers induced by different final demand categories. Moreover, at the regional level, Zhang et al. (2015) investigated the embodied energy flows among China's 30 provinces, and identified Zhejiang and Henan provinces as the largest embodied energy importer and exporter, respectively. At the sectoral level, Hong et al. (2016) estimated the embodied energy use of the construction industry in China, and demonstrated that this sector contributed 29.6% to total national energy consumption. Those embodiment studies have greatly deepened people's understanding of the overall energy performance of China.

However, to properly address the energy problems in China, the literature list of embodied energy analysis for Chinese economy is still very short. Particularly, the investigation with the most recent statistics is in great need, in view of the new challenges met by China in current world. The input-output analysis (IOA) offers an efficient way to track the complex relationship between sectors and regions, and is therefore regarded as the major method for embodied energy calculation. The economic input-output table is the essential data in this method. In December 2015, the input-output table of Chinese economy 2012 is released as the sixth national basic table, which is the most recent available data. Compared with previous tables, the newest table records many changes in China during the period of rapid economic development. For example, a structural change in the economy is witnessed with an increased share of the tertiary industry in GDP, from 38.7% in 2007 to 44.8% in 2012, which is viewed as a main source of change in energy use. Hence, the target of the present work is to present a detailed energy inventory for Chinese economy with the latest data, and to systematically reveal the energy use embodied in production, consumption and trade.

Different from previous researches adopting the equal intensity assumption of imports, this study concretely accounts for the differences of the production technology between domestic and foreign sectors. Limited by available data, the existing studies have generally assumed that imported products have the same embodied intensities as the domestic ones. However, there is a large gap between China and foreign countries in economic structure and production technologies, which are the major determinants of embodied intensity. For example, as revealed by our recent study on global energy use, the embodied energy intensity of the machinery industry in China is shown to be twice that of the world average level. Therefore, it is necessary to differentiate the embodied energy flows from different economies at different scales. Next, energy resources are essentially natural resources, and cannot be simply taken as economic commodities. Most embodiment studies focus on the technical consumption of these commodities. There are many different ways of technical consumption of primary and secondary energies, such as the combustion of coal to provide heat, the conversion of wind kinetic energy to provide power, and the utilization of electricity. However, energy resources belong to the environmental system, which provides the economic system with natural resources as exogenous and external support for economic development. These resources' initial use by the economic system occurs when they are exploited from the earth, because that is when the resources are removed from the environmental system and inputted into the economic system. In these regards, embodied energy intensity of foreign imports of China is calculated based on our previous work on the world economy (Section 1.1) to distinguish the imported commodity from the commodity produced locally, and to highlight the cross-scale effect between China and the rest of the world. The energy use in Chinese economy is tracked from the source of energy exploitation to the sink of embodied energy in final use, to explore an all-inclusive energy budget for China.

1.3.2 Methodology and Data

1.3.2.1 Cross-scale Input-output Model

The input-output analysis (IOA) method has shown an advantage of uncovering the complex interactions between components in the economic system since its introduction in 1930s. In environmental analysis, this advantage of the IOA method is made use of and amplified to measure both the direct and indirect environmental impacts of different economic activities. So far, the IOA method has found wide application in embodiment accounting for ecological endowments such as energy, water, land, carbon emissions, mercury releases and so forth.

Based on the idea of "conservation of embodied energy", a systems IOA method is developed to evaluate the embodiment performance of both final use and intermediate production activities in economies. Due to lack of data for imported products, the single-scale systems IOA model was firstly built with an assumption that the imported and domestic products from the same industry are produced via the same technology and these products have an equal embodied intensity. This assumption to get around the cross-scale effect between local economy and the rest of the world, however, leads to serious errors when there exist great differences between the domestic and foreign production technologies. This problem offers new possibilities for accounting improvement, and a cross-scale model is therefore introduced. In line with the general model for multi-scale input-output analysis, a cross-scale diagram of energy use in Chinese economy is illustrated in Figure 1.3.1.

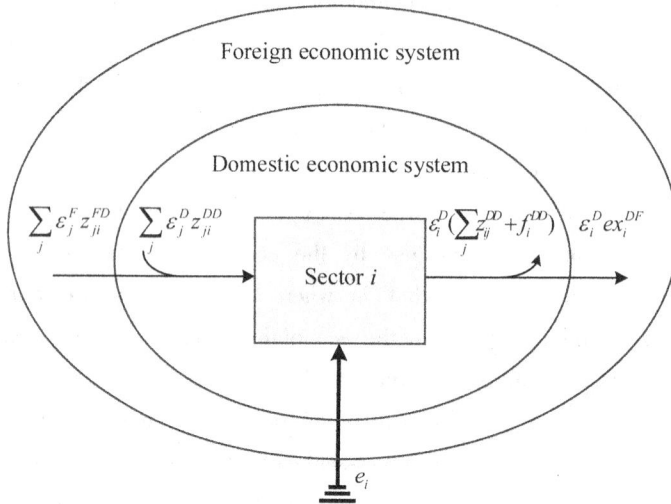

Figure 1.3.1   Cross-scale Energy Use Diagram for Chinese Economy

For a specific sector in domestic economy, it receives direct energy resources inputs (e_i) from local environment, and indirect energy resources inputs embodied in intermediate goods from domestic sectors ($\sum_j \varepsilon_j^D z_{ji}^{DD}$) and foreign sectors ($\sum_j \varepsilon_j^F z_{ji}^{FD}$). The superscripts of D and F are used here to distinguish between the two systems of domestic economic system and foreign economic system. ε_j^D denotes the embodied energy intensities of goods or services from Sector j in domestic economic system, corresponding to z_{ji}^{DD}, which is defined as the intermediate inputs from domestic Sector j to domestic Sector i. Similarly, z_{ji}^{FD} represents the foreign intermediate inputs, which have an embodied intensity of ε_j^F. Owing to these inputs, this sector can produce goods or provide services to sustain domestic intermediate production (z_{ij}^{DD}) and final demand (f_i^{DD}), and to meet the requirements from foreign markets as exports (ex_i^{DF}). ε_i^D describes the embodied energy intensity of the outputs from this sector. Therefore, an input-output balance of embodied energy flows can be induced as

$$e_i + \sum_j \varepsilon_j^F z_{ji}^{FD} + \sum_j \varepsilon_j^D z_{ji}^{DD} = \varepsilon_i^D \left(\sum_j z_{ij}^{DD} + f_i^{DD} \right) + \varepsilon_i^D ex_i^{DF} \qquad (1.3.1)$$

In fact, the economic input-output tables of competitive imports type for Chinese economy are regularly constructed by statistics departments, as shown in Table 1.3.1. In the table, the economy is divided into n industrial sectors. The definitions of symbols of z_{ij}, f_i and ex_i are the same as those in Figure 1.3.1, but without superscripts as indicators to identify where they are from. This is because the imported goods are not clearly differentiated from those produced locally in this table. To integrate concerned environmental, foreign and domestic energy flows, a cross-scale input-output table (see Table 1.3.2) for Chinese economy is compiled on basis of the conventional economic input-output table released. The information associated with environmental resources (e_i) is covered in the table and the value-added part in the conventional table is replaced. Moreover, the intermediate exchange (z_{ij}), final demand (f_i) and exports (ex_i) are all divided into two parts according to the proportion of local total outputs to foreign imports as in many other studies. The related equations are:

Table 1. 3. 1　Scheme of the Economic Input-output Table for Chinese Economy

Sale ╲ Purchase		Intermediate use			Final use		Imports
		Sector 1	$\cdots$	Sector n	Final demand	Exports	
Intermediate input	Sector 1						
	$\cdots$			z_{ij}	f_i	ex_i	im_i
	Sector n						
Value added				v_j			

Table 1. 3. 2　Scheme of the Cross-scale Energy Input-output Table for Chinese Economy

Sale ╲ Purchase		Intermediate use			Final use	
		Sector 1	$\cdots$	Sector n	Final demand	Exports
Domestic intermediate input	Sector 1					
	$\cdots$			z_{ij}^{DD}	f_i^{DD}	ex_i^{DF}
	Sector n					
Foreign imported intermediate input	Sector 1					
	$\cdots$			z_{ij}^{FD}	f_i^{FD}	ex_i^{FF}
	Sector n					
Direct energy input				e_j		

$$z_{ij}^{DD} = z_{ij}(x_i / (x_i + im_i)) \tag{1.3.2}$$

$$z_{ij}^{FD} = z_{ij}(im_i / (x_i + im_i)) \tag{1.3.3}$$

$$f_i^{DD} = f_i(x_i / (x_i + im_i)) \tag{1.3.4}$$

$$f_i^{FD} = f_i(im_i / (x_i + im_i)) \tag{1.3.5}$$

$$ex_i^{DF} = ex_i(x_i / (x_i + im_i)) \tag{1.3.6}$$

$$ex_i^{FF} = ex_i(im_i / (x_i + im_i)) \tag{1.3.7}$$

where $x_i (= \sum_j z_{ij} + f_i + ex_i - im_i)$ stands for the local total outputs of Sector i.

1.3.2.2   Algorithm

After the cross-scale input-output table is complied, the next step is to obtain the domestic sectoral embodied energy intensity. When all sectors in Chinese economy are considered, a matrix form of the input-output balance equation (Equation (1.3.1)) can be deduced as

$$\mathbf{E} + \boldsymbol{\varepsilon}^F \mathbf{Z}^{FD} + \boldsymbol{\varepsilon}^D \mathbf{Z}^{DD} = \boldsymbol{\varepsilon}^D \hat{\mathbf{X}} \tag{1.3.8}$$

in which $\mathbf{E} = [e_i]_{1 \times n}$, $\boldsymbol{\varepsilon}^F = [\varepsilon_i^F]_{1 \times n}$, $\mathbf{Z}^{FD} = [z_{ij}^{FD}]_{n \times n}$, $\boldsymbol{\varepsilon}^D = [\varepsilon_i^D]_{1 \times n}$, $\mathbf{Z}^{DD} = [z_{ij}^{DD}]_{n \times n}$ and $\mathbf{X} = [x_i]_{n \times 1}$ ($\hat{\mathbf{X}}_{n \times n}$ is the corresponding diagonal matrix). The embodied intensities of domestic sectors are calculated as

$$\boldsymbol{\varepsilon}^D = (\mathbf{E} + \boldsymbol{\varepsilon}^F \mathbf{Z}^{FD})(\hat{\mathbf{X}} - \mathbf{Z}^{DD})^{-1} \tag{1.3.9}$$

In this way, energy embodied in final use (EEF), can be obtained as the sum of energy use embodied in final demand and exports of each sector (EEF_i).

$$EEF = \sum_i EEF_i = \sum_i (\varepsilon_i^D(f_i^{DD} + ex_i^{DF}) + \varepsilon_i^F(f_i^{FD} + ex_i^{FF})) \tag{1.3.10}$$

Energy use embodied in imports (EEI), exports (EEX) and trade balance (EEB) can be calculated as

$$EEI = \sum_i EEI_i = \sum_i (\varepsilon_i^F(\sum_j z_{ij}^{FD} + f_i^{FD} + ex_i^{FF})) \tag{1.3.11}$$

$$EEX = \sum_i EEX_i = \sum_i (\varepsilon_i^D ex_i^{DF} + \varepsilon_i^F ex_i^{FF}) \tag{1.3.12}$$

$$EEB = \sum_i EEB_i = \sum_i (EEI_i - EEX_i) \tag{1.3.13}$$

EEI_i indicates the energy use embodied in imports of Sector i for both intermediate production ($\sum_j z_{ij}^{FD}$) and final use ($f_i^{FD} + ex_i^{FF}$). In contrast, EEX_i represents the energy use embodied in goods or services exported by Sector i, and these exports can be produced locally (ex_i^{DF}), or imported from international market (ex_i^{FF}). Accordingly, a sector receives positive EEB_i (embodied energy surplus) when its EEI_i exceeds EEX_i, and receives negative EEB_i (embodied energy deficit) vice versa.

1.3.2.3   Data Sources

At the domestic scale of Chinese economy, the economic input-output table 2012 is adopted in this study. In the table, Chinese economy is simulated as a 139-sector coupled system, as provided in Appendix F. The economic flows are expressed in producers' prices in 2012 with a unit of Ren Min Bi (RMB hereafter). Additionally, included seven sources for direct energy input are divided into two groups as fossil fuels (coal, crude oil and natural gas) and non-fossil fuels (biomass, hydroenergy, nuclear energy and other renewable energy). The statistics of energy exploitation are collected from China Energy Statistical Yearbook by calorific value calculation and Tian's study (Tian, 2014). Nuclear electricity production efficiency is assumed to be 33%. Because part of the fossil fuels is used as raw materials for industrial production instead of energy sources, they are excluded from energy statistics. The non-energy use portions of coal, crude oil and natural gas in China are calculated as 1.22%, 14.15% and 9.94%, separately. In total, the primary energy resources exploited by Chinese economic system in 2012 amount to 9.58E + 07 TJ. In recognition of the fact that coal resources are generally exploited by the mining sectors, the coal exploitation data are allocated into Sector 6 (Mining and washing of coal) based on the physical entry scheme originated in embodied energy accounting. Likewise, the production data of crude oil, natural gas, biomass, hydroenergy, nuclear energy and other renewables are allocated into corresponding primary energy sectors, respectively. Detailed distribution is listed in Table 1.3.3.

Table 1.3.3 Sectoral Distribution of Direct External Energy Inputs for Chinese Economy (Unit: TJ)

Sector	Coal	Crude oil	Natural gas	Biomass	Hydroenergy	Nuclear energy	Others	Total
1				3.83E+06				3.83E+06
2				2.13E+06				2.13E+06
3				3.29E+05				3.29E+05
6	7.35E+07							7.35E+07
7		7.42E+06	3.69E+06					1.11E+07
9						1.10E+06		1.10E+06
96				3.19E+06			6.24E+05	3.81E+06

At the global scale, the Eora input-output database and the energy database by International Energy Agency (IEA) are employed to calculate the sectoral embodied energy intensities in foreign regions of 2012 according to the method introduced in our previous work. The relevant data of China are excluded from the calculation and the sectoral average embodied intensities of the rest of the world are taken as embodied intensities of the corresponding sector's imports. To comply with Chinese economic input-output table, the 26 sectors recorded in global economy are broken down into 139 sectors, as displayed in Appendix G.

1. 3. 2. 4   Uncertainties

In the cross-scale input-output model, two economic systems are taken into consideration. One is Chinese economy embracing 139 sectors, and the other is the foreign economy composed of 26 sectors in 188 countries or regions. It should be noted that there are 189 countries or regions in total in the input-output table from the Eora database, and the region of China is excluded when thinking about the foreign economy. In combining Chinese economy with the foreign economy, sectoral aggregation and spatial aggregation have resulted in uncertainties. In the economic input-output table, small industries and areas are aggregated into broad sectors and regions respectively based on the homogeneous assumptions, for a trade-off between data quality and compilation time. As a result, Chinese economy is simplified as a 139-sector economy, while the foreign economy as a 188-region, 26-sector economy. The imports of the 139 sectors in China are from the foreign economy in the cross-scale input-output model, in order to adjust the equal intensity assumption of imports adopting in previous studies. However, due to data constraints, the embodied energy intensity of the imports is just the weighted average value of the 188 foreign regions, rather than the figure of the region where the imports are from. The average intensity assumption of imports is a major limitation of the model, and a more accurate statistic of external trade information of China can fix the problem.

In addition, the Eora database provides the most recent data for the world economy, so it is chosen in this research. But it is noted that the level of sector detail provided by Eora is much lower than that by our government, as there are 26 sectors in the foreign economy but 139 sectors in Chinese economy. Therefore, it is also a main source of uncertainty to aggregate the imported commodities of the 139 sectors into 26 foreign industries. Although such uncertainties are witnessed in the cross-scale input-output model, this study improves the treatment of foreign imports and shed light on the exchanges between different economies at different scales, which will contribute to high-quality embodied energy accounting.

The information on energy use is another source of uncertainty. To match the energy use data with economic input-output data, energy use flows are allocated to economic sectors. In our research, each kind of energy resource is allocated to the corresponding mining sector according to the physical entry scheme. For example, three kinds of biomass are considered here, including straw, fuelwood and biogas. The straw biomass is allocated to the farming sector as it is produced originally by this sector. However, different farming activities with large variances are aggregated into this sector. Therefore, this allocation scheme could yield an underestimate for straw-related industries, and an overestimate for the other ones.

1.3.3 Results

1.3.3.1 Embodied Energy Intensity

Illustrated in Figure 1.3.2 are embodied energy intensities of the 139 sectors in Chinese economy. The embodied energy intensity represents an important indicator for evaluating the environmental pressure caused by the sector's economic activities. In Chinese economy, Sector 6 (Mining and washing of coal) holds the top volume of embodied energy intensity as 3.97E-01 TJ/10,000 RMB, followed by Sector 40 (Manufacture of coke products), Sector 96 (Production and supply of electricity and steam) and Sector 39 (Manufacture of refined petroleum products, processing of nuclear fuel). But there are differences between the four sectors in terms of their roles in the energy supply chains. Sectors 6 and 96 are energy miners that impose direct stress on resources during the exploitation process. In contrast, Sectors 40 and 39 are downstream processing sectors that are supplied with energy by other sectors via domestic and foreign trade, and impose indirect stress on resources along supply chains. As indicated in Equation (1.3.8), sectoral embodied energy intensity is induced by three sources, respectively corresponding to the three terms on the left side of the equation. First is related to the direct exploitation as direct energy input, and its contribution is represented by the white triangles in the figure. Direct exploitation occurs merely in the seven primary energy sectors as listed in Table 1.3.3 above. Second is the foreign imported energy input as embodied energy in imports from foreign regions, and is represented by the black triangles. The remaining is contributed by the domestic trade.

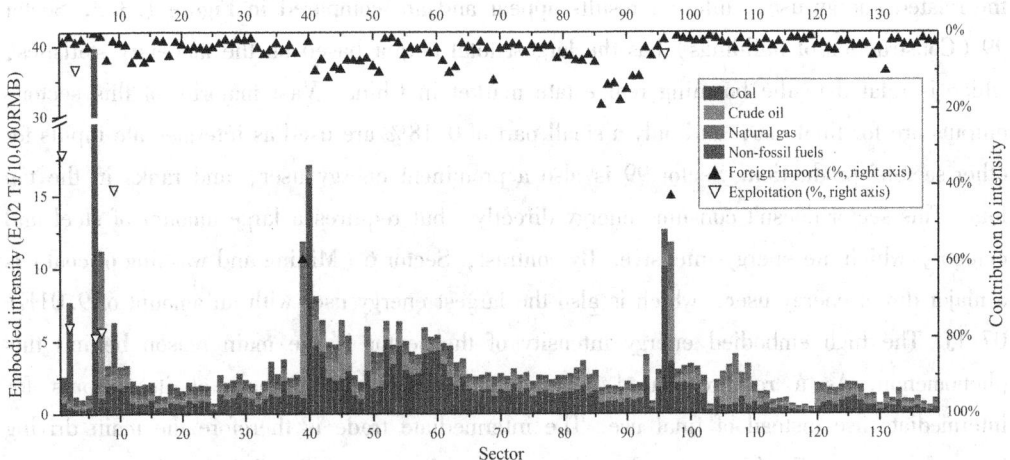

Figure 1.3.2 Sectoral Embodied Energy Intensity for Chinese Economy (Sectoral information corresponding to the sector code is provided in Appendix F.)

The results show that the direct exploitation contributes 81. 52% to the embodied energy intensity of Sector 6, while domestic trade and foreign trade are respectively the major contributors to the intensities of Sectors 40 and 39 with fractions of 97. 60% and 59. 64%. Therefore, different measures should be taken in sectoral regulation with respect to different contributors to their embodied energy intensity. For Sector 6, mining optimization and coal price adjustment could reduce the environmental stress, while the adjustment of domestic and external trade structure should be attached due importance in Sectors 40 and 39, separately.

With the help of trade, the sectors without direct energy use or consumption can own the usefulness of energy resources and exert pressure on the environment. Some sectors, such as some tertiary industries, are regarded as the zero-energy sectors or clean sectors based on the traditional direct accounting, but from the embodiment perspective, a considerable number of energy resources are hidden in their supply chains. For example, Sector 121 (Business services) has an embodied energy intensity of 2. 05E-02 TJ/10,000 RMB, which is even larger than that of some light manufacturing sectors, like Sector 32 (Manufacture of leather, fur, feather and its products). Many works have been conducted to examine the life cycle environmental burdens of specific projects, like power plants and buildings. The sectoral embodied energy intensities obtained here can therefore serve to build a latest and unified database for such systems ecological evaluations.

1. 3. 3. 2   Energy Embodied in Total Output

Total output reflects the general scale of production activities in the region. According to the statistics, the total output of Chinese economy is 160 trillion RMB. When thinking about the related energy use, different results appear and are compared in Figure 1. 3. 3. Sector 99 (Construction of buildings) has the largest total output based on the monetary statistics, which is related to the booming real estate market in China. Vast majority of this sector's outputs are for final use, and only a small part of 0. 18% are used as intermediate inputs for other sectors' production. Sector 99 is also a prominent energy user, and ranks in the top four. This sector doesn't consume energy directly, but requires a large amount of steel and cement, which are energy-intensive. By contrast, Sector 6 (Mining and washing of coal) is a major direct energy user, which is also the largest energy user with an amount of 9. 01E+ 07 TJ. The high embodied energy intensity of the sector is the main reason behind this phenomenon. As a resource-based sector, Sector 6 provides most of its outputs for intermediate use instead of final use. The intermediate trade is therefore the main driving force of energy use in this sector. In order to reduce its energy use, it is important to control the energy demand of the trade partners of the sector. The optimization of production processes in other sectors therefore relieves the stress of Sector 6 on energy resources. Similarly, the outputs of both Sectors 96 (Production and supply of electricity and steam) and 39 (Manufacture of refined petroleum products, processing of nuclear energy use fuel) are also dominated by outputs for intermediate use. In contrast, the outputs of Sector 99 are mainly for final use, which is the primary cause for energy use in this sector. The energy demand related to the consumption activities of households and governments, and the investment and export activities of enterprises become the keys to energy use reduction in this sector.

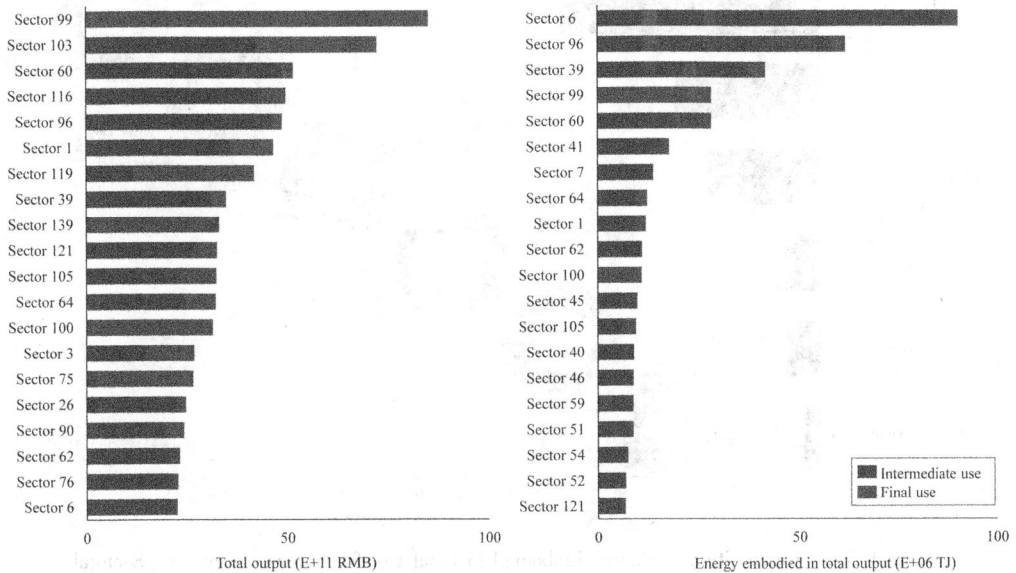

Figure 1.3.3   Sectoral Energy Use Embodied in Total Output (Sectoral information corresponding to the sector code is provided in Appendix F.)

1. 3. 3. 3   Energy Embodied in Final Use

In total, the energy embodied in final use (EEF) is equal to the sum of local energy resources exploited and embodied energy in imports, amounting to 1.50E+08 TJ. Based on Chinese input-output table, final use can be divided into six categories, namely, rural household consumption, urban household consumption, government consumption, gross fixed capital formation, changes in inventories and exports. As illustrated in Figure 1.3.4, gross fixed capital formation causes 6.46E+07 TJ of energy use, with the top fraction as 43.06% of the total, 76% larger than the total household consumption. Exports also occupy a remarkable proportion of 23.97%, approximately equal to that of total household consumption. As the largest developing country, China is still in the process of industrialization and urbanization, which requires substantial resources in its domestic infrastructure construction. Consequently, most energy use in this country is not for consumption, but for investment and production. Energy embodied in urban household use is 2. 85E+07 TJ, 3. 45 times of that embodied in rural household use. In China, the urban residents make up 52. 57% of the population, slightly outnumber the rural population. In per capita terms, the energy use in rural areas just reaches one-third of that in urban areas, revealing the striking gap in living conditions between rural and urban areas.

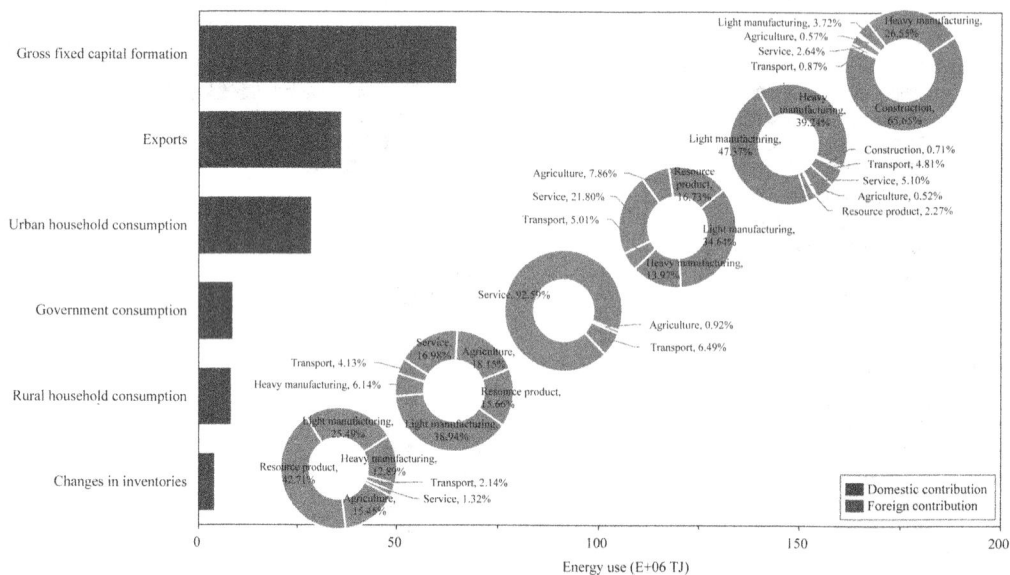

Figure 1. 3. 4   Composition of Energy Embodied in Final Use for Chinese Economy (Sectoral information is provided in Appendix F.)

Energy use in the six categories is originated from two sources referring to Equation (1. 3. 10): goods produced by domestic sectors and goods imported from foreign sectors. In the whole, domestic sectors are responsible for most of the final use. The sectoral energy use for different final use categories is also displayed in the plot. For clarity, the sectors are divided into seven groups, and detailed information can be found in Appendix F. The construction industry occupies the largest portion of 65. 65% in gross fixed capital formation, followed by the industry of heavy manufacturing. The rapid increase of estate prices in China greatly stimulates estate sales, and hence promotes the development of construction industry.

1. 3. 3. 4   Energy Embodied in Trade

Figure 1. 3. 5 portrays the embodied energy in imports and exports by sector. The energy embodied in total imports is 5. 42E + 07 TJ, of which 90. 20% is imported for intermediate production, and 9. 80% is for final use. Sector 7 (Extraction of crude petroleum and natural gas) is the largest importer, and 2. 91E+07 TJ of energy is embodied in its imports, above half of the total imports. Domestic production of crude oil in China has been recognized as being in the plateau stage, but the country's demand for oil is still growing rapidly in the industrialization process. Hence, China depends heavily on the imported oil. The imports of the tertiary industry are relatively small, and zero import can even be found in some sectors, such as Sector 124 (Technique promotion and application services).

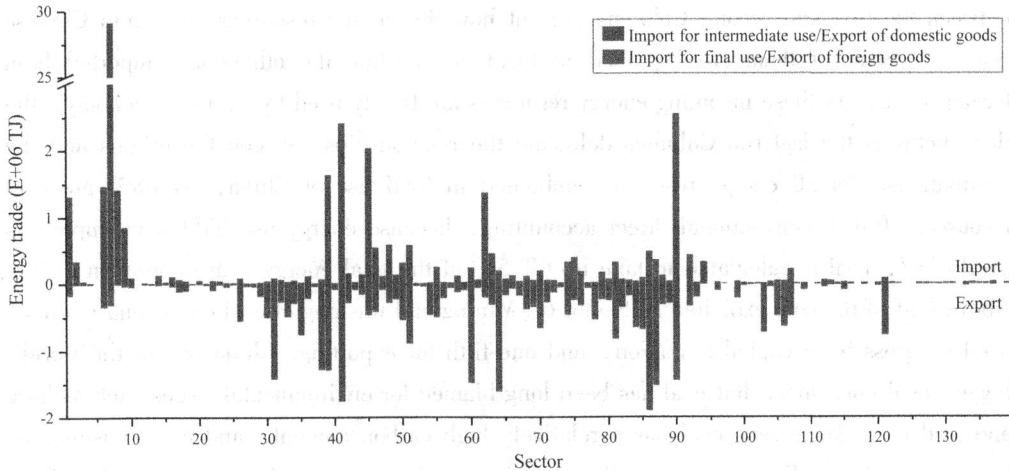

Figure 1. 3. 5　Energy Embodied in Imports and Exports of Chinese Economy (Sectoral information corresponding to the sector code is provided in Appendix F.)

The energy embodied in total exports is 3. 59E+07 TJ, of which 93. 00% is related to the exports produced by domestic sectors, and 7. 00% is embodied in re-export trade. Sector 86 (Manufacture of computer) is the leading exporter, accounting for 5. 28% of the total exports, followed by Sector 41 (Manufacture of basic chemicals) and Sector 64 (Manufacture of fabricated metal products, except machinery and equipment).

China acts as a net importer of embodied energy with a net import volume of 1. 83E+07 TJ. Among the 139 sectors, 37 sectors are net importers and 90 sectors are net exporters. Sector 7 has the largest net import volume of 2. 88E + 07 TJ, followed by Sectors 45 (Manufacture of synthetic materials) and 8 (Mining of ferrous metal ores), in contrast to Sectors 86, 64 and 31 (Manufacture of textile wearing apparel) as the top three biggest net exporters.

1. 3. 4　Discussion

1. 3. 4. 1　Energy Security

In the recent report of the Thirteenth Five-year Plan, developing a secure, clean, efficient and low-carbon energy system is a top priority for our government. In this section, the energy problems in China are discussed from an embodiment perspective. The energy use in China is tracked from the source where the energy resources are exploited, to the sink where the final use occurs, as shown in Figure 1.3.6. The energy resources investigated in this study are classified into four types, which are listed in the first Column in the figure. The second Column describes the origin of the energy resources used by Chinese economy, while the third Column corresponds to the destination of these energy resources. The flows between the first and second Columns present how the energy resources enter into Chinese economy. Some of them are exploited in local areas while the others are imported from foreign areas. As these incoming energy resources are finally used by Chinese economy, the flows between the last two Columns delineate the relationships between the origins and the destinations. For all energy resources embodied in final use of China, 54.08% are coal resources. But in conventional direct accounting, because energy use hidden in imports is overlooked, coal is calculated to take up 68.5% of the total energy consumption in China. Above half of the coal exploited by Sector 6 (Mining and washing of coal) in China is finally used for gross fixed capital formation, and one-fifth for exporting. China is now the world's biggest coal consumer, but coal has been long blamed for environmental issues such as haze and acid rain. Moreover, coal has a relatively high carbon content, and coal consumption has become the leading source of anthropogenic greenhouse gas emissions. In 2015, China promised to peak carbon emissions by around 2030 in the climate conference in Paris. Therefore, to fulfill the commitment, the energy structure should be adjusted and optimized in the aspects of both source and sink. More efforts need to be made toward the reduction of the share of fossil fuels in the energy supply, as well as the control of final use.

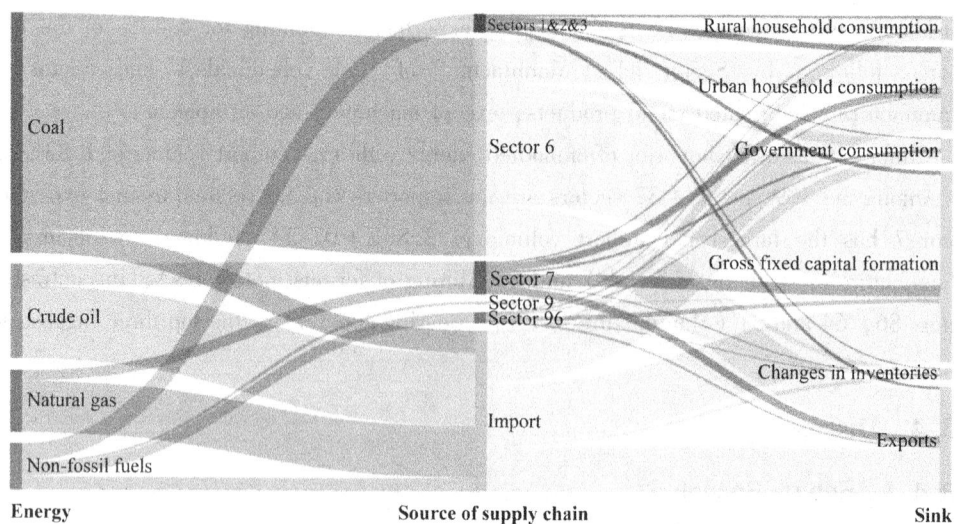

Figure 1.3.6   A Source-to-sink Budget for Energy Use in Chinese Economy

With the rapid economic growth, China becomes increasingly dependent on energy imports, especially oil imports. According to the national statistics, the share of energy imports in China's total energy consumption grows from 9. 75% in 2000 to 17. 08% in 2012. The external dependence degree of oil, which is defined as the ratio of net oil imports over total oil consumption, is reported to reach 61. 10% in 2012, far exceeding the critical threshold of 50% recognized by the international society. From the embodiment viewpoint, 36. 13% of the energy resources embodied in final use are foreign resources. In Chen and Chen's (2013) study on the world economy 2007, the foreign resources' share in China's total energy requirements was reported to be 42%, in contrast to 30% in 2010. Such differences can be attributed to the different study years chosen in these researches and the data resolution, especially sectoral aggregation in their input-output tables. Regarding crude oil, this ratio reaches 76. 78%, one-fourth in magnitude larger than the conventional external dependence degree of oil. These foreign resources are imported directly and indirectly (as embodied in non-energy imports) by China. But the indirect imports aren't taken into account by conventional direct energy accounting. In order to enhance energy security, direct energy imports have been widely discussed. But it is also worth noting that indirect energy imports have caused indirect energy dependence and indirect energy insecurity, which cannot be neglected in the course of sustainable energy development. This embodiment analysis can supplement the existing works on direct accounting and illuminate the energy security issue.

1. 3. 4. 2 Energy Trade Imbalance

Sector 7 (Extraction of crude petroleum and natural gas) has the largest effect on China's energy trade imbalance. The net import volume of embodied energy of this sector is 1. 57 times of that of the whole country. The hefty oil imports of China and the high embodied intensity of the sector are the major causes. The imports of Sector 7 grew from 0. 58 trillion RMB in 2007 to 1. 43 trillion RMB in 2012, and its share in China's total imports reached 11. 71% in 2012, 1. 50 times of the level five years ago. Such growth in oil and gas imports records the increasing energy demand in China, and turns China from a net exporter of embodied energy in 2007 (Chen and Chen, 2013) into a net importer in 2012. In the foreign economy, Sector 7 has the largest embodied energy intensity among the 139 sectors as shown in Appendix G, and there are two reasons for it. One is the massive oil and gas exploitation in foreign regions. According to IEA statistics, 60. 44% of total primary energy supply in the foreign market came from crude oil and natural gas in 2012. The other is the physical entry scheme adopted in the present study. The direct energy inputs are taken as natural resources exogenous to the economy, and are distributed to the mining sectors, which record the resources' original entry into the economy. The role of primary energy exploitation sectors is therefore strengthened in the physical entry scheme, making Sector 7 own a remarkable intensity. In contrast, the technical consumption scheme in previous researches assumes the direct energy input occurs at the point of energy combustion/conversion. All purchased energy resources are considered as economic commodities, and the sectors consuming these commodities are highlighted. Tang et al. (2016) calculated the embodied energy intensity for Chinese economy based on the technical consumption scheme, and reached the conclusion that China was a net exporter in 2012. In their study, the embodied intensity of Sector 7 measures the amount of energy consumed to sustain the sector's economic activities, while all energy resources that are mined or consumed by the sector are assessed in this study. The physical entry scheme reflects the physical cost of the sectors, and is adopted here to shed light on the interaction between the environmental and economic systems, and track the environmental impacts of all the economic activities.

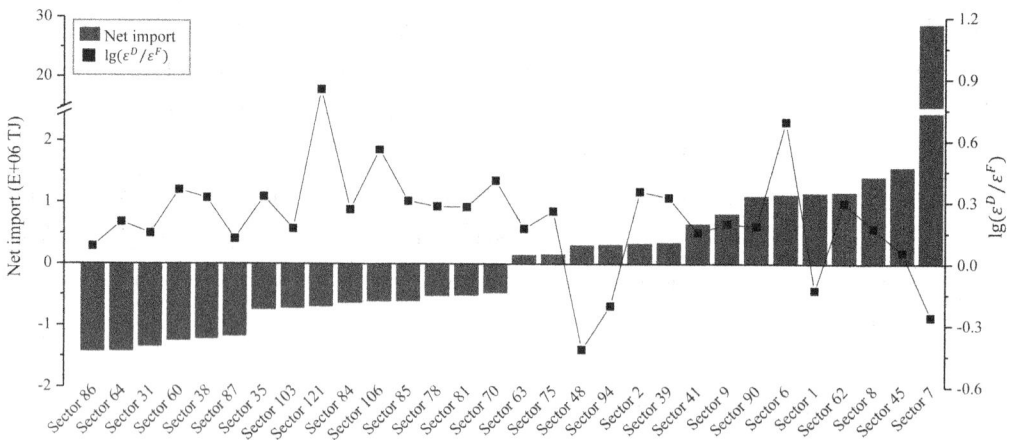

Figure 1.3.7   Sectoral Trade Imbalance and Embodied Energy Intensity (Sectoral information corresponding to the sector code is provided in Appendix F.)

In classical economics, the comparative advantage theory points out that each country can benefit if it exports the goods for which it has a comparative advantage, and imports the other goods. This theory is also true in the fields of resources and environment. The country with a relative lower embodied energy intensity can produce the goods at a lower energy cost, and thus shows an advantage in resources conservation over other countries. Trade between parties with different comparative advantages can therefore make the global production more efficient. Based on this theory, Kander et al. (2015) proposed an improved consumption-based accounting framework by considering the disparity between the domestic and foreign embodied intensities. It shows that if a certain exported commodity of a country has a lower embodied intensity than the world average level, the country should be encouraged to produce and export this commodity, because the alternative production it replaces in the world market wound consume more resources and produce more pollution.

For the leading sectors contributing to China's trade imbalance in terms of embodied energy, their embodied intensities are compared to those of the relevant foreign sectors, respectively, in Figure 1.3.7. Sector 86 (Manufacture of computer) is the largest net exporter. But it is noted that this sector in China has an embodied intensity of 1.78E-02 TJ/ 10,000 RMB, 21.74% larger than the foreign average level, which is due to the inferior production technology in China. In total, China exports 1.10 trillion RMB worth of computers to other foreign regions, and requires 1.96E + 06 TJ of energy resources to produce these exports. But if these computers are manufactured in foreign regions, 1.61E+ 06 TJ of energy resources on average would be enough. Therefore, for the global benefit of resources conservation, the exports of computer from China needs to be reduced. But as China has an advantage in the labor source and raw-material prices, its export of computer is the result of the law of comparative advantage in economics. So it is now back to the fundamental and difficult problem, how to choose between the economic profit and the environment. This problem can also be witnessed in other sectors, as well as in other low and middle income countries. In this context, the sharing of the efficient and clean technologies among countries is of essential importance for the realization of the global common goal of energy conservation and emissions reduction.

1.3.5   Conclusions and Policy Implications

As the largest developing country in the world, China has gained wide attention in the academic field, particularly on topics regarding its huge energy consumption and massive carbon emissions. The present study aims to provide a comprehensive overview for the energy resources required by Chinese economy with the latest data. A systems cross-scale input-output analysis is adopted to track the energy use from the source of exploitation to the sink of final use.

Sector-wise, a latest database of embodied energy intensity is built in this study, which can serve as the basic data for systems ecological evaluations regarding industries' energy performance. Some tertiary industries are regarded as the zero-energy sectors in the traditional direct accounting, but are found with a considerable amount of energy use in their supply chains, as indicated by their embodied energy intensities. Moreover, sectoral contributions to the total output, the final use and the trade are analyzed, respectively, to examine how energy use in the sector is driven by economic activities, and to help reduce the energy use at the sectoral scale. For the resource-based sectors, the energy requirements from their trade partners for intermediate production are the keys for energy reduction, while the requirements related to final use activities deserve close attention for the service-oriented sectors.

Nearly forty percent of the energy resources embodied in final use in China are found to be foreign resources, twice in magnitude the share of direct energy imports in total energy consumption reported by national statistics. China faces a more serious energy security challenge from the embodiment perspective. Therefore, the indirect dependence hidden in non-energy imports should be attached due importance, in order to enhance energy security. Not only the energy imports and exports, but also the energy-intensive commodity trade of the country needs to be controlled. The relationships between sectoral embodied intensities and the trade imbalance are discussed based on the comparative advantage theory. It suggests that the region with economic advantages may not show advantages in environmental conservation at the same time. For example, due to the low price, the manufacturing industry of computer in China is revealed with the largest trade surplus, but the energy use required to produce these computer exports in China is one-fifth more than the foreign average level. In view of the global benefit of resources conservation and environmental protection, such exports need to be reconsidered. Both the economic performance and the environmental impacts should be taken into account in trade structure adjustment for governments and administrators.

In addition to direct energy consumption and trade, indirect ones are also worthy of attention given their remarkable impacts on the environment and resources. This embodiment analysis on energy use can contribute to recent efforts to better understand Chinese economy.

References

Chen, Z. M., Chen, G. Q., 2013. Demand-driven Energy Requirement of World Economy 2007: A Multi-region Input-output Network Simulation. *Communications in Nonlinear Science and Numerical Simulation*, 18, 1757-1774.

Hong, J. K., Shen, G. Q., Guo, S., Xue, F., Zheng, W., 2016. Energy Use Embodied in China's Construction Industry: A Multi-regional Input-output Analysis. *Renewable and Sustainable Energy Reviews*, 53, 1303-1312.

Kander, A., Jiborn, M., Moran, D. D., Wiedmann, T. O., 2015. National Greenhouse Gas Accounting for Effective Climate Policy on International Trade. *Nature Climate Change*, 5, 431-435.

Liu, Z., Geng, Y., Lindner, S., Zhao, H. Y., Fujita, T., Guan, D. B., 2012. Embodied Energy Use in China's Industrial Sectors. *Energy Policy*, 49, 751-758.

Tang, X., McLellan, B. C., Zhang, B. S., Snowden, S., Höök, M., 2016. Trade-off Analysis Between Embodied Energy Exports and Employment Creation in China. *Journal of Cleaner Production*, 134, 310-319.

Tian, Y. S., 2014. Development Status and Trend of Rural Energy in China. *Energy of China*, 36, 10-14.

Zhang, B., Qiao, H., Chen, Z. M., Chen, B., 2016. Growth in Embodied Energy Transfers via China's Domestic Trade: Evidence from Multi-regional Input-output Analysis. *Applied Energy*, 184, 1093-1105.

Zhang, Y., Zheng, H. M., Yang, Z. F., Su, M. R., Liu, G. Y., Li, Y. X., 2015. Multi-regional Input-output Model and Ecological Network Analysis for Regional Embodied Energy Accounting in China. *Energy Policy*, 86, 651-663.

Chapter Two
Economic Analysis on Environmental Pollution

2.1 Concentration of Industrial Pollution in China[①]

2.1.1 Introduction

This study uses the Theil index to measure the concentration of pollution in China during 2003-2015. This index measures the disproportionality of a population distribution relative to a predetermined reference distribution. It is primarily used to measure the regional imbalance in income, employment, or industry; or the racial segregation. Applying it to measure the concentration of pollution has not drawn much attention.

While most discussions are on reducing the level of pollution, lowering the concentration of pollution is equally important. Millimet and Slottje (2002) argue that if pollution is highly concentrated, the citizens would suffer adverse health effects by exposing to a threshold level of toxins and face disproportionately increasing health risk. From an economic perspective, if income is "good" and pollution is "bad", society may wish to distribute the cost of pollution evenly across regions just as it may wish to distribute the benefit of income equally. As suggested by Wu and Heberling (2013), the level of pollution has become a less critical environmental issue and environmental justice for a less concentrated pollution is the next goal to achieve.

The case of China is of particular interest. Initiated in the 10th Five-Year Plan (2001-2005), the "Great Western Development" and the "Northeast China Revitalization" strategies provoke moving the center of the economy to the inland from the advanced east-coast region. The plan is believed to be on the right track in reducing the concentration of industries (Lemoine et al., 2015; Long and Zhang, 2012). While most discussions are on the redistribution of income and industries, our purpose is to assess the effectiveness of this initiative on the redistribution of pollution.

---

① Published on *Applied Economics Letter*, Volume 26, pp. 1339-1344, with a few modifications due to space constraints. Reuse permission has been obtained from Taylor & Francis.

We take advantages of two methodological features of the Theil index to investigate the over-time changes of pollution concentration. The first is the relative measure. The relative concentration of pollution with respect to the concentration of industrial output allows us to assess the impact of diversions of industries on the concentration of pollution. The second is the decomposition of the index into the between-region concentration and the within-region concentration, which distinguishes itself from the popular Gini coefficient as a measure of regional inequality as it suggests the relative importance of spatial dimension of inequality. This decomposition is of particular interest in that the between-region concentration reveals whether the decline in the regional imbalance of industries since the mid-2000s has changed the regional distribution of pollution as well.

2. 1. 2 Methodology

Consider the following Theil index:

$$
Theil = \sum_{i=1}^{n} \frac{\frac{E_i}{\Pi_i}}{\sum_i \frac{E_i}{\Pi_i}} \ln \left(\frac{\frac{E_i}{\Pi_i}}{\sum_i \frac{E_i}{\Pi_i}} \right) \tag{2.1.1}
$$

where E_i is the measure of pollution, i represents cities and n the number of cities, and Π_i is the reference distribution. The existence of concentration is indicated by a deviation of E from Π. The absolute measure assumes that the reference distribution is uniform. For the relative measure it is the distribution of industrial output. A zero measure means the pollutant is distributed the same way as the industry across cities.

To decompose the Theil index, let $E_{r,i}$ be the pollution in City i of Region r and n_r be the number of cities in Region r. The Theil index of an individual region is $Theil_r = \frac{1}{n_r} \sum_{i=1}^{n_r}$ $\frac{E_{r,i}}{\bar{E}_r} \ln \left(\frac{E_{r,i}}{\bar{E}_r} \right)$, where $\bar{E}_r = \frac{1}{n_r} \sum_{i=1}^{n_r} E_{r,i}$ is the mean pollution in Region r across cities. Assume R disjoint regions and $N \equiv R \times n_r$ cities. Let $\bar{E}$ be the overall mean pollution across all cities. The entire concentration explained by the Theil index can be decomposed as:

$$
\frac{1}{N} \sum_{r=1}^{R} \sum_{i=1}^{n_r} \frac{E_{r,i}}{\bar{E}} \ln \left(\frac{E_{r,i}}{\bar{E}} \right) = \sum_{r=1}^{R} \left(\frac{n_r \cdot \bar{E}_r}{N \cdot \bar{E}} \times Theil_r \right) + \sum_{r=1}^{R} \left(\frac{n_r}{N} \frac{\bar{E}_r}{\bar{E}} \ln \left(\frac{\bar{E}_r}{\bar{E}} \right) \right) \tag{2.1.2}
$$

The first term on the right-hand side is the within-region concentration, measuring the concentration as a result of the differences concerning the city-level pollution concentration in these R regions. It is the weighted arithmetic mean of the regional Theil indices, with the weight being the share of each region's pollution in total pollution. The second term is the measure of between-region concentration, which quantifies the part of pollution concentration due to the differences of concentration that exist between these R regions. It is a Theil index for the average pollution at the regional level.

For inference, since the index is a non-linear function of a random variable, Mills and Zandvakili (1997) suggest using bootstraps. To test the statistical significance of the changes of an index over time, we follow their methodology, which is analogous to comparing means from two samples.

2.1.3　Empirical Results

Data for industrial output, wastewater, and soot-dust emissions are from the *China City Statistical Yearbook*, including 287 cities from 2003 to 2015. Wastewater is the amount of water discharged by factories at the end of the pipes, and soot-dust emission is the mass of suspended particulate emitted into air. The industrial output is deflated by the GDP deflator. Table 2.1.1 reports the summary statistics. While industrial outputs continue to grow, the levels of wastewater and soot-dust emissions behave differently over time. Wastewater pollution remains stable, possibly due to the utilization of sewage treatment technology. On the other hand, soot-dust emissions shoot up after 2010, indicating a disproportional acceleration of air pollution compared to economic growth.

Table 2.1.1　Summary Statistics

Year	Industry outputs (100 million RMB)				Wastewater (10,000 tons)				Soot-dust (10,000 tons)			
	Mean	Std.	Min.	Max.	Mean	Std.	Min.	Max.	Mean	Std.	Min.	Max.
2003	807	1566	14	16,926	7178	10,035	157	81,973	2.7	3.0	0.005	25.0
2004	1004	1896	6	19,731	7490	10,440	139	83,031	2.9	3.0	0.005	20.3
2005	1269	2364	5	23,147	8033	11,540	133	85,735	3.2	3.9	0.007	43.2
2006	1543	2790	26	26,295	7976	10,834	150	85,347	2.9	2.6	0.020	16.4
2007	1825	3160	8	29,304	8500	12,074	22	91,260	2.5	2.2	0.010	13.0
2008	2114	3440	10	30,797	8186	10,783	17	75,585	2.2	1.9	0.005	12.2
2009	2308	3551	14	29,527	7915	10,655	25	79,959	1.9	1.7	0.008	10.9
2010	2779	4096	18	34,784	7954	9928	23	80,468	1.9	1.8	0.009	10.2
2011	3098	4257	22	34,684	7881	9423	78	86,804	3.5	4.5	0.020	50.6
2012	3299	4372	37	33,023	7430	7950	72	70,754	3.2	4.0	0.030	41.0
2013	3598	4620	40	32,443	7197	7626	69	66,916	3.2	4.1	0.020	47.9
2014	3870	4863	49	32,191	6851	7346	46	61,438	4.4	5.0	0.070	53.6
2015	3826	4867	53	31,323	6648	7231	53	60,506	3.8	4.3	0.090	46.7

Figures 2. 1. 1 (a)-2. 1. 1 (c) plot the absolute measures along with their 90% confidence intervals. The concentration of industrial output starts at a very high level, arguably caused by the "open door" strategy in the early 1980s that drives a fast development in the east coast. It continuously declines up to 2011 and remains stable afterwards, reflecting that the strategic plan successfully narrows the disparities between the east coast and the inland. Panel (A) of Table 2. 1. 2 reports that the decreasing concentration of industry is statistically significant for both 5-year sub-periods (2005-2010, 2010-2015) and the whole sample period. The concentration of wastewater also has a significant declining trend. The concentration of soot-dust emissions slightly decreases up to 2010, but jumps to a higher level afterwards, although the changes over time are statistically insignificant.

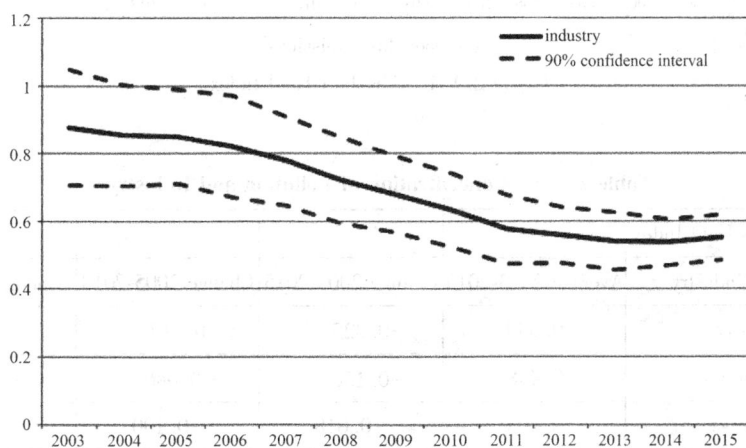

(a) Industry

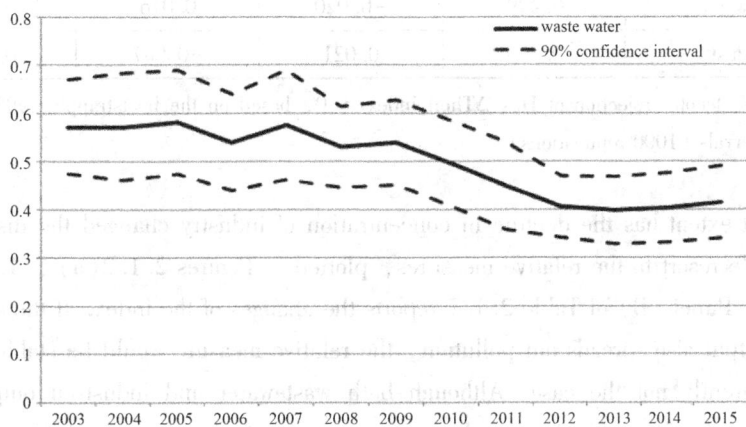

(b) Wastewater

69

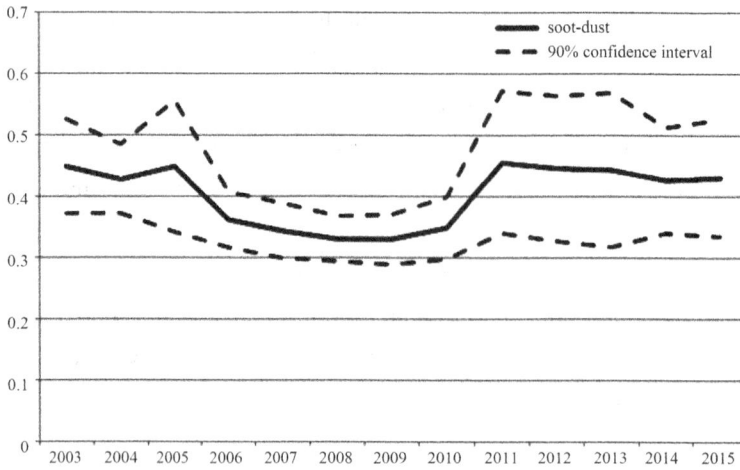

(c) Soot-dust emissions

Figure 2. 1. 1   Absolute Theil Index

Table 2. 1. 2   Concentration of Pollution and Industry

(A) Absolute Theil Index				
Pollution/industry	Average 2003-2015	Change 2003-2015	Change 2005-2010	Change 2010-2015
Industry	0. 690	$-0. 325^{***}$	$-0. 217^{***}$	$-0. 081^{*}$
Wastewater	0. 498	$-0. 156^{***}$	$-0. 086^{**}$	$-0. 080^{*}$
Soot-dust	0. 403	-0. 018	-0. 100	0. 082
(B) Relative Theil Index				
Wastewater	0. 499	-0. 020	0. 076	-0. 128
Soot-dust	0. 575	0. 021	-0. 087	$0. 130^{**}$

$^{***}/^{**}/^{*}$ denotes rejection of H_0: ΔTheil index = 0, based on the bootstrapping 99%/95%/90% confidence intervals (1000 replications).

To what extent has the decline in concentration of industry changed the distribution of pollution? We resort to the relative measures, plotted in Figures 2. 1. 2(a)-2. 1. 2(b), for the answers. Panel (B) of Table 2. 1. 2 reports the changes of the index. If the spreading of industrial output also spreads out pollution, the relative measure would be stable over time. This is apparently not the case. Although both wastewater and industrial output show a downward trend of concentration, the concentration of wastewater relative to industry increases in the early sample, especially from 2006 to 2008. This implies that when the overall industry experiences a decreasing concentration, the concentration of wastewater-generating firms does not change as much. This is because water-polluting industries are subject to geographical constraint (water source) and do not relocate as quickly as other industries. After the water source is found and the constraint is unchained, these industries begin to spread more widely and the relative concentration falls back to the original level.

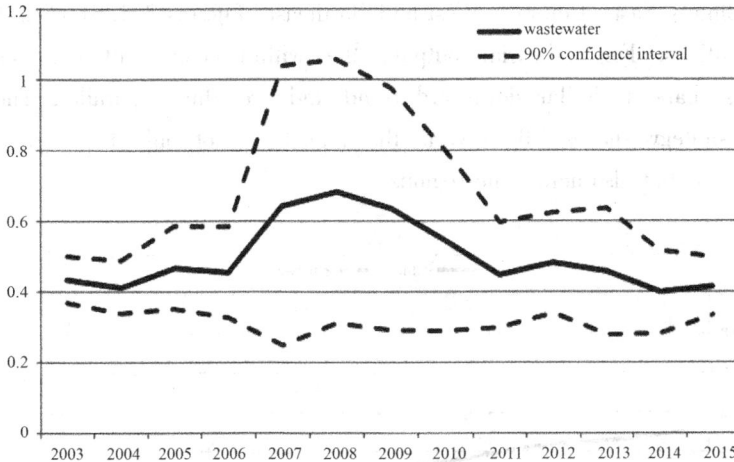

(a) Wastewater

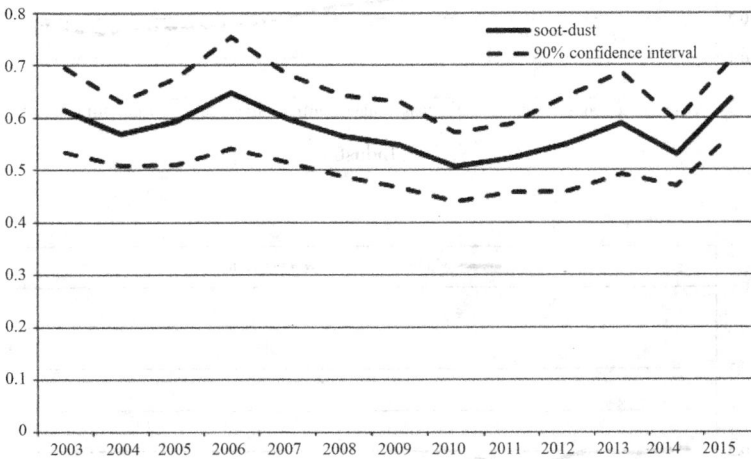

(b) Soot-dust emissions

Figure 2. 1. 2   Relative Theil Index

The relative measure for soot-dust emissions shows an opposite pattern to that of wastewater. It declines from 2006 to 2010, then rises back to the original level afterwards. Soot-dust emissions are not perceived as a critical issue until substantial jumps in the latter period. The plan does have an impact on spreading soot-dust emissions more widely in earlier years when the issue is not severe. After 2010 the air pollution shoots up along with the expansion of industrial outputs, but at the same time, the concentration of industry stops to decline. While relocating of air polluting industries is completed in the early period, restructuring the facilities fails to control the increase in soot-dust emissions.

The decomposition analysis is based four regions characterized by the National Bureau of Statistics of China: East, Central, West and Northeast. Figures 2.1.3(a)-2.1.3(c) plot the decompositions. For industrial output, the within-region and the between-region concentrations share a similar downward trend and are almost parallel. Therefore, the development strategy successfully diverts the industries not only to other cities within individual regions but also across the regions.

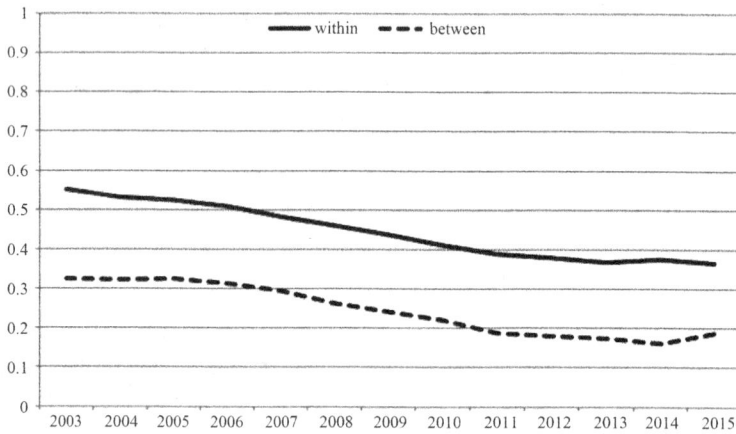

(a) Industry

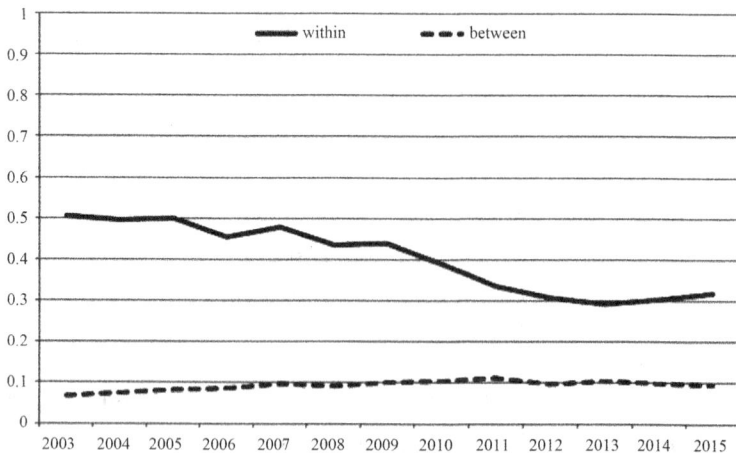

(b) Wastewater

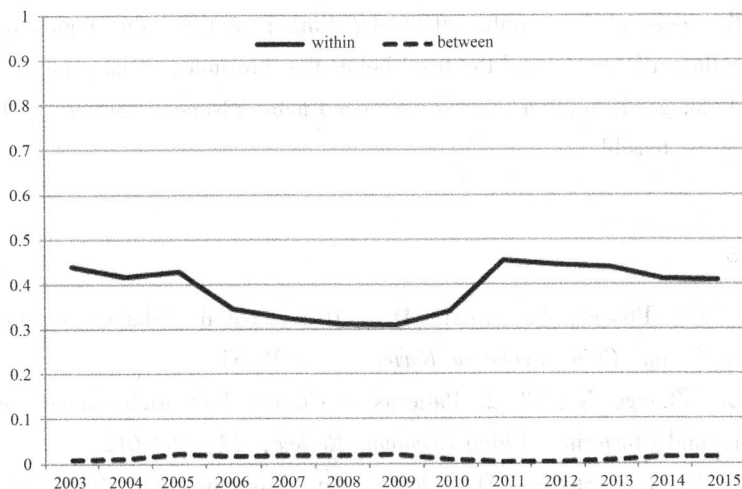

(c) Soot-dust emissions

Figure 2. 1. 3   Decomposed Absolute Theil Index

Figures 2. 1. 3 (b)-2. 1. 3 (c), on the other hand, tell a different story about the effects of the development plan on pollution. The between-region pollution concentrations over time are very low and stable. It is understandable that there is no significant movement of water-polluting industries across regions over time. Water-polluting industries are more likely to site within the watershed. For example, many factories in these industries are located in the Yangtze Delta. This geographical constraint makes most of the decline of the wastewater concentration over time to be within-region.

On the other hand, soot-dust emissions have been evenly distributed across regions because the between-region concentration is very low. The improvement and deterioration of the concentration of soot-dust emissions all happen within each region. Compared to wastewater, soot-dust emissions are more common to all industries. While the relocation of air polluting firms within the region may follow the overall trend, restructuring their facilities is not very successful.

2. 1. 4   Discussion

We pioneer the application of the Theil index to pollutants and take advantages of its two special features. It is definitely not the only statistical tool available for this type of research. Comparisons of the Theil index and other inequality measures are out of the scope of this study, and we leave it for future research. Another extension is to identify the industries that generate specific pollutants, providing a more direct link between pollution and industrial output to assess the effectiveness of policies aiming at relocating and restructuring these industries. Finally, there is no decisive scientific measure of the threshold level and accelerating the speed of the harmful effect of pollution. If the within-region reduction and diversion of pollution have lowered the level below the threshold, it may not be necessary to spread the inferior goods to other regions. We need more advanced studies in other fields for this research to be feasible.

References

Lemoine, F., Poncet, S., Ünal, D., 2015. Spatial Rebalancing and Industrial Convergence in China. *China Economic Review*, 34, 39-63.

Long, C., Zhang, X., 2012. Patterns of China's Industrialization: Concentration, Specialization, and Clustering. *China Economic Review*, 23, 593-612.

Millimet, D. L., Slottje, D., 2002. An Environmental Paglin-Gini. *Applied Economics Letters*, 9, 271-274.

Mills, J. A., Zandvakili, S., 1997. Statistical Inference via Bootstrapping for Measures of Inequality. *Journal of Applied Econometrics*, 12, 133-150.

Wu, S., Heberling, M. T., 2013. The Distribution of Pollution and Environmental Justice in Puerto Rico: A Quantitative Analysis. *Population and Environment*, 35, 113-132.

2. 2   The Distribution of Pollution and Environmental Justice in Puerto Rico: A Quantitative Analysis[①]

2. 2. 1   Introduction

Environmental justice has recently been highlighted as an important research issue. The research needs to address inequities facing minority and low-income communities. An important step related to the goals is assessing the distribution of environmental and health hazards in a country or region. An unequal distribution of environmental hazards implies local communities may suffer different levels of environmental hazards across locations, which therefore contributes to environmental injustice. Linking the inequity to important socio-economic and demographic indicators can then be used to identify subpopulations impacted by the hazards.

---

① Published on *Population and Environment*, Volume 35, pp. 113-132, with a few modifications due to space constraints. Reuse permission has been obtained from Springer.

2. 2. 1. 1　Environmental Justice Research

Much research has been published studying subpopulations and the distribution of pollution to highlight inequalities (e. g. , Mohai et al. , 2009; Chakraborty et al. , 2011). Brooks and Sethi (1997) broadened previous studies by considering a larger number of air toxics for the continental United States and found that race was significantly related to air emissions. They also found income, education, property values, and voter participation were significant. Using the same data source, Arora and Cason (1998) suggested that race, income, and unemployment were important determinants of releases in non-urban areas.

Early research on the distribution of environmental hazards relied on a specified geographic unit to compare those units with a hazard to those without (Mohai et al. , 2009). Explanatory variables representing demographic or socioeconomic characteristics were analyzed for unequal distributions (Mohai et al. , 2009; Chakraborty et al. , 2011). Limitations of this approach led to alternatives such as analyses using the quality or quantity of emissions, but these also required restrictive assumptions related to the boundaries of the geographic unit (Chakraborty et al. , 2011). To improve these analyses, distance-based and risk-based approaches were developed (Mohai et al. , 2009). Distance-based approaches incorporated geographic information systems (GIS) to confine the population affected near the hazardous sites (Chakraborty et al. , 2011).

2. 2. 1. 2　Environmental Justice Case Study: Puerto Rico

The aim of this study is to provide insights into the distribution of toxic releases and environmental justice in Puerto Rico. We examined Puerto Rico for two reasons. Since the 1940s, the island has experienced rapid changes in human activities, population distribution, and environmental systems due to industrialization and urbanization. Industrialization and urbanization also have resulted in a population migration from rural areas to urban areas (Center for Sustainable Development Studies, 2009) and led to increasing public participation in environmental issues.

Another reason we chose the archipelago is due to the limited studies on environmental justice in Puerto Rico. Martinuzzi et al. (2009) used historical information and long-term landscape analyses to investigate potential impacts of human activities on mangrove areas and found that past human activity altered the original proportion of mangrove species. Miranda and Hale (2005) investigated solid waste management, one of the biggest challenges in Puerto Rico, and found environmental costs of waste management options do vary across locations. This indicates that various socioeconomic and demographic characteristics in local communities may play an important role. However, we are aware that environmental justice issues are different in the Caribbean, and distributional issues and environmental justice in Latin America and the Caribbean do not always follow the patterns found in the United States. Relationships between race or poverty and environmental hazards are not always found in these regions.

Current methodologies applied to environmental justice issues include visual displays (e. g. , geographic information system), summary statistics, regression analyses, visual ranking tools (e. g. , Lorenz curves), and inequality indices (Maguire and Sheriff, 2011). We use regression analyses for environmental justice research and inequality indices for assessing the distribution of toxic releases. We measure the distribution using the Gini coefficient, which is one of the best known and most frequently used inequality measures (e. g. , typically with income distribution).

This study makes the following contributions. First, we develop an empirical foundation for Puerto Rico's distribution of toxic releases and environmental justice research. Our exploratory study adds to the limited number of environmental justice studies in Puerto Rico. Second, we employ an environmental Gini coefficient. Finally, according to the previous literature on environmental justice, our econometric model tests several socioeconomic and demographic indicators that may be related to toxic releases. These indicators include race, income and poverty level, education levels, age structure, unemployment, housing rental, vehicle ownership, and income measures. We assess whether certain subpopulations defined by the indicators face higher levels of toxic releases in Puerto Rico. This particular aspect of the study finds mixed evidence compared with findings in the existing literature where linkages between environmental risk and poverty or race are not typically found in Latin American cities. We recognize the number of observations (discussed in the data section) for our empirical model is a potential limitation; however, we are performing the best analysis we can based on the information available.

2. 2. 2   Data Description

For our analysis, we chose the Toxics Release Inventory (TRI) database. TRI data are reported for stationary sources only and are available by facility, county, specific chemical, and industry. We designed the study as a regional-level analysis using TRI data for counties (called municipios in Puerto Rico). Puerto Rico has 78 municipios that range in area from approximately 5-126 square miles (see Figure 2. 2. 1).① Because TRI data are available at smaller scales, we recognize the limitations in our approach; however, in this exploratory

---

① Accessed at http://factfinder2. census. gov/faces/tableservices/jsf/pages/productview. xhtml? pid = DEC _ 10 _ SF1 _ GCTPH1. ST05&prodType = table on January 3, 2013. The US census defines a municipio as the primary legal division of Puerto Rico. The census treats municipios as equivalent to US counties for data purposes (Accessed at: http://www.census.gov/geo/www/tiger/glossary.html on January 3, 2013). Our dataset excluded municipios without TRI data. In those municipios, no facilities reported releases.

analysis, we focused on the environmental injustice for municipios (i. e., environmental Gini coefficient and regression analysis are on a consistent scale). In addition, TRI data are limited to stationary sources which means mobile sources (i. e., vehicle emissions) are excluded from the analysis; we also recognize this as a limitation.① The TRI list of reportable toxic chemicals can vary year to year by USEPA adding or deleting chemicals. In order to control for these changes, we chose a time period from 2000 to 2008. In 2000, the USEPA added seven chemicals and one chemical category to the TRI reporting list, but since then it remained unchanged until 2011.② We note that TRI data do not include information about public exposure to chemical releases, but releases in conjunction with industrial site-specific characteristics can be used as a proxy for exposures.

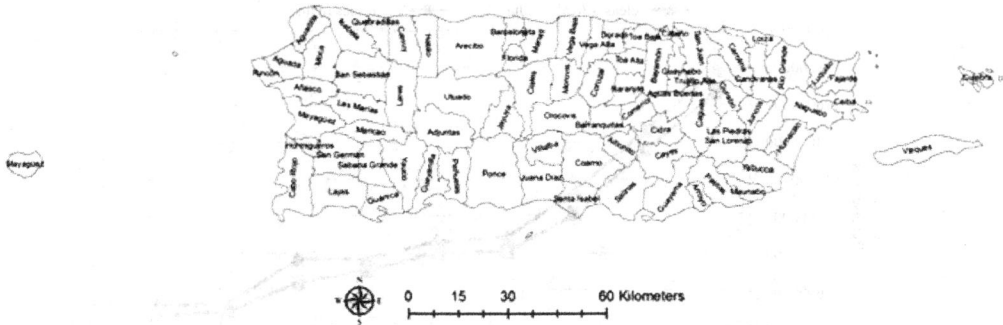

Figure 2. 2. 1   Puerto Rico municipios. Municipios are legal divisions of Puerto Rico and are similar to US counties.

TRI data can be categorized into air, land, water, and underground releases. Facilities in Puerto Rico typically only have releases to air and usually do not emit to water because most water bodies are too small. We only found a few releases on land, in water, or underground; therefore, our study focused on releases to all media combined and their distribution. We also examined releases to air because they are a large percentage of releases to all media combined.

Releases to all media and releases to air, expressed either as total or per capita

---

① By contrast, the National-Scale Air Toxics Assessment (NATA) is a comprehensive study of health risks from inhaling air pollutants (Accessed at: http://www.epa.gov/nata/ on February 25,2013). It is a national inventory of stationary and mobile sources, but it is updated only every 3 years (1996, 1999, 2002, 2005). Although NATA covers Puerto Rico, changes in the methodology across the four assessments make it difficult to compare results. This suggests we could not use NATA for the types of analyses presented here.

② Accessed at http://www.epa.gov/tri/trichemicals on January 3,2013.

amount, declined steadily over the period 2000-2008; these declines were statistically significant (Figure 2.2.2, Figure 2.2.3). We used Puerto Rico TRI data to investigate the distribution of releases. To perform the regression analysis for environmental justice, we also collected socioeconomic and demographic data from the American Community Survey (ACS, US Census Bureau) for Puerto Rico municipios where facilities actually report releases. The analysis was limited to 2005-2008 due to the availability of ACS data. To clarify, we used the TRI data from 2000-2008 for distribution analysis and used the TRI and ACS data from 2005 to 2008 for the regression analysis on environmental justice (see Figure 2.2.4 for municipios where both TRI and sociodemographic data are available).

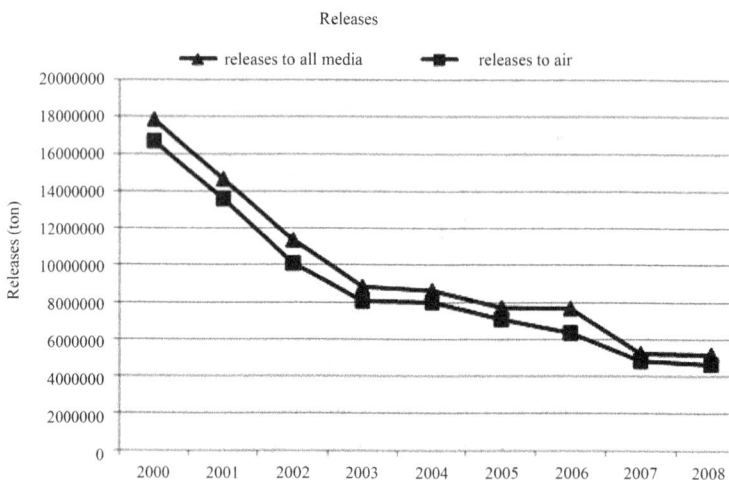

Figure 2.2.2   Toxic Releases, All Municipios 2000-2008

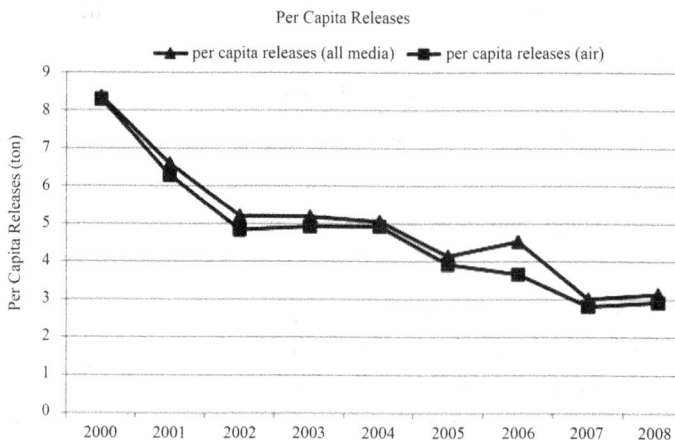

Figure 2.2.3   Per Capita Releases, All Municipios 2000-2008

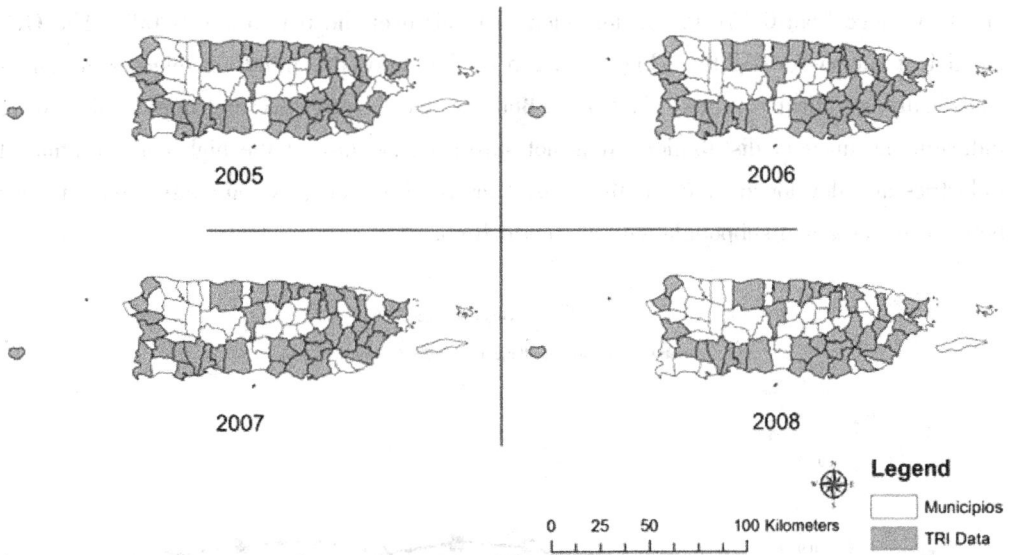

Figure 2. 2. 4   Availability of Toxics Release Inventory Data for Puerto Rico Municipios, 2005-2008

2. 2. 3   The Distribution of Toxic Releases in Puerto Rico

2. 2. 3. 1   Methodology

The Gini coefficient is an inequality measure that quantifies the distribution effect. When applied to measure the distribution of releases, it is referred to the environmental Gini coefficient (Millimet and Slottje, 2002). The exact formulation is as follows:

$$G = \frac{2cov(E, \ F)}{\mu} \qquad (2.2.1)$$

where G is the environmental Gini coefficient, E is per capita releases to all media or to air, F is the cumulative distribution of per capita releases, and μ is per capita releases averaged across municipios. The cumulative distribution of per capita releases is obtained by ranking all municipios in terms of per capita releases and then dividing the rank of each municipio by the total number of municipios. We estimated the Gini coefficient for the time period 2000-2008. Similar to the income Gini, the environmental Gini coefficient is bounded between zero and one, where zero implies perfect equality and one implies perfect inequality. We only examined between-municipio inequality and assume zero inequality within each municipio. Another assumption and limitation is that the adverse impacts of toxic releases are confined only to municipio boundaries, and people in a given municipio are not affected by the toxic releases in an adjacent municipio.

2. 2. 3. 2   Results

The estimates of the Gini coefficient range from 0. 867-0. 894 for releases to all media,

79

and they range from 0. 876-0. 906 for releases to air over the period 2000-2008. The Gini coefficient increased slightly (Figure 2. 2. 5), but only the trend of releases to air is statistically significant (Table 2. 2. 1). Both of these estimates are approaching one, indicating an unequal distribution. It is not surprising because of the high concentration of industries and developed lands in the coastal areas. Therefore, we are interested in links between releases and subpopulations in Puerto Rico.

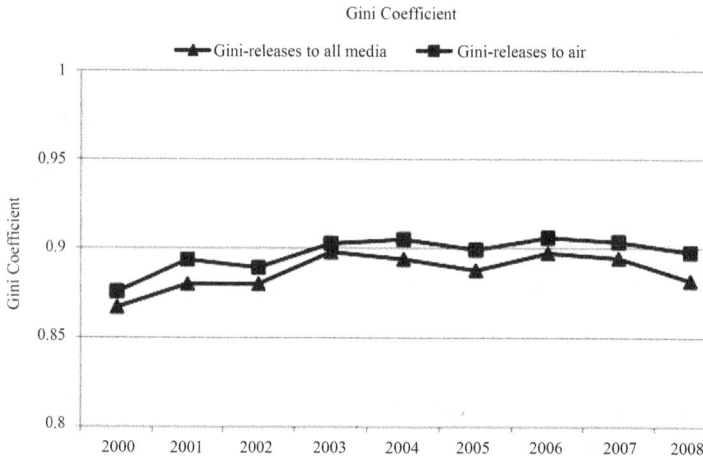

Figure 2. 2. 5   Environmental Gini Coefficient 2000-2008

Table 2. 2. 1   Environmental Gini Coefficient, 2000-2008

Year	Environmental Gini Coefficient	
	Total releases	Air releases
2000	0. 867	0. 876
2001	0. 880	0. 893
2002	0. 880	0. 889
2003	0. 898	0. 903
2004	0. 894	0. 905
2005	0. 888	0. 899
2006	0. 897	0. 906
2007	0. 894	0. 904
2008	0. 882	0. 898
Year(t)	0. 002 (1. 796)	0. 002 (2. 566) [**]

t-statistics in parentheses; [**] significant at 95% level.

2. 2. 4   Environment Justice Analysis in Puerto Rico

2. 2. 4. 1   Econometric Methodology

Table 2. 2. 2 lists the municipio-level indicators of interest for Puerto Rico. The selection of the indicators is based on the literature where the empirical evidence shows a relationship with toxic releases.

We ran a Spearman's rank correlation test to examine the correlations between toxic releases and selected indicators (i. e. race, poverty, education indicators, age indicators, unemployment, and car ownership) and found the relationships were not uniform across the municipos; the most significant effects existed in the municipios with more releases.

Because of the non-uniformity, we used quantile regression approach that can examine the relationships between indicators and releases at different municipios. We estimated the following quantile regression model:

$$Q_\theta(y_i \mid x_i) = x_i \beta_\theta \qquad (2.2.2)$$

where θ represents the appropriate quantile, y is log per capita releases at the municipio (i) level, x is a vector of municipio-level socio-demographic indicators, and β_θ is a vector of parameters to be estimated. The coefficients of the quantile regressions can be interpreted in a similar way to ordinary least squares (OLS) coefficient estimates. The detailed specification is as follows:

$$\ln(1+e_i) = \beta_1 + \beta_2 White_i + \beta_3 Black_i + \beta_4 Asian_i + \beta_5 Otherhispanic_i + \beta_6 Popden_i$$
$$+ \beta_7 Poverty_i + \beta_8 School_i + \beta_9 College_i + \beta_{10} Rent_i + \beta_{11} Under14_i \qquad (2.2.3)$$
$$+ \beta_{12} Over65_i + \beta_{13} Unemployed_i + \beta_{14} Vehicle_i + \delta_t + \varepsilon_i$$

where the subscript i refers to the municipio, ε_i is the error term associated with each municipio i, and δ_t denotes time effects. Using $\ln(1 + e)$ as the dependent variable allows inclusion of those municipios where releases are zero. Independent variables include the socioeconomic and demographic indicators introduced in Table 2. 2. 2.

Because of the potential similarities of independent variables, we tested for multicollinearity (i. e., independent variables that are highly correlated). When independent variables are highly correlated, it becomes difficult to determine which independent variable is actually producing the effect on the dependent variable. When multicollinearity is present, the standard errors will be greater and t statistics will tend to be small as a consequence. We ran regression collinearity diagnostic procedures. The procedures provided the condition index (Table 2. 2. 3) and variance-decomposition proportions that identify source of collinearity among variables (not reported). According to the literature, when the condition index is larger than 30, there may be collinearity problems. In Table 2. 2. 3, condition index numbers 9-14 have condition indices considered high. When investigating the source, population density, poverty, school, and under 14 have large variance-decomposition proportions (larger than 0.5), which indicated these variables are the major source of collinearity. We need to pay close attention to these relevant variables when analyzing the regression results.

Although quantile regression may be the right technique for this work, it is not commonly applied in environmental economics. Most studies still choose standard regression approaches based on the mean of the conditional distribution of the dependent variable. These approaches already assume that impacts of the independent variables are homogeneous along the entire distribution of the dependent variable. Among these approaches, we used OLS to compare results. In addition, when the dependent variable is censored (in this work, no releases below 0 are allowed), the OLS estimates may be biased and inconsistent. Therefore, we also used Tobit for the censored dependent variable.

Finally, environmental justice studies are using spatial regression techniques to address spatial autocorrelation (Chakraborty, 2011). When spatial data are used, spatial autocorrelation occurs when variables are influenced by their neighbors, a fact that will cause errors in regression analysis not to meet independence assumptions. As a consequence, the spatial regression techniques that account for spatial autocorrelation should be used. For example, two spatial regression models, spatial lag models and spatial error model, have been applied by several environmental justice studies. Because we have an unbalanced panel dataset (different municipios across four years), we have run into problems using spatial regression. Whether we drop municipios to make a balanced panel or use analyses that can estimate unbalanced models, the number of observations seems to be too small for results.[1] We recognize this as a limitation and potential problem for our results (Chakraborty, 2011). We will consider it as a future research direction.

Table 2.2.2 Summary of Socioeconomic and Demographic Indicators

Indicator	Measurement	Expected sign	Variable names in the model
Race	The percentage of population which is white, black, Asian and other Pacific, and other Hispanic (non-Puerto Rican such as Mexican, Cuban and other Hispanic and Latino)	Nonwhite percentages are expected to be positive	*white*, *black*, *Asian and other Hispanic*
Population density	Total population divided by the size of each municipio	Positive	*popden*

----

① Dropping observations for a balanced panel leaves 15 municipios for 4 years.

82

Continued

Indicator	Measurement	Expected sign	Variable names in the model
Poverty	The percentage of population which lives below an acceptable poverty level	Positive	*poverty*
Education	The percentage of population which has high school education or has a bachelor's degree or higher	Percent of high school education is expected to be positive; percent of bachelor's degree is expected to be negative	*school*, *college*
Housing rental status	The percentage of total housing units which is renter occupied in a municipio	Positive	*rent*
Age	The percentage of population which is under 14 or over 65	Both percentages are expected to be negative	*under* 14, *over* 65
Unemployment	The percentage of civilian labor force which is unemployed	Positive	*unemployed*
Car ownership	The percentage of workers over 16 driving alone to work	Negative	*vehicle*

Table 2. 2. 3   Multicollinearity Test Results

Condition index number	Condition index
1	1. 00
2	2. 84
3	5. 07
4	6. 75
5	10. 87
6	11. 26
7	18. 67
8	20. 84
9	28. 45
10	36. 68
11	52. 16
12	79. 60
13	109. 74
14	215. 00

STATA command "coldiag 2" was applied to test multicollinearity.

2. 2. 4. 2   Results

Table 2.2.4 presents the results using per capita releases to all media as the dependent variable.① We found estimates from both regressions are very similar. The variables Black, Popden, College, Under 14, Over 65, and Vehicle are significant and negative, while Other Hispanic, School, and Unemployed are significant and positive. Both regressions help predict the mean of dependent variable across the entire distribution. However, we want to know whether the strong effects found in these models only exist at certain points of the distribution of releases.

Table 2. 2. 4   Ordinary Least Square and Tobit Estimates, Releases to All Media

ln (1+per capita releases)	OLS	Tobit
White (%)	1. 265	1. 573
	(1. 05)	(1. 18)
Black (%)	−2. 709	−2. 663
	(−2. 42) **	(−2. 44) **
Asian (%)	22. 684	23. 283
	(0. 73)	(0. 77)
Other Hispanic (%)	16. 707	17. 275
	(2. 68) ***	(2. 82) ***
Population density	−0. 0004	−0. 0004
	(−3. 59) ***	(−3. 74) ***
Poverty	2. 491	2. 705
	(1. 26)	(1. 37)
School	19. 215	19. 625
	(4. 74) ***	(4. 69) ***
College	−14. 573	−14. 486
	(−4. 69) ***	(−4. 45) ***
Rent	−0. 257	−0. 034
	(−0. 15)	(−0. 02)
Under 14	−35. 503	−35. 908
	(−5. 18) ***	(−5. 30) ***

---

①   Results for per capita releases to air available upon request.

Continued

ln (1+per capita releases)	OLS	Tobit
Over 65	−35. 509	−36. 357
	(−5. 38) ***	(−5. 49) ***
Unemployed	5. 644	4. 975
	(3. 40) ***	(2. 81) ***
Vehicle	−7. 752	−9. 227
	(−3. 09) ***	(−3. 49) ***
Constant	15. 775	3. 419
	(0. 14)	(0. 03)
R^2/Pseudo R^2	0. 41	0. 17
Number of Obs.[a]	166	166

t-statistics in parentheses; * significant at 10% level; ** significant at 5% level; *** significant at 1% level.

Our data for regression analysis cover 4 years with a different set of municipios for each year (unbalanced panel). The TRI has data for about 50 municipios for each year in Puerto Rico. When ruling out missing values, the total number of observations remains 166.

We present our quantile regression results in Table 2. 2. 5, Table 2. 2. 6 with releases to all media and to air (per capita) separately as the dependent variables. We reject the hypothesis that all the coefficients are constant across quintiles based on the F test (equality) results. Quantile regressions provide a clear picture of the entire distribution where the strong relationships between the indicators and releases mainly exist in the municipios with the fewest and largest releases (the extreme lower and upper quintiles).[1]

Table 2. 2. 5   Quantile Regression Results, Releases to All Media, Municipio Level, 2005-2008

ln(1+per capita releases)	0. 2 Quintile	0. 4 Quintile	0. 6 Quintile	0. 8 Quintile
White (%)	0. 193	0. 848	1. 504	−1. 920
	(0. 65)	(1. 18)	(0. 64)	(−0. 59)
Black (%)	−0. 323	−0. 565	0. 924	−3. 272
	(−0. 74)	(−0. 56)	(0. 48)	(−1. 78) *

①   Based on TRI 2008, Puerto Rico municipios with the largest releases are Guayanilla, Salinas, Guayama, Las Piedras, Penuelas, Barceloneta, Yabucoa, Toa Baja, Yauco, and San Juan.

Continued

ln(1+per capita releases)	0. 2 Quintile	0. 4 Quintile	0. 6 Quintile	0. 8 Quintile
Asian (%)	14. 932	52. 113	48. 189	36. 230
	(0. 77)	(1. 71) *	(0. 89)	(0. 62)
Other Hispanic (%)	10. 360	10. 388	4. 343	26. 244
	(3. 10) ***	(2. 43) **	(0. 45)	(1. 92) ***
Population density	−0. 0002	−0. 0002	−0. 0002	−0. 0006
	(−3. 02) ***	(−2. 62) ***	(−0. 91)	(−3. 25) ***
Poverty	−0. 874	−1. 053	1. 657	5. 443
	(−1. 33)	(−0. 80)	(0. 58)	(1. 44)
School	2. 206	4. 348	8. 999	19. 988
	(1. 64) *	(1. 69) *	(1. 32)	(2. 54) **
College	−2. 812	−3. 863	−4. 995	−16. 952
	(−2. 07) **	(−1. 57)	(−0. 94)	(−2. 94) ***
Rent	0. 661	1. 401	1. 511	−9. 767
	(1. 33)	(1. 54)	(0. 54)	(−1. 90) *
Under 14	−6. 341	−7. 571	−18. 152	−50. 239
	(−2. 19) **	(−1. 28)	(−1. 29)	(−3. 70) ***
Over 65	−8. 257	−11. 299	−16. 486	−27. 475
	(−2. 45) **	(−1. 85) *	(−1. 15)	(−1. 93) *
Unemployed	0. 600	1. 252	3. 589	7. 546
	(1. 02)	(0. 95)	(1. 51)	(2. 32) **
Vehicle	−0. 683	−0. 865	−0. 865	−13. 102
	(−0. 87)	(−0. 52)	(−0. 21)	(−3. 21) ***
Constant	2. 160	5. 799	11. 421	21. 309
	(0. 13)	(0. 15)	(0. 14)	(0. 20)
Pseudo R^2	0. 06	0. 12	0. 17	0. 38
F-test (Equality)			1. 81 (0. 005)	
Number of Obs.			166	

Bootstrap t-statistics in parentheses (1000 repetitions); * significant at 10% level; ** significant at 5% level; *** significant at 1% level.

Table 2.2.6   Quantile Regression Results, Releases to Air, Municipio Level, 2005-2008

ln(1+per capita releases)	0. 2 Quintile	0. 4 Quintile	0. 6 Quintile	0. 8 Quintile
White (%)	0. 063	0. 453	−0. 149	−1. 133
	(0. 25)	(0. 78)	(−0. 08)	(−0. 34)
Black (%)	−0. 115	−0. 198	1. 242	−0. 421
	(−0. 32)	(−0. 23)	(0. 71)	(−0. 21)
Asian (%)	5. 244	23. 543	47. 994	44. 033
	(0. 40)	(0. 85)	(0. 99)	(0. 78)
Other Hispanic (%)	4. 045	9. 476	3. 344	11. 238
	(1. 51)	(2. 57) **	(0. 43)	(0. 84)
Population density	−0. 00007	−0. 0002	−0. 00008	−0. 0005
	(−1. 53)	(−1. 68) *	(−0. 50)	(−2. 29) **
Poverty	−0. 409	−0. 812	1. 463	8. 040
	(−0. 73)	(−0. 78)	(0. 60)	(1. 97) **
School	0. 845	3. 038	6. 160	20. 176
	(0. 67)	(1. 32)	(0. 90)	(2. 33) **
College	−1. 151	−3. 091	−3. 954	−10. 356
	(−1. 06)	(−1. 49)	(−0. 80)	(−1. 67) *
Rent	0. 307	1. 264	1. 505	−5. 189
	(0. 73)	(1. 53)	(0. 72)	(−1. 05)
Under 14	−2. 901	−6. 587	−19. 745	−42. 847
	(−1. 31)	(−1. 41)	(−1. 77) *	(−3. 15) ***
Over 65	−3. 027	−8. 735	−16. 900	−26. 830
	(−1. 13)	(−1. 70) *	(−1. 30)	(−1. 85) *
Unemployed	0. 082	1. 211	3. 298	4. 695
	(0. 17)	(0. 89)	(1. 81) *	(1. 22)
Vehicle	−0. 267	0. 265	2. 000	−10. 364
	(−0. 31)	(0. 13)	(0. 46)	(−2. 13) **
Constant	0. 995	0. 592	23. 731	110. 343
	(0. 08)	(0. 02)	(0. 41)	(1. 07)
Pseudo R^2	0. 04	0. 09	0. 15	0. 35
F-test (Equality)		1. 56 (0. 03)		
Number of Obs.		168		

Bootstrap t-statistics in parentheses (1,000 repetitions); * significant at 10% level; ** significant at 5% level; *** significant at 1% level.

Across the entire island, 96.4% of the population is Puerto Rican (Hispanic and Latino of any race) and 3.6% is other Hispanic and Latino (Non-Puerto Rican such as Mexican, Cuban, and other Hispanic or Latino). Within the Puerto Rican population, 83% are white, 13% are black, and 0.4% are of Asian and other Pacific origin.[1] The analysis from the US Census Bureau (Puerto Rico Census 2000 Responses to the Race and Ethnicity, Final Report, July 2003) showed that the residents of Puerto Rico identified themselves as overwhelmingly of Hispanic origin and of a single race. In terms of race, the great majority identified themselves as White, and a substantial minority reporting Black or African American.

We found population of non-Puerto Rican Hispanic was positively related to air releases and releases to all media, although the relationship was not significant in every quintile. This indicates the non-Puerto Rican Hispanic subpopulation is more likely to live in municipios with more releases. The percent of Asian and other Pacific origin was positively related to all releases, but only in the 0.4 quintile (or relatively clean municipios). We also found that, while living in those municipios with the largest releases to all media, the percent of black population was more likely to stay in the relatively clean municipios (negative sign of Black in 0.8 quintile). Furthermore, we found no significant relationship between white population and releases. One reason that race may not present a relationship similar to that of the United States is the mixed categories of races in Puerto Rico. The racial mixing of the population has been acknowledged in Puerto Rico for a long time.

Releases were lower in more densely populated municipios, and the negative relationships between releases and population density were significant in most municipios (i.e., most quintiles). Population has gradually migrated from urban to suburban areas. The urban land cover also has increased, which results in a decreasing population density in urban Puerto Rico. Since TRI facilities are located in the metropolitan areas, it is not surprising to find that releases were lower in those suburban areas where population density tends to increase.

Among the municipios with the largest releases to air (0.8 quintile), releases were larger in municipios where poverty levels were high (positive and significant sign of poverty). This relationship between poverty and releases to air is similar to findings for the United States. Releases to all media were important in municipios where education levels were either low or high (i.e., positive and significant sign of school and negative and significant sign of college across most quintiles). The relationship between releases and education was much stronger in the municipios with larger releases given the larger coefficients of education variables. Also among the municipios with the largest releases to all media (0.8 quintile),

---

[1]   Data source: ACS (American Community Survey) data. Race categories are defined in the ACS.

there were more renter-occupied housing units in relatively clean municipios (negative and significant sign of Rent). This differs from findings in the United States where more polluted counties were likely to have more renter-occupied housing units.

Generally speaking, families with children under the age of 14 or individuals over 65 were more likely to live in municipios with fewer releases (i. e., negative and significant age variables in most quintiles). Among the municipios with larger releases (0. 6 and 0. 8 quintiles), unemployment rate was higher in those less clean municipios (positive and significant sign of Unemployed), but unemployment was not related to releases in municipios with lower releases (0. 2 and 0. 4 quintiles). Local authorities may allow polluting industries to locate nearby in order to create job opportunities, which may explain the link between unemployment and releases (Deily and Gray, 1991; Cole et al., 2008). Last, among the municipios with the largest releases (0. 8 quintile), fewer cars were associated with the less clean municipios. This is consistent with the literature (Mitchell and Dorling, 2003). As mentioned previously, TRI does not report emissions from mobile sources, so car ownership here was included only as a control variable.

2. 2. 4. 3 Sensitivity Analysis

We also perform a sensitivity analysis using two income measures (per capita income and average weekly wage) to capture the effects of socioeconomic and demographic measures. Low-income areas were sometimes characterized by larger pollution releases. We examined the sensitivity of the results by dropping several socio-demographic indicators and replacing them with two income variables, per capita income and average weekly wage.[1] We dropped the variables of poverty, educational indicators, housing rental type, age indicators, unemployment, car ownership, which all relate to income differentials. In the OLS and Tobit models, average weekly wage was significant and positive while per capita income was insignificant. In the quantile model, average weekly wage was significant and positively related to releases to all media only in the 0. 6 quintile, and there was no relationship between income variables and releases in most quintiles. This result suggests that Puerto Rico's income differentials were not strongly related to the level of releases. This weak relationship was identified as a possibility by previous studies.

2. 2. 5 Conclusion

This study has carefully studied two environmental issues in Puerto Rico, toxic releases distribution, and environmental justice. We calculated the Gini coefficient from 2000 to 2008; it remained close to one and fairly stable over time while the level of releases to all media declined. This indicates that even though the environmental quality seems to be

---

[1] Regression results are available upon request.

improving in terms of level of releases to all media, the distribution of toxic releases remains unequal.

We estimated a quantile regression model to provide empirical evidence for the potential relationships between pollution releases and subpopulations. We used municipio-level TRI data from USEPA and socioeconomic and demographic indicators from American Community Survey.

Our results have highlighted some findings among the subpopulations and releases. For example, the municipios that have a large percentage of well-educated subpopulations (bachelor's degree or above) or municipios that have large populations under 14 or over 65 have lower releases. Some of our findings need more study. In the municipios with more releases, two negative relationships were different from existing environmental justice literature for the United States. They were between releases and the percent of black residents and between releases and renter-occupied housing units.

We point out that more indicators were significant in the highest quintiles. Based on the results, a focus on education and unemployment policies may be important because of the connections with the level of releases. We finish on a note of caution. We are aware of the limitations of assuming the releases are distributed equally within each municipio (Chakraborty et al., 2011), but we see this work as an initial attempt to examine the pollution distribution and environmental justice issues for an island region such as Puerto Rico. Inevitably, the study would have benefited from a richer dataset with a longer time series (e. g., to avoid problems of multicollinearity and the limitations for spatial analyses). In addition, we identified a number of limitations in our approach and potential future research activities for Puerto Rico environmental justice studies. There are a few directions from which we might improve our current research. First, we may work on pollutants other than toxics releases. Considering the concerns about solid wastes in Puerto Rico (Miranda and Hale, 2005), this may have important environmental justice issues. In a similar way, we could include sources that are not stationary or focus on a facility-level analysis. Finally, we may improve the technique by incorporating spatial variables (GIS technique) as suggested by several studies (Chakraborty et al., 2011; Maguire and Sheriff, 2011).

References

Arora, S., Cason, T. N., 1998. Do Community Characteristics Influence Environmental Outcomes? Evidence from the Toxic Release Inventory. *Journal of Applied Economics*, I (2), 413-453.

Chakraborty, J., 2011. Revisiting Tobler's First Law of Geography: Spatial Regression Models for Assessing Environmental Justice and Health Risk Disparities. In: Maantay, J.,

McLafferty, S. (ed.)Geospatial Analysis of Environmental Health. Springer, Netherlands.

Cole, M. A., Elliott, R. J., Wu, S. S., 2008. Industrial Activity and the Environment in China: An Industry-level Analysis. China *Economic Review*, 19 (3), 393-408.

Deily, M. E., Gray, W. B., 1991. Enforcement of Pollution Regulations in a Declining Industry. *Journal of Environmental Economics and Management*, 21, 260-274.

Maguire, K., Sheriff, G., 2011. Comparing Distributions of Environmental Outcomes for Regulatory Environmental Justice Analysis. *International Journal of Environmental Research and Public Health*, 8, 1707-1726.

Martinuzzi S., Gould, W. A., Lugo, A. E., Medina, E., 2009. Conversion and Recovery of Puerto Rican Mangroves: 200 Years of Change. *Forest Ecology and Management*, 257, 75-84.

Millimet, D. L., Slottje, D., 2002. An Environmental Paglin-Gini. *Applied Economics Letters*, 9(4), 271-274.

Miranda, M. L., Hale, B., 2005. Paradise Recovered: Energy Production and Waste Management in Island Environments. *Energy Policy*, 33, 1691-1702.

Mitchell, G., Dorling, D., 2003. An Environmental Justice Analysis of British Air Quality. *Environment and Planning A*, 35, 909-929.

Mohai, P., Pellow, D., Roberts, J. T., 2009. Environmental Justice. *The Annual Review of Environment and Resources*, 34, 405-430.

2. 3 Industrial Activity and the Environment in China: An Industry-level Analysis[1]

2.3.1 Introduction

In recent years, the rapid industrial growth of China has placed increased pressure on the country's natural environment. With economic growth rates consistently above 8% since 2000 (World Bank, 2007), there is a pressing need to find ways to minimise the resultant environmental impact. This impact is already evident. Seventeen of the twenty-five most polluted cities in the world can be found in China.[2] In terms of global warming, China is likely to be the world's largest emitter of carbon dioxide by 2009-2010 when it surpasses the emissions of the USA; and an estimated 300, 0000 people die prematurely each year as a

[1] Published on *China Economic Review*, Volume 19, pp. 393-408, with a few modifications due to space constraints. Reuse permission has been obtained from Elsevier.

[2] *China Environment Yearbook* (2000).

result of air pollution. If future economic growth is to be "greener" in nature, policymakers require a detailed understanding of the complex linkages between industrial activity, environmental regulations and pollution emissions.

To date, studies examining such linkages at the firm or industry-level have often focused on developed economies. For example, Kahn (1999) and Gray and Shadbegian (2004) examine the relationship between emissions, abatement activity and production levels using US plant and industry level data. Similarly, Cole et al. (2005) use industry-level data for the UK to identify the determinants of pollution emissions and the extent to which regional characteristics may influence regulations and, in turn, emissions. The minority of firm or industry studies to have examined developing economies include Pargal and Wheeler (1996) who undertake a plant-level study of the determinants of water pollution in Indonesia and Dasgupta et al. (1999) who examine the effect of regulation and plant-level management policies on environmental compliance in Mexico. As far as we are aware, studies specifically examining the determinants of firm or industry level emissions in China are non-existent, although both Dasgupta et al. (2001) and Wang et al. (2003) examine the factors that influence firms' compliance with environmental standards.

The aim of this study is to identify the industrial characteristics that determine industry-level emissions intensity in China, thereby providing a greater understanding of the linkages between industrial characteristics, environmental regulations and pollution intensity. Following Pargal and Wheeler (1996) and Cole et al. (2005), we work within a framework of the demand for, and supply of, environmental services. The characteristics of an industry determine its demand for such services, whilst society, through environmental regulations, supplies environmental services at a price. The equilibrium level of emissions for a given industry will therefore reflect both demand and supply-side considerations. This provides us with a theoretical framework to explore the possible determinants of industry specific emissions intensity.

The study makes the following contributions. First, we examine the extent to which an industry's use of factor inputs influences its emissions intensity. Specifically, we assess whether Chinese pollution intensive industries are typically more or less intensive in the use of physical and human capital. Several studies have suggested a positive link between physical capital and pollution intensity in US and UK industries (Antweiler et al., 2001; Cole et al., 2005), but this has never been demonstrated for a developing or newly industrialised economy. We also assess whether a firm's productivity levels extend to resource efficiency and hence pollution intensity; whether the size of the average firm within an industry affects pollution; and whether R&D expenditure and the age of plant and machinery within an industry affect pollution intensity. Our analysis enables us to compare the relative magnitude of these effects and the extent to which they vary across different pollutants.

Second, we investigate the role of Chinese regulations. Following Pargal and Wheeler (1996) and Cole et al. (2005) we argue that there may be both a formal and an informal component to regional regulation levels. We define formal regulations as those that operate through national government or local authorities. In contrast to formal regulations, informal regulations may occur when communities regulate firms or industries through lobbying and petitioning. This may arise due to a perception that formal regulations are weak or absent.[①]

2.3.2   Background to the Chinese Economy and Natural Environment

Despite average annual industrial value added growth rates in excess of 16% over the period 1997-2004, Figure 2.3.1 illustrates that emissions of dust, soot and sulphur dioxide (SO_2), actually fell for at least part of this period.[②] However, SO_2 and soot appear to have increased since around the year 2002. Nevertheless, in the face of such economic growth rates the absence of rapidly rising pollution levels suggests that Chinese environmental regulations and energy efficiency gains may have proved reasonably effective. Figure 2.3.2 provides further evidence to support this assertion by illustrating the emissions of our three pollutants in the form of intensities i. e. per unit of value added. All three intensities can be seen to fall over time.

Whilst the aggregate country level trends are interesting, in this study we are concerned with the examination of pollution patterns at the industry-level where we classify industries

---

① Pargal and Wheeler (1996) investigate the role of informal regulations in plant-level emissions of water pollution in Indonesia. They find water pollution to be an increasing function of output and state ownership and a decreasing function of productivity and local (informal) environmental regulations. Whilst interesting, Pargal and Wheeler's study differs from ours in that it examines a single pollutant for a developing country using cross-sectional data only. Nevertheless, some interesting commonalities are found between our results and those of Pargal and Wheeler.

② Value added data from *China Industrial Yearbook* 1997-2004. Data on non-industrial dust emissions are not available. Sulphur dioxide emissions refer to the volume of sulphur dioxide emitted by industrial production processes. Soot and dust differ both in terms of the source of emissions and in the size of the particles. The diameter of soot particles is less than 0.1μm (often referred to as PM_{10}) and these finer particles are more damaging to health, particularly in the form of respiratory problems, than the larger (> 0.1μm) dust particles. Soot emissions emanate specifically from the process of fuel burning by industrial activity. Dust emissions refer to the volume of particulates emitted by industrial production processes more widely. Industry-level emissions of SO_2, Soot and Dust, as reported in the *China Statistical Yearbooks*, are based upon the emissions of over 71,000 firms and in the majority of cases stem from direct measures of pollution. Where such direct measures are not available, emissions are estimated using emissions ratios applied to fuel use. Note that the *China Statistical Yearbooks* only provide the aggregated industry data rather than the firm specific data.

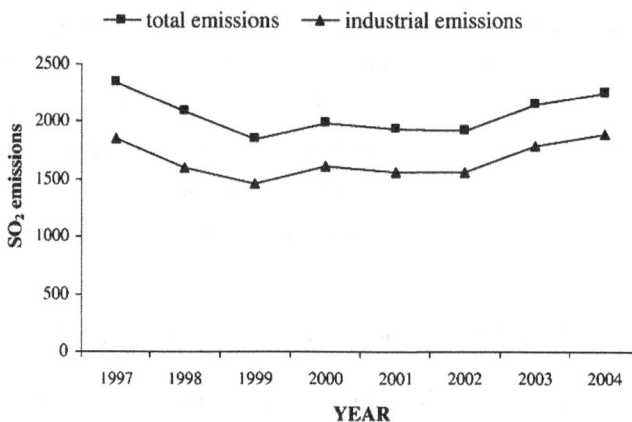

(a) SO$_2$ emissions

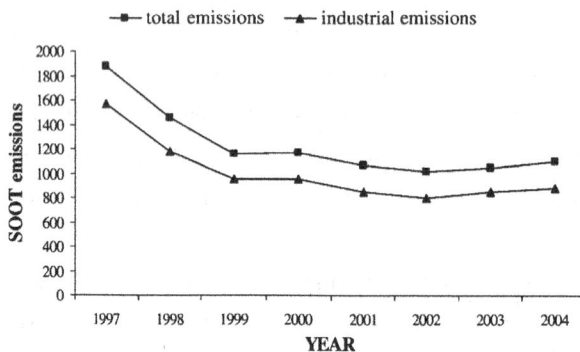

(b) Soot emissions

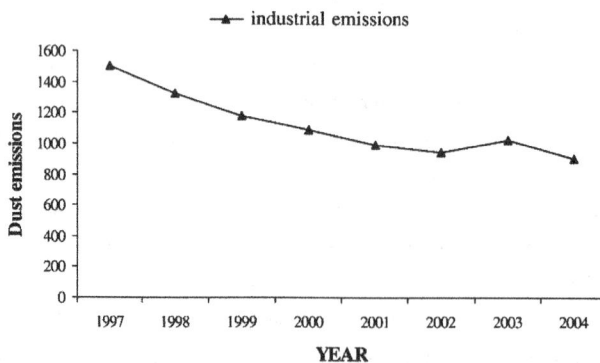

(c) Dust emissions

Figure 2.3.1   Emissions of Sulphur Dioxide (SO$_2$), Soot and Dust 1997-2004 (tonnes)

according to the International Standard of Industrial Classification (ISIC). Due to differences between the ISIC classification and the classification for which Chinese data are reported, it proved necessary to aggregate several 3-digit ISIC industries together. The result is that three of our Chinese "industries" each comprise more than one ISIC industry.①

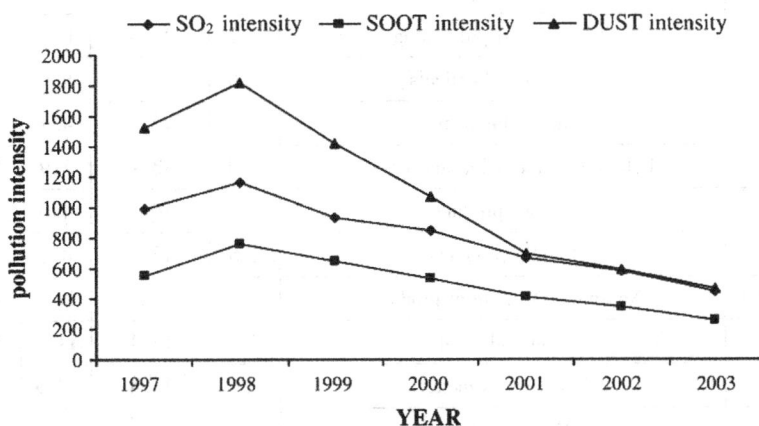

Figure 2. 3. 2   Pollution Intensities (tonnes per million yuan of value added) for SO_2, Soot and Dust, 1997-2003

Table 2. 3. 1 presents the average pollution intensities for our three air pollutants for a range of Chinese sectors for the period 1997 to 2003. Also provided is each industry's contribution towards total manufacturing value added. In each Column the five largest values are highlighted in bold. Considering the value added data first, we see that over the period 1997-2003 the five largest manufacturing industries were Food Beverages and Tobacco, Textiles and Wearing Apparel, Industrial Chemicals, Iron and Steel and the various Machinery Industries. With regard to the growth of value added, we note that all manufacturing sectors grew rapidly over this period with Iron and Steel, Non-Ferrous Metals, and Machinery Industries growing particularly rapidly.

Table 2. 3. 1   Average Pollution Intensities and Share of Total Value Added, 1997-2003

ISIC	Industry	%VA	ΔVA (%)	SO_2	Soot	Dust
311+313+314	Food, beverage and tobacco	**15. 1**	10. 8	2. 6	2. 0	0. 1
321+322	Textiles and wearing apparel	**9. 6**	9. 8	2. 7	1. 3	0. 02
323	Leather products	1. 8	11. 8	0. 9	0. 6	0. 02
341	Paper and products	2. 2	11. 3	**15. 8**	**11. 2**	**2. 8**

① Food, beverage and tobacco consists of ISIC311 + 313 + 314, textiles and wearing apparel is ISIC321+322, non-metallic mineral products ISIC361+362+369 and machinery except electrical, electrical machinery, transport equipment, professional and scientific equipment comprise ISIC382+383+384+385.

Continued

ISIC	Industry	%VA	ΔVA (%)	SO$_2$	Soot	Dust
342	Printing and publishing	1. 1	10. 4	0. 5	0. 3	0. 05
351	Industrial chemicals	**7. 6**	11. 5	**9. 9**	**6. 2**	**10. 8**
352	Other chemicals	4. 4	**13. 6**	4. 7	2. 3	0. 3
353	Petroleum processing and coking	4. 0	**13. 4**	7. 9	5. 1	2. 1
355	Rubber products	1. 2	10. 4	4. 0	1. 6	0. 09
356	Plastic products	2. 5	13. 2	0. 6	0. 3	0. 3
361+362+369	Non-metallic mineral products	5. 9	8. 2	**29. 8**	**30. 0**	**124. 7**
371	Iron and steel	**7. 3**	**17. 1**	**11. 0**	**5. 2**	**13. 1**
372	Non-ferrous metals	2. 6	**17. 4**	**27. 9**	**7. 6**	**6. 0**
381	Metal products	3. 3	10. 4	1. 4	1. 0	1. 9
382+383+ 384+385	Machinery except electrical; electrical machinery; transport equipment; professional and scientific equipment	**31. 5**	**18. 4**	0. 8	0. 5	0. 2
Manufacturing overall		100	13. 7	8. 0	5. 0	10. 8

Note: All Columns report the average annual value over the years 1997-2003. %VA measures each industry's share of total manufacturing value added. ΔVA provides the average annual growth rate of value added over the period 1997-2003. Pollution intensities are measured as tonnes per million yuan of value added. For each Column, the industries with the five highest values are highlighted in bold.

Turning to the pollution data we see that for all three pollutants the five dirtiest sectors are the same, namely Paper and Products, Industrial Chemicals, Non-Metallic Mineral Products, Iron and Steel and Non-Ferrous Metals. We also note that, of the five dirtiest industries, two are also amongst the five largest industries. It can also be seen that two of the dirtiest industries, Iron and Steel and Non-Ferrous Metals, are amongst the five industries that are growing most rapidly suggesting that the composition of Chinese manufacturing may be becoming increasingly pollution intensive.

In order to examine industry-specific changes in pollution intensity, Figure 2. 3. 3 plots pollution intensity over time for the 5 dirtiest industries for each pollutant, and reveals that even the dirtiest Chinese industries have become cleaner over the period 1997-2003 when pollution is measured per unit of value added. Figure 2. 3. 3 also illustrates the differences in pollution intensity across sectors. Non-metallic mineral products (ISIC361+362+369) stand out as the largest polluter but also the sector that has seen the largest fall in its emissions. However, the "spike" in pollution intensities for non-metallic mineral products in 1998 appears to be largely driven by a reduction in value added in that year, rather than an increase in pollution.

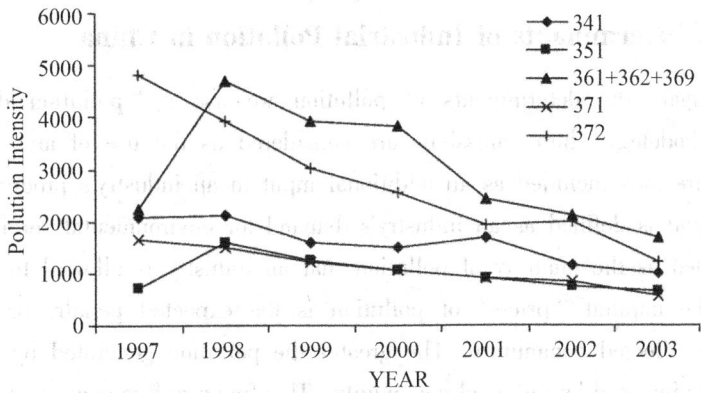

(a) SO$_2$ pollution intensity

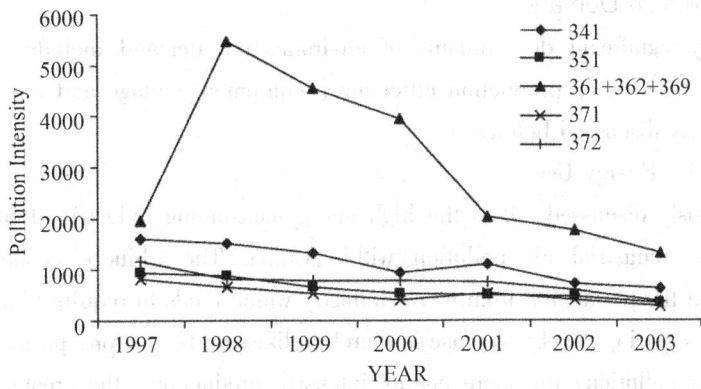

(b) Soot pollution intensity

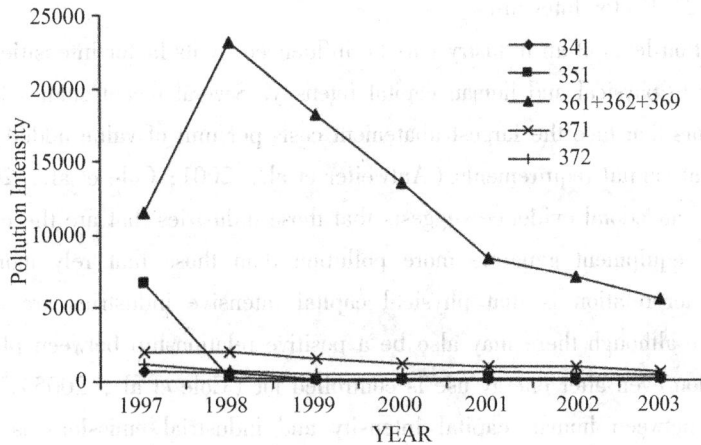

(c) Dust pollution intensity

Figure 2. 3. 3 Pollution Intensity of SO$_2$, Soot and Dust for the Five Dirtiest Manufacturing

Sectors (tonnes per million yuan of value added)

2.3.3   The Determinants of Industrial Pollution in China

To investigate the determinants of pollution we use a " pollution demand-supply schedule" methodology where emissions are considered as the use of an " environmental service" and are thus included as an additional input in an industry's production function. Pollution demand is defined as an industry's demand for environmental services; pollution supply is defined as the quantity of pollution that an industry is allowed to emit within a community. The implicit " price" of pollution is the expected penalty or compensation exacted by the affected community. The greater the pollution generated by industries the higher the costs imposed by the local community. This framework is consistent with that used by Pargal and Wheeler (1996) and Cole et al. (2005).

2.3.3.1   Pollution Demand

Potentially significant determinants of environmental demand include energy, factor intensities, industry size, production efficiency, equipment vintage and innovation. These factors are briefly discussed below.

2.3.3.1.1   Energy Use

As previously discussed, it is the high energy-consuming industries that generate the majority of the industrial air pollution within China. The Chinese economy is highly dependent upon the production from heavy industry which tends to require high levels of raw material and energy inputs. Energy use is therefore likely to be a strong positive determinant of industrial air pollution; the more energy intensive production, the greater an industry's demand for pollution.

2.3.3.1.2   Factor Intensities

The pollution level of an industry may be influenced by its factor intensities where factor intensities refer to physical and human capital intensity. Several recent studies have suggested that those sectors that face the largest abatement costs per unit of value added also have the greatest physical capital requirements (Antweiler et al., 2001; Cole et al., 2005).

In China, anecdotal evidence suggests that those industries that are the most reliant on machinery and equipment generate more pollution than those that rely more heavily on labour. One interpretation is that physical capital intensive industries are also the most energy intensive although there may also be a positive relationship between physical capital use and pollution even after energy use is controlled for (Cole et al., 2005).

The link between human capital intensity and industrial emissions is less straight-forward. Cole et al. (2005) argue that, on the one hand, high technology, human capital-intensive sectors are likely to be more efficient and less energy intensive and therefore relatively clean compared to lower skilled sectors. On the other hand, relatively low skilled, labour-intensive sectors could be fairly clean whilst those industries which typically generate greater volumes of pollution are more likely to be based on complex industrial processes that require higher levels of human capital (skilled labour) to maintain them. Interestingly, Cole et al. (2005) find a statistically significant positive relationship between pollution intensity and human capital intensity, suggesting that the latter explanation may be correct at least for developed countries.

2. 3. 3. 1. 3   Size

Size is measured by the value added per firm in an industry. Pollution intensity is expected to diminish as output increases; moreover, most empirical studies of the relationship between firm size and pollution abatement suggest scale economies in abatement are to be expected, reflecting the benefits of economies of scale both in resource and in pollution abatement. Conversely, larger firms may be more visible targets for regulatory authorities which may offset these economies of scale in abatement.[1] The relationship between an industry's gross value added per firm and its pollution intensity is therefore indeterminate.

2. 3. 3. 1. 4   Efficiency

We might expect an industry that is more productive to be more resource efficient and better managed and hence to be less energy intensive per unit of output. Furthermore, highly productive industries should also be better placed to respond relatively quickly to any change in pollution control incentives.

2. 3. 3. 1. 5   Vintage

Defined as the use of modern production processes. It is generally expected that a newer plant or one that uses modern production processes will be cleaner. As environmental regulations have become increasingly stringent, modern production processes have become more resource efficient and therefore produce less waste per unit of output. Since China's wide scale economic reforms began in the early 1980s all industries have had increased access to modern production processes and have developed many of the technological capabilities for implementing them throughout their production processes.

2. 3. 3. 1. 6   Innovation

Innovation within firms, as measured by research and development expenditure, will often result in improvements to the firm's production processes, often resulting in the need for fewer inputs per unit of output. Thus, we might expect innovation expenditure to reduce a firm's demand for pollution.

2. 3. 3. 2   Pollution Supply

The " environmental supply schedule " is determined by environmental regulations. Environmental regulations ensure that the greater the use of environmental services (i. e. the

---

[1]   We thank a referee for raising this point.

larger the emission of pollution) the higher the costs imposed on any firm or industry. Environmental regulations can be defined in terms of formal and informal environmental regulations. In terms of formal regulations, the regulatory authority imposes pollution controls on the community's behalf, e. g., command and control, pollution taxes and tradable permits. Informal regulations are those that act to compensate for weak, weakly enforced or even missing formal regulations. When this is the case, there is now significant evidence to suggest that communities "informally" regulate polluters themselves through protests, bargaining and lobbying.

Formal environmental regulations have been in place in China for many years. In 1979, the National People's Congress adopted the Environmental Protection Law (EPL), which was officially enacted in 1989. The EPL provides the basic principles governing environmental protection and the prevention of pollution and imposes criminal responsibility for serious environmental pollution. In addition, the pollution levy system was formally introduced by the Chinese government in 1978 with the intention that the levy should be imposed on pollution discharges which exceed national pollution discharge standards. Although the Chinese central government establishes the level and structure of the levy, it is the responsibility of local government to collect the levy from firms. Article 16 of Chapter Three of the EPL states that "the local people's governments at various levels shall be responsible for the environmental quality of areas under their jurisdiction and shall take measures to improve the quality of the environment" (quoted in Wang et al. 2003). As such, local authorities are required to take measures to ensure the air quality in their own jurisdiction meets the prescribed national standard. Not surprisingly, the level of the levy actually paid by firms varies considerably from one region to another and has been shown to be influenced by the level of development (Wang and Wheeler, 2000).

There are two main policy strategies on the prevention and control of industrial air pollution in China. The first strategy is to change industry production patterns; the second one is to strengthen the prevention and control of SO_2. Regulators in China thus perceive that changing the structure of the economy can significantly reduce air pollution, a perception at least partially supported by Table 2.3.1. The primary source of SO_2 and acid rain is coalmines and electricity generation by power stations. A cornerstone of Chinese environmental policy is to close down coal mines with sulphur content more than 3% and small power stations with capability less than 50,000 KW (kilowatt). By the end of 1999, such closures contributed to a remarkable and significant reduction in SO_2 emission and acid rain. Besides the above source of SO_2 and acid rain, other sources include small-scale glass factories, cement factories, and oil refining factories. By shutting down those factories that have a low level of capability, regulators can reduce SO_2 emission and acid rain by significant amounts.

The second pollution strategy has been to attempt to limit emissions in designated high-emission areas (*China Environment Yearbook*, 2000). These areas are vast and refer to 175 cities over 27 provinces where there is a geographic concentration of population and industry. The areas cover 11. 4% of China's surface area and contain sources responsible for 60% of total SO_2 emissions. In the controlled areas, a variety of environmental regulations are implemented to reduce SO_2 emissions. For instance, a pollution permit scheme is in operation; there are policies to try to encourage the use of cleaner energy sources rather than the traditional reliance on coal; and there is an increase in the standard levy for SO_2 emissions. As a result of these policies air quality within these areas appears to be gradually improving.

Despite formal regulations, a level of informal regulation appears to be present in China. According to the State Environmental Protection Administration there were 51,000 disputes over environmental pollution in 2005. Furthermore, between 2001 and 2005 China's environmental authorities received over 2. 53 million letters and 430,000 visits from 597,000 individuals seeking action to mitigate an environmental problem. There are also numerous anecdotal examples of environmental lobbying proving to be effective. For example, local people repeatedly reported to local officials a smelting plant in western China that was believed to have poisoned hundreds of villagers by dumping lead into the air and water. This lobbying eventually attracted a significant amount of national and even worldwide press attention and ultimately led the environmental protection administration to relocate the plant to a more appropriate area.[1] Secondly, in 2002 there was a proposal to build a large coal-fired power plant in the metropolitan area of Chongqing which was strongly opposed by the public. A newly formed non-governmental organisation, the Green Union of Environment Protection, led the campaign against the construction of the power plant and vociferously lobbied the local government to suspend the project. By the end of 2003 the project was finally cancelled.[2]

2. 3. 3. 3　Pollution Equilibrium

With the above discussion in mind, we define an industry's pollution demand as:

$$e_{it} = f(p_{it}, \ n_{it}, \ pci_{it}, \ hci_{it}, \ s_{it}, \ tfp_{it}, \ vin_{it}, \ innov_{it}) \tag{2.3.1}$$

where, subscripts i and t denote industry and year, e denotes air emissions, p denotes the expected price of pollution as a result of environmental regulations, n denotes energy use, *pci* is physical capital intensity, *hci* is human capital intensity, s is the size of the average

---

[1]　For the full story see ENN "Smelting Plant Blamed for Poisoning Hundreds in China Reported Many Times", September 12, 2006.

[2]　Although in these examples the public lobbied the regulators, normally local government, informal regulation may also be "direct" where the community directly lobbies the firm.

firm in the industry, *tfp* is an industry's total factor productivity, *vin* is a measure of the vintage of production process and finally *innov* represents innovation. All variables are defined in the next section.

The expected price of pollution in Equation (2.3.1) can be identified through the industry's pollution supply schedule. It is in turn a function of the quantity of pollution and the stringency of formal and informal environmental regulations.

$$p_{it} = f(e_{it}, \ FRegs_{it}, \ IRegs_{it}) \qquad\qquad (2.3.2)$$

where p and e are already defined, *FRegs* refers to formal environmental regulations, whilst *IRegs* refers to informal regulations.

In equilibrium, substituting p in Equation (2.3.1) with Equation (2.3.2) and formulating our pollution function, then we can define emission intensity as:

$$e_{it} = f(n_{it}, \ pci_{it}, \ hci_{it}, \ s_{it}, \ tfp_{it}, \ vin_{it}, \ innov_{it}, \ FRegs_{it}, \ IRegs_{it}) \quad (2.3.3)$$

2.3.4　Data and Econometrics

Our estimating equation originates from Equation (2.3.3),

$$E_{it} = \alpha_i + \delta_t + \beta_1 N_{it} + \beta_2 PCI_{it} + \beta_3 HCI_{it} + \beta_4 SIZE_{it} + \beta_5 TFP_{it} + \beta_6 CAP_{it} + \beta_7 RD_{it} + \lambda REG + \varepsilon_{it}$$

$$(2.3.4)$$

Our dependent variable, E_{it}, is pollution emission intensity measured as pollution emission per unit of value added. We estimate Equation (2.3.4) separately for three different sorts of air pollution, namely SO_2, soot and dust. The variable α_i with subscript i denotes industry specific effects whilst δ_t with subscript t denotes year specific effects. Equation (2.3.4) is estimated for 15 three-digit ISIC manufacturing industries, and the period covers 7 years from 1997 to 2003. All monetary variables are deflated to 1990 prices by a GDP deflator. See Appendix H for details on the data.

2.3.4.1　"Demand" Variable Considerations

With regard to our "demand" variables, N_{it} denotes total energy consumption per unit of value added, including consumption of coal, coke, crude oil, gasoline, kerosene, diesel oil, fuel oil, natural gas and electricity. PCI_{it}, physical capital intensity, is measured as non-wage value added per worker. HCI_{it}, human capital intensity, is defined as an average wage paid to staff. Our size variable, $SIZE_{it}$, is defined as value added per firm, calculated as the ratio of an industry's value added to the number of enterprises in that industry. The variable total factor productivity, TFP_{it}, is estimated using a Cobb-Douglas production function.① The variable CAP_{it} is an industry's capital expenditure scaled by total physical capital stock, and we measure the capital expenditure using data on investment in

---

① Details regarding our estimation of TFP are available upon request. The coefficient on TFP in Equation (2.3.4) is robust to a number of alternative specifications of production functions.

capital construction reported in the *China Statistical Yearbook*.① Under the assumption that the greater such investment within an industry, the newer the industry's equipment and machinery is likely to be, such investment can act as a good measure for the vintage of production processes. The variable RD_{it} is an industry's research and development expenditure scaled by value added. RD_{it} is measured as investment in innovation, including innovation investment in new construction projects, expansion projects and reconstruction projects within an industry.②

2.3.4.2 "Supply" Variable Considerations

REG in Equation (2.3.4) denotes a vector of variables capturing formal and informal regulations. Since direct measures of regulations are not available, we argue that these variables are locally determined and hence capture regulations by using their regional determinants.

Since formal regulation is weak or even absent in developing countries like China, many communities have struck bargains for pollution abatement with local factories. Without recourse to legal enforcement of existing regulations (if any), they must rely on the leverage provided by social pressure on workers and managers, adverse publicity, the threat (or use) of violence, recourse to civil law, and pressure through politicians, local administrators, or religious leaders. This process is distinct from national or local formal regulation in that it uses other channels to induce compliance with community-determined standards of acceptable performance.

Also, formal regulation is likely to have a regional component. As already outlined, China's legislation on the prevention and control of air pollution endows local authorities with the power to establish their own standards for those items that are not specified by national standards. Local policymakers can take into account local conditions when implementing environmental policy.

With the above arguments in mind, we need to investigate the local determinants of formal and informal regulations. Our first attempt to capture formal regulations is to use a measure of regional pollution prosecutions, defined as the number of pollution related prosecutions in a region scaled by a region's industry output.

Since the emphasis placed on formal regulations by local authorities may depend upon

① Capital construction refers to the new construction projects or extension projects, and related work of the enterprises, institutions or administrative units, only covering projects with a total investment of 500,000 RMB yuan and over. The purpose of capital construction is mainly for expanding production capacity or improving project efficiency.

② Investment in innovation refers to the renewal of fixed assets and technologies. It also includes investment in the corresponding supplementary projects and the related work. This measure only covers projects with a total investment of 500,000 RMB yuan and over.

the social problems within a region, a region's unemployment rate is included to reflect the social status of that region. The unemployment rate might affect local pollution regulations for two reasons. First, a high unemployment rate in a region might attract more attention from the local authorities and force them to devote more resources to dealing with unemployment hence devoting fewer resources to pollution control. Second, communities in a region may tolerate the existence of a polluting plant nearby if it provides employment. Such an effect is more likely to occur in regions with a high level of unemployment. Both arguments suggest that a region with a high unemployment rate will tend to have lax environmental regulations and attract more pollution intensive industries.

With regard to informal regulation, we postulate that these are also likely to be determined by regional characteristics. There is likely to be a positive link between a region's income and the stringency of its regulations. An affluent neighbourhood might be more concerned about the impact of pollution on property prices than a relatively poor neighbourhood. Similarly, a neighbourhood with a greater proportion of professional workers might be more able to mobilise opposition to pollution intensive plants. We rely upon the unemployment rate to capture wealth, although we do use per capita income in our sensitivity analysis.①

Furthermore, regional environmental regulations may be a function of a region's population density. On the one hand, a densely populated area may have more people adversely affected by pollution and hence opposition to a pollution intensive plant may be greater. On the other hand, within a densely populated area a pollution intensive plant may be less "visible" and hence less likely to come to local people's attention. Our estimation will examine which of these competing effects is dominant.

There are a number of other factors that may determine regional regulations, including demographic factors such as a region's age structure and the population's level of education. Demographic factors may influence the extent to which a region lobbies for cleaner industries, for instance, a younger population may be expected to be more concerned about pollution issues and better placed to lobby against polluters. We measure a population's age structure in terms of the number of people under the age of 15.

The level of education in a region may also play a role in determining regional regulations. Communities that consist of people with a low level of education and with little ability to acquire information may give an inappropriately low weight to pollution matters simply because they are not aware of the consequences. Moreover, people in such communities may be incapable of using the available regulatory channels. Hence, polluting

① Since regional formal and regional informal regulations are likely to be driven by the same determinants (e. g. wealth) we are unable to separate these two components.

plants may locate to areas with a larger percentage of poorly educated people or incumbent firms may simply face less regulatory pressure in areas with below average educational attainment. Our education variable is defined as the share of a region's population that has acquired a college or higher level of education.

In sum, the determinants discussed above for both formal and informal regulations incorporate a region's pollution prosecutions, unemployment rate, population density, age structure, and level of education. As we can see, all of these determinants are region specific. However, our pollution data and industrial characteristic data are industry specific and not region specific. We therefore have to transform our regulation data from region specific to industry specific. To take the example of our pollution prosecutions variable, we do this as follows:

$$REGpros_{it} = \sum_r (s_{irt} * PROS_{rt}) \qquad (2.3.5)$$

where subscripts i, r, and t denote industry, region and year, respectively, s is the output of industry i in region r as a share of total national output of industry i, and $PROS_{rt}$ is pollution prosecutions in region r scaled by that region's total industry output. Therefore, industries that have a higher share of output in regions with high pollution prosecutions will have higher values of $REGpros$. Equivalent variables for regional unemployment rate, population density, population under the age of 15 and level of education are also calculated in the same way and denoted by $REGunem$, $REGpd$, $REGagapop$, $REGedu$, respectively. These variables are calculated using data for 31 regions in China, including 22 provinces, 5 autonomous districts and 4 municipalities.[1]

Table 2.3.2 Determinants of Industrial Pollution (Fixed and Random Effects)

	FIXED EFFECTS			RANDOM EFFECTS		
	(1) SO_2emi	(2) Sootemi	(3) Dustemi	(4) SO_2emi	(5) Sootemi	(6) Dustemi
Energy	92. 9	85. 1	518. 3	90. 0	64. 2	298. 7
	(2. 48) **	(2. 09) **	(2. 67) ***	(3. 30) ***	(2. 17) **	(2. 27) **
PCI	1. 24	0. 933	4. 50	0. 722	1. 02	0. 0412
	(1. 30)	(0. 97)	(1. 14)	(1. 01)	(1. 74) *	(1. 65) *
HCI	0. 026	0. 405	1. 581	0. 049	0. 202	0. 854
	(0. 16)	(2. 30) **	(2. 13) **	(0. 45)	(1. 67) *	(1. 65) *
SIZE	50. 2	20. 2	68. 9	−5. 25	−9. 72	−73. 3

---

[1] Hong Kong, Macao and Taiwan are excluded due to lack of data.

Continued

	FIXED EFFECTS			RANDOM EFFECTS		
	(1)SO$_2$emi	(2)Sootemi	(3)Dustemi	(4)SO$_2$emi	(5)Sootemi	(6)Dustemi
	(1.91)*	(1.05)	(0.63)	(−0.32)	(−0.62)	(−1.02)
TFP	−20.1	−19.1	−31.4	−84.5	−12.9	−40.8
	(−1.88)*	(−2.16)**	(−0.96)	(−1.58)	(−2.45)**	(−2.10)**
CAP	−1.46	4.11	2.75	−4.35	2.42	−3.26
	(−0.52)	(1.94)*	(0.29)	(−0.81)	(0.90)	(−0.29)
RD	−0.26	−1.60	−7.54	−3.55	−4.61	−22.19
	(−0.18)	(−1.25)	(−1.24)	(−2.36)**	(−2.00)**	(−2.19)**
REGpros	−38.4	−23.2	−107.9	−14.5	−14.4	−98.4
	(−1.05)	(−1.06)	(−1.11)	(−0.46)	(−0.70)	(−1.13)
REGunem	24.7	−10.9	107.5	113.8	26.3	75.3
	(0.38)	(−0.32)	(0.70)	(1.36)	(0.89)	(0.62)
REGpd	5.90	2.42	−2.04	−0.493	0.00668	−0.235
	(2.24)**	(1.42)	(−0.25)	(−0.73)	(0.020)	(−0.11)
REGagapopi	−13.2	7.46	18.5	2.77	29.2	156.6
	(−0.33)	(0.27)	(0.16)	(0.08)	(0.99)	(1.27)
REGedu	61.3	−10.8	−16.2	−26.1	−56.1	−20.8
	(1.65)	(−0.40)	(−1.59)	(−1.07)	(−2.39)**	(−2.13)**
R^2	0.60	0.40	0.42	0.61	0.51	0.10
Hausman				140.8	11.0	0.39
(FE. V RE.)				(0.000)	(0.754)	(1.000)
D-M Exog.	0.20	0.61	0.14			
(REGpd)	(0.66)	(0.44)	(0.71)			
D-M Exog.	2.81	0.28	0.70			
(REGunem)	(0.10)	(0.60)	(0.40)			
n	105	105	105	105	105	105

Our dependent variables are expressed in terms of pollution intensities, measured as emissions per unit of value added. t-statistics in parentheses for fixed effects and z-statistics in parentheses for random effects. Time dummies are included. * significant at 10% level; ** significant at 5% level; *** significant at 1% level. D-M Exog is the Davidson and Mackinnen test for exogeneity, this test cannot be performed for random effects estimations.

Endogeneity is a potential problem with some of our regulation variables. The regional unemployment rate, for example, could be endogenously determined by pollution intensity rather than the other way around. It could be argued that high wage individuals will choose not to live in a highly pollution intensive region and hence such a region will have a high percentage of low-income or unemployed individuals. The population density in a region may also be determined by that region's pollution intensity. Individuals would choose not to reside in close proximity to a pollution intensive plant and hence the surrounding population density could be lower. Such endogeneity concerns are examined in our Results section.

Table 2.3.3　Estimated Elasticities from Table 2.3.2

	FIXED EFFECTS			RANDOM EFFECTS		
	(1)SO_2	(2)SOOT	(3)DUST	(4)SO_2	(5)SOOT	(6)DUST
Energy	1.002**	1.47**	4.14***	0.971***	1.11***	2.38***
PCI	0.509	0.613	1.359	0.296	0.672*	1.25
HCI	0.160	3.97**	7.10**	0.302	1.98*	3.83*
SIZE	0.578*	0.372	0.586	−0.0600	−0.179	−0.622
TFP	−3.50*	−5.35**	−4.04	−1.476	−3.61***	−5.23**
CAP	−0.059	0.268*	0.0820	−0.177	0.158	−0.0970
RD	−0.0450	−0.431	−0.933	−0.598**	−1.24***	−2.74***
REGpros	−0.569	−0.550	−1.17	−0.215	−0.343	−1.07
REGunem	0.660	−0.465	2.09	3.03	1.12	1.47
REGpd	3.43**	2.26	−0.872	−0.287	0.00612	−0.100
REGagepop	−0.340	0.308	0.349	0.0710	1.21	2.96*
REGedu	3.36	−0.947	−6.482	−1.43	−4.92***	−8.31**

* significant at 10% level; ** significant at 5% level; *** significant at 1% level.

Since China's formal environmental regulations are not entirely regional in nature, we rely upon industry effects to capture regulations which are industry specific and which do not change over time and on year dummies to capture effects which are common to all industries but do change over time.

Equation (2.3.4) is estimated using both fixed and random effects specifications and year dummies are included in all specifications. As outlined previously our prior expectations are as follows: we expect the sign of $\beta1$, the coefficient on energy use per unit of value added and $\beta2$, the coefficient on physical capital intensity, to be positive. The coefficient on human capital intensity, $\beta3$, could be positive or negative depending on whether human capital intensive industries are clean or dirty subject to the industrial features in a particular country. $\beta4$, the coefficient on value added per firm within industry i (SIZE) could be positive or negative depending on the potentially competing effects of economies of scale in abatement and increased visibility to regulatory authorities. $\beta5$ the coefficient on total factor productivity (TFP), $\beta6$ the coefficient on capital expenditure (CAP) and $\beta7$ the coefficient on R&D expenditure (RD), should all be negative. We expect the sign on *REGpros* to be negative and that on *REGunem* to be positive. The sign on *REGpd* may be negative due to the lobbying power of a densely populated region or positive if a plant in a densely populated area is less visible and hence escapes informal regulation. Finally, we expect the signs on *REGagepop* and *REGedu* to both be negative.

2.3.5   Estimation Results

2.3.5.1   Main Results

We present our main results in Table 2.3.2 for both fixed and random effects specifications. The dependent variable is the pollution intensity of SO_2, SOOT and DUST, denoted by SO_2, SOOT and DUST, respectively. The Hausman specification test rejects the null of consistency when using SO_2 as the dependent variable, but the null cannot be rejected when using SOOT or DUST. Random effects results may therefore be considered consistent for SOOT and DUST. Since a random effects specification captures variation both within and between industries we place greater emphasis on random effects results given that a reliance on only within industry variation, as provided by fixed effects, is not ideal given our limited time series. For SO_2, random effects results are not consistent and hence for this pollutant we place greater emphasis on fixed effects results.

Focusing our discussion on fixed effects SO_2 and random effects SOOT and DUST, and concentrating on statistically significant coefficients, we see that all three pollutants have a positive relationship with energy use and a negative relationship with total factor productivity (TFP). In addition, soot and dust are both positive functions of physical and human capital intensity (PCI and HCI) suggesting that those industries reliant upon large amounts of physical capital such as machinery and equipment are typically more pollution intensive. With regard to HCI, it appears that in China, high skilled, human capital-intensive industries are dirtier than low skilled, labour intensive industries, at least in terms of soot and dust emissions. Table 2.3.2 also indicates that soot and dust are both negative functions of research and development expenditure, RD, suggesting that innovation within firms can reduce pollution intensity.

Turning to our regulation variables, we find that SO_2 emissions are a positive and significant function of *REGpd* (our regulation proxy based upon population density) suggesting that industries located in regions with high population density will tend to have higher pollution, other things being equal. This is consistent with the 'visibility' argument raised earlier i. e. plants located in densely populated areas may be less visible to the local population and hence less likely to face lobby pressure. In addition, we find that soot and dust are both negative and significant functions of *REGedu* (our regulation measure based upon education) suggesting that regions with greater levels of education may have more stringent regulations.[1]

Table 2.3.4　Sensitivity Analysis

RANDOM EFFECTS	(7) SOOT	(8) DUST	(9) SOOT	(10) DUST	(11) SOOT	(12) DUST	(13) SOOT	(14) DUST
Energy			57.1**	269.5**	58.2**	274.6**	58.9**	287.1**
			(2.02)	(2.15)	(2.01)	(2.16)	(2.19)	(2.36)
PCI	1.77**	8.26**	00.781	4.21*	0.827	3.95	1.08	5.12*
	(2.10)	(2.07)	(1.30)	(1.67)	(1.40)	(1.57)	(1.56)	(1.73)
HCI	0.251*	1.29**	0.202*	0.623	0.168	0.616	0.345**	1.26**
	(1.73)	(1.97)	(1.79)	(1.41)	(1.56)	(1.38)	(2.12)	(1.84)
SIZE	−7.83	−73.0	−10.5	−93.1	−11.7	−99.9	−20.7	−89.9
	(0.49)	(1.02)	(0.72)	(1.44)	(0.74)	(1.47)	(0.70)	(1.10
TFP	−21.1**	−78.1**	−10.3*	−29.2*	−0.00991**	−0.0274*	−0.0094**	−0.0276
	(2.31)	(1.97)	(1.95)	(1.65)	(2.08)	(1.70)	(2.22)	(2.11)
CAP	5.78***	13.9	2.13	−5.33	2.00	−5.18	2.66	2.03
	(3.26)	(1.14)	(0.80)	(0.52)	(0.72)	(0.51)	(1.13)	(0.25)
RD	−2.80	−12.1*	−3.38**	−16.8**	−3.51*	−17.5**	−3.70**	−14.3**
	(1.61)	(1.69)	(2.04)	(2.07)	(1.88)	(2.02)	(2.13)	(2.27)
REGpros	−19.9	−137.8*					3.04	−56.0
	(0.98)	(1.66)					(0.8)	(1.19)
REGunem	47.3	135.6						
	(1.04)	(0.85)						

---

　①　To test for the potential endogeneity of *REGpd* and *REGunem* we perform the Davidson-Mackinnon exogeneity test. The null hypothesis for this test states that OLS estimates would be consistent and hence a rejection of the null suggests that endogenous regressors are having an impact on estimated coefficients and hence instrumental variables should be used. We use lagged values of *REGpd* and *REGunem* as instruments in order to perform the test. As Table 2.3.2 indicates, we are unable to reject the null of consistency for either *REGpd* or *REGunem* suggesting that endogeneity is not a problem.

Continued

RANDOM EFFECTS	(7) SOOT	(8) DUST	(9) SOOT	(10) DUST	(11) SOOT	(12) DUST	(13) SOOT	(14) DUST
REGpd	0.125	1.03						
	(0.25)	(0.34)						
REGagepop	−10.1	−48.5						
	(0.52)	(0.69)						
REGedu	−51.3**	−189.0*					−22.6**	−93.3**
	(2.28)	(1.92)					(2.13)	(2.19)
REGpcy					−0.0685	−0.396		
					(0.34)	(0.50)		
R^2	0.31	0.16	0.29	0.33	0.33	0.34	0.36	0.23
n	105	104	105	104	105	104	105	104

Our dependent variables are expressed in terms of pollution intensities, measured as emissions per unit of value added. t-statistics in parentheses. * significant at 10% level; ** significant at 5% level; *** significant at 1% level.

In order to assess and compare the economic significance of our estimated results, Table 2.3.3 provides estimated elasticities from the results in Table 2.3.2. Asterisks denote the statistical significance of the elasticities and hence indicate which should receive the greatest emphasis. In our three preferred models of fixed effects SO_2 and random effects soot and dust, we find that TFP has the greatest elasticity, together with REGpd for SO_2 and REGedu for soot and dust. The elasticities on energy use, HCI and RD vary by pollutant. Taking the random effects soot model as an example, these results suggest that a 10% increase in energy use will lead to an 11.09% increase in soot intensity, equivalent to an increase of 55.6 tonnes per unit of value added. Conversely, a 10% increase in TFP will reduce soot intensity by 36.14%, equivalent to 181.17 tonnes per unit of value added. Perhaps a greater policy implication stems from the RD result. A 10% increase in R&D expenditure per unit of value added will reduce soot intensity by 12.44%, equivalent to 62.36 tonnes per unit of value added.

2.3.5.2   Sensitivity Analysis

To check the sensitivity or our results to changes in our specification Table 2.3.4 presents a number of robustness checks. For reasons of space we focus on random effects results and two of our three pollutants, SOOT and DUST.

Models (7) and (8) begin our sensitivity analysis by dropping energy use from our standard model. We now find an increase in the statistical significance of PCI, indicating that physical capital intensive firms are more pollution intensive, ceteris paribus, because they tend to be more energy intensive. This accords with prior expectations although it is worth emphasising that our main results, together with those of Cole et al. (2005), do find physical capital intensity to be significant even once energy use is controlled for, suggesting that physical capital intensive firms are pollution intensive for reasons unrelated to their use of energy. The sign and significance of the other explanatory variables are similar to those in Table 2. 3. 2, although one notable exception is *REGpros* which remains negative but becomes weakly significant for dust emissions.

Models (9) and (10) drop all of the regulation variables and rely upon the industry and year effects to capture the effects of environmental policy. The sign and significance of our results remain very similar to those in Table 2. 3. 2, suggesting that the regulation variables are not unduly influencing the coefficients on the non-regulation variables.

Models (11) and (12) use an alternative measure of regional regulations, namely regional per capita income (*REGpcy*). We might expect both formal and informal regulatory pressure to be correlated with per capita income. In light of endogeneity concerns we again perform Davidson-Mackinnon exogeneity tests which are unable to reject the null of consistency, suggesting endogeneity is not present.[①] For both pollutants, we find income to be a negative but statistically insignificant determinant of pollution.

Finally, models (13) and (14) limit our regulation variables to *REGedu*, a key proxy for informal regulatory pressure and the only regulation variable that appears to be consistently significant for soot and dust, and *REGpros* our most direct measure of formal regulatory pressure. *REGedu* remains negative and significant while *REGpros* is insignificant and is not consistently signed.

2. 3. 6　Conclusions

This study has carefully examined the possible factors that may influence industrial pollution emissions in China. Our panel of 15 industries covering the period 1997-2003 has provided a number of insights into what determines industrial pollution intensity. For three air pollutants, SO_2, soot and dust, we have found energy use, physical capital intensity and human capital intensity to be positive and generally significant determinants of pollution intensity. On the other hand, pollution intensity turned out to be a negative function of the productivity of an industry and an industry's expenditure on innovation. Other factors such as average firm size and capital expenditure do not have statistically significant relationships

---

　① Davidson-Mackinnon test results using lagged *REGpcy* as an instrument are 0. 11 (0. 74) and 2. 75 (0. 11) for DUST and SOOT, respectively.

with pollution intensity.

In our model we have no direct measure of pollution regulations. Instead, we have attempted to capture the effects of regulations using year and industry effects, together with those regional characteristics that are likely to influence the stringency of regulation. Our proxies for informal regulations do not perform particularly well in our model. The majority of our regional characteristic variables have an insignificant effect on pollution intensity except the level of education that has a significant effect on the pollution intensity of soot and dust.

Our results suggest that for both firms and pollution regulators in China, the most fruitful ways in which to reduce industry pollution are to reduce energy use, to stimulate industrial productivity and to increase research and development expenditure. Tax credits or other incentives to stimulate R&D expenditure may be something Chinese policy makers may wish to emphasize. With regard to productivity, our results indicate that "environmental productivity", perhaps with associated reductions in environmental compliance costs, is a positive side-effect of traditional productivity gains.

We finish on a note of caution. We see this study as a first attempt to examine the complex linkages between pollution intensity and industrial characteristics for a large developing country such as China. Inevitably the study would have benefited from a richer dataset with a longer time series, greater industry coverage and smaller regional units to capture regional regulatory effects. In time such data may be forthcoming therefore allowing more sophisticated analyses of even greater benefit to Chinese policymakers.

References

Antweiler, W., Copeland, B. R., Taylor, M. S., 2001. Is Free Trade Good for Environment? *American Economic Review*, 91, 877-908.

Cole, M. A., Elliott, R. J. R., Shimamoto, K., 2005. Industrial Characteristics, Environmental Regulation and Air Pollution: An Analysis of the UK Manufacturing Sector. *Journal of Environmental Economics and Management*, 50, 121-143.

Dasgupta, S., Hettige, H., Wheeler, D., 1999. What Improves Environmental Performance? Evidence from Mexico. *Journal of Environmental Economics and Management*, 38, 39-66.

Dasgupta, S., Laplante, B., Mamingi, N., Wang, H., 2001. Inspections, Pollution Prices and Environmental Performance: Evidence from China. *Ecological Economics*, 36, 487-498.

Hamilton, J., 1993. Politics and Social Costs: Estimating the Impact of Collective Action on Hazardous Waste Facilities. *Rand Journal of Economics*, 24, 101-125.

Helland, E., Whiford, A. B., 2001. Pollution Incidence and Political Jurisdiction:

Evidence from the TRI. Presented at the American Economic Association Meetings (2001), and the Western Economic Association Meetings.

Kahn, M. E., 1999. The Silver Lining of Rust Best Manufacturing Decline. *Journal of Urban Economics*, 46, 360-376.

Pargal, S., Wheeler, D., 1996. Informal Regulation of Industrial Pollution in Developing Countries: Evidence from Indonesia. *Journal of Political Economy*, 104, 1314-1327.

Wang, H., Wheeler, D., 2000. Endogenous Enforcement and the Effectiveness of China's Pollution Levy System. World Bank Policy Research Department, Working Paper 2336.

Wang, H., Mamingi, N., Laplante, B., Dasgupta, S., 2003. Incomplete Enforcement of Pollution Regulation: Bargaining Power of Chinese Factories. *Environmental and Resource Economics*, 24, 245-262.

Chapter Three
Sustainability Measures

3. 1　Ecological Accounting for an Integrated "Pig-biogas-fish" System Based on Emergetic Indicators[①]

3. 1. 1　Introduction

Since fossil fuels are limited and consumption of these fuels casts a negative impact on the environment, renewable energy is playing a crucial role in sustainable energy development. In 2012 alone, global investment in renewables has reached 244 million dollars, 8% above the 2010 level. As the world's fourth largest source of energy (following oil, coal, and natural gas), biomass is expected to become the most promising renewable energy source. Biogas production, a primary way of using biomass to provide modern energy services, has continued to increase, especially in developing countries.

China has an enduring history of biogas utilization with the first test of biogas fermentation that was undertaken in the 1880s. Afterwards to address challenges from energy shortage in rural areas, China has been on a constant endeavor to promote the biogas construction. In 2007, the government published the *Medium and Long-Term Development Plan for Renewable Energy*, predicting that some 80 million household biogas digesters would have been installed with a total output of 30 billon m^3 by the end of 2020. In recent years, with the expansion of rural urbanization in China, waste disposal is becoming a troublesome roadblock in the way. A promising biogas technology is expected to offer energy supply, as well as to achieve multi-level utilization of organic waste. In this context, the integrated biogas-utilization system, which incorporates biogas fermentation technology into crop production and animal husbandry, has arrested extensive attention.

In the integrated biogas-utilization system, the substrate for anaerobic digestion is from

---

① Published on *Ecological Indicators*, Volume 47, pp. 189-197, with a few modifications due to space constraints. Reuse permission has been obtained from Elsevier.

agricultural and household wastes, thus drastically preventing environmental pollution that stems from the wastes discharged directly. After fermentation, biogas finds its application as a clean fuel in households, and biogas residue is recycled to agriculture as an organic fertilizer. The integrated biogas-utilization system has thus realized the maximization of recycling and declared its sound environmental and economic advantages. However, though the integrated system yields energy and goods, it demands materials and work force, particularly free resources from nature as its subsystems of crop production and animal husbandry are heavily dependent on environmental conditions. Therefore, systematic accounting on the integrated system is imperative to be undertaken in order to guarantee a sustainable future. Extensive studies on the ecological accounting of typical biogas systems have been carried out with methods of life cycle assessment (LCA) and exergy. These studies have contributed significantly to the development of accounting for renewable energy projects. However, these methods are rarely implemented in full consideration of the resource use due to human labor and environmental work. In contrast, the emergy method that was first proposed by Odum on the basis of a combined system of humanity and nature, could offer an insightful perspective into production system evaluation from a systematic point of view (Brown and Ulgiati, 2004).

Emergy is defined as the available energy of one kind of previously used up in transformations directly and indirectly to make a product or service (Odum, 1996). It tracks the total amount of resources required to produce something by tracing all energy flows back to the conventionally accepted Earth's ultimate energy source: solar radiation, thus integrating the value of environmental investments, goods, services and information on a common foundation of solar emjoule (abbreviated seJ) and devising scientific indicators to measure its ecological performance. Till now, the emergy method has been performed on the region scale, the nation scale, and the world scale. In addition, some renewable energy technologies have also been evaluated with emergy, such as the hydropower plant, the wind power plant and the solar power system. A few studies have been conducted so far to assess typical biogas systems via the emergy approach. Wei et al. (2009) compared the efficiency and sustainability between a "four in one" peach production system in Beijing and a conventional solar greenhouse peach production system by emergy-based ecological analysis. Ciotola et al. (2011) evaluated a small scale biogas production and electricity generation system in Costa Rica on aspects of sustainability and environmental impacts with emergy indices. Chen and Chen (2012) undertook an emergy evaluation of the efficiency and emission mitigation effect of a biogas-linked agricultural ecosystem in Gongcheng County, China. These studies serve as a reflection for the developments of both the emergy analysis and ecological biogas system.

Hubei Province is located along the Yangtze River with developed aquaculture industry, and the "pig-biogas-fish" system, a common integrated biogas mode in Hubei is chosen as a case in this study. As an extension for our work on fossil energy cost of purchased goods in the "pig-biogas-fish" system, this study presents systematic accounting and indicators of the "pig-biogas-fish" system via the emergy method to estimate environmental and economic inputs and to assess the sustainability of this system. Nowadays, the latest systematic multi-scale embodied ecological elements databases including different kinds of productions in China have been published by Chen and his research group (Chen and Chen, 2010; Zhou, 2008), and are thus applied in this research to improve the accuracy and avoid repeatability of emergy accounting. Besides, the operational time of the biogas digester is assumed as 21 years or 20 years in previous researches, but actually, it does not always tally with the fact. In this case, this study tries to take account of the impact of the lifespan on sustainability for a more accurate analysis.

3.1.2　Materials and Methods

3.1.2.1　The Case Biogas System Description

The household biogas system under consideration is the biogas energy and animal husbandry linked agro-ecosystem in Zhongzhouzi fishery, Jinzhou City (111°15′-114°05′E, 29°26d-31°37′N), Hubei province, which we call a "pig-biogas-fish" system. Jinzhou is an important port city and freshwater fishery base along the Yangtze River, and is known as "the land of plenty" in China, with an annual average sunlight time of 1978 h. The annual average temperature is 17.8℃, with the lowest winter temperature going down to -3.0℃ and the highest temperature climbing up to 38.4℃ in summer. The annual average precipitation is 1,300 mm. In recent years, Jinzhou is committed to developing ecological agriculture, and chooses Zhongzhouzi fishery as an exemplary demonstration area for the household "pig-biogas-fish" system. Up to 2010, the demonstration area has been extended to 0.6 million m² and the income of residents has increased by 6.2 million RMB in total compared to the year 2008.

As shown in Figure 3.1.1, the "pig-biogas-fish" system consists of a pigsty, a biogas pool and a fishpond. The workflow is as follows: through raising pigs, residents put the pig manure into the digester as the fermentation crude to produce biogas for everyday lighting and cooking. Meanwhile, the biogas slurry and residue can be used as a base fertilizer and top dressing for the fishpond. This system is designed with an operational life of 20 years. Given the poor management, however, it is not capable of working for 20 years. In China, the government has offered local residents sufficient technological guidance and subsidy for biogas promotion at the beginning of the construction, but subsequent management guidance is often neglected.

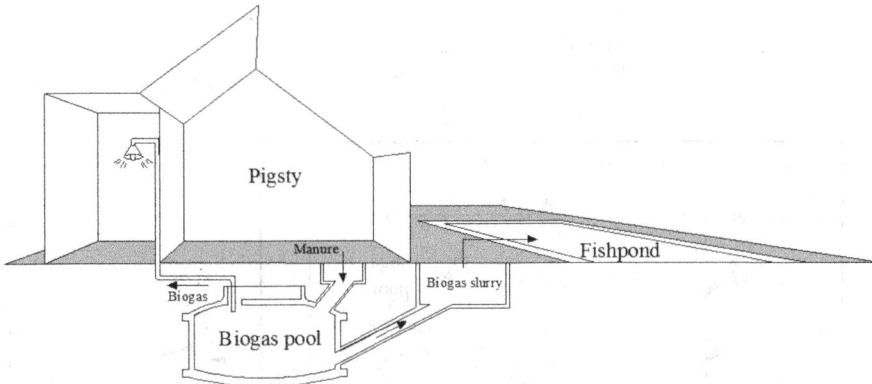

Figure 3. 1. 1 Schematic Diagram of the "Pig-biogas-fish" System

3. 1. 2. 2 Emergy Analysis

Odum's emergy synthesis is a thermodynamic approach for the ecological evaluation of resources, products and services by accounting the total natural work. On the one hand, the emergy method focus on the role of the environment in support of human-dominated processes, which can be used as a supplement to the money-based economic evaluation that takes only the contribution from social economy into consideration. On the other hand, totally different from conventional energy analysis which merely accounts for the remaining available energy at present, the emergy method expands the time scale of the evaluation to include the memory of resource flows converging to the system. Detailed process of emergy accounting has been given by some researchers. For the "pig-biogas-fish" system, the first step is to draw an overview emergy diagram to define the boundary of the given system and identify the inputs and outputs to be evaluated on basic symbols presented by Odum. As described in Figure 3. 1. 2, the total emergy inputs are generally aggregated into four categories: free environmental renewable resources (RR), free environmental nonrenewable resources (NR), purchased social renewable inputs (RP) and purchased social nonrenewable inputs (NP). The total emergy use (U) is equal to the sum of emergy inflows ($RR+NR+RP+NP$). Correspondingly, produced energy (Ep) denotes the output of total energy produced by the "pig-biogas-fish" system. Besides, pig manure and biogas residues are recycled in this system, and these two intermediate materials are regarded as the internal force that drives emergy to transfer from pigsty to biogas pool and then from biogas pool to fishpond, hence system feedback emergy (SF) represents the communication emergy within this system.

The second step for emergy analysis is to obtain the emergy value of each item considered in the "pig-biogas-fish" system. In this step, all inputs with raw data such as

117

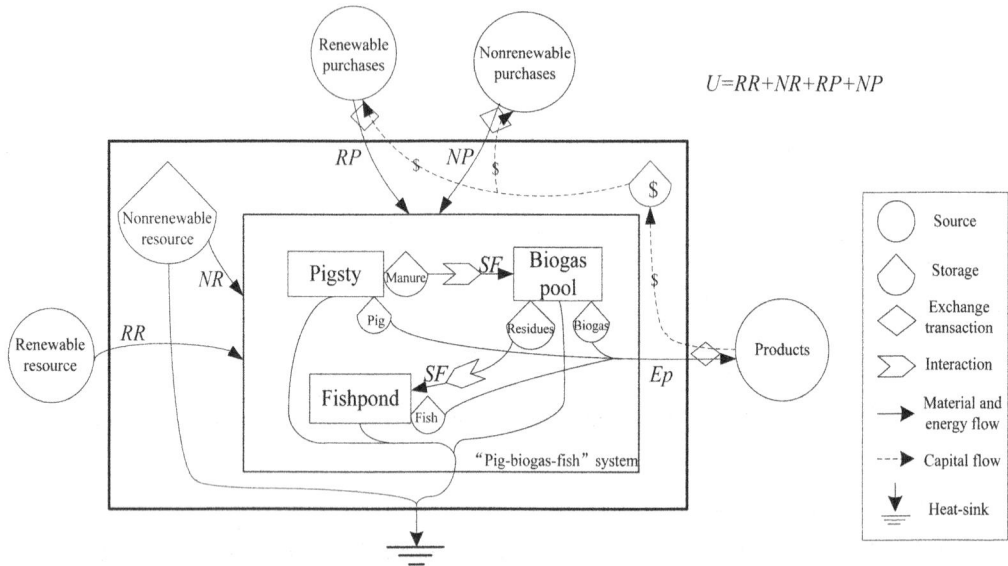

Figure 3. 1. 2   Aggregated Emergy Flow Diagram for the "Pig-biogas-fish" System

joules, kilograms or dollars are converted into solar emergy with the unit of seJ. And for this conversion, Unit Emergy Value (UEV), also regarded as emergy intensity, is defined as the solar emergy required to make per unit (joule or mass or money) of a product or service, thus total emergy use (U) in the biogas system can be calculated as

$$U = \sum u_i = \sum p_i \cdot UEV_i \qquad (3.1.1)$$

where u_i denotes the emergy associated directly and indirectly with the production of the ith product, p_i, to the entire process of the system. It should be noted that UEVs for a wide variety of goods and services can be obtained from previous studies to facilitate the emergy analysis. However, UEV of a given object may have different values due to the specific geographic location and production process. As the first endeavor in embodied ecological elements accounting of Chinese national economy, Zhou (2008) offered a systematic UEV database consisting of 151 physical goods by combining the input-output analysis with ecological thermodynamics. To avoid dispersed and inappropriate UEVs and to guarantee the accuracy of emergy analysis in this study, UEVs of materials and resources associated with the investigated biogas system are mainly from Zhou's database.

The final step is to establish an emergetic indicator framework and to quantify ecological behaviors of the "pig-biogas-fish" system, which will be elucidated in detail below.

The global emergy sustaining the biosphere is also regarded as the emergy base of reference, which was previously calculated as 9. 44E + 24 seJ/yr, and then updated as

1. 58E+25 seJ/yr and 1. 52E+25 seJ/yr (Brown and Ulgiati, 2010). In the following we adopt the Brown and Ulgiati (2010) baseline, and *UEV*s prior to the year 2010 are multiplied by 1. 61 (the ratio of 1. 52E+25/9. 44E+24) or 0. 96 (the ratio of 1. 52E+25/1. 58E+25) for conversion to the new baseline.

3. 1. 2. 3 Emergetic Indicators

On the basis of the fluxes mentioned above (*RR*, *NR*, *RP*, *NP*, *U*, *Ep*, *SF*), a series of indicators are introduced as follows to present the system performance of the "pig-biogas-fish" system.

$$\text{Transformity } (Tr) = \frac{U}{Ep} \qquad (3.1.2)$$

Transformity (*Tr*), a type of *UEV*, is defined as the emergy input per unit of available energy output with a unit of seJ/J. It is obtained by the ratio of total emergy used in a process to the energy yielded by the process. *Tr* is an expression of the quality of the output itself. The higher the transformity, the more emergy is required to make the product flow.

$$\text{Renewable percentage index } (Pr) = \frac{RR + RP}{U} \qquad (3.1.3)$$

Different from the percent renewable index as the ratio of *RR* to *U* presented by Brown and Ulgiati (1997), a modified renewable percentage index (*Pr*) is defined as the ratio of all renewable emergy inputs free or purchased to the total emergy inputs and it illustrates renewable contribution in the total inputs of the given system. A system with higher *Pr* is considered more sustainable in the long run.

$$\text{Emergy yield ratio } (EYR) = \frac{U}{RP + NP} \qquad (3.1.4)$$

EYR is the ratio of total emergy cost to the purchased emergy from the outside economy, which represents the efficiency of a process using purchased inputs to exploit natural resources. The higher the index, the greater the return is obtained per unit of emergy invested.

$$\text{Environmental load ratio } (ELR) = \frac{NR + NP}{RR + RP} \qquad (3.1.5)$$

ELR is the ratio of the total emergy of nonrenewable inputs to the total emergy of renewable inputs, which indicates the stress of the given system on the environment. And the lower the ratio, the lower the stress is on the environment.

$$\text{Environmental sustainability index } (ESI) = \frac{EYR}{ELR} \qquad (3.1.6)$$

ESI takes both ecological and economic compatibility into account, and it indicates whether a process provides due contribution to the user with a low environmental pressure, reflecting the overall sustainability of a production process. The higher the index, the higher

119

the sustainability of the system is.

$$\text{Emergy feedback ratio } (EFR) = \frac{SF}{RP + NP} \tag{3.1.7}$$

It is the ratio of system feedback yield emergy to the purchased emergy from the economy, which represents the self-organization ability of the system. The higher the index, the stronger the inner drive is in the system.

3.1.3   Results and Discussion

3.1.3.1   Emergy Accounting

Corresponding to Figure 3.1.2, Table 3.1.1 lists the evaluated emergy values of the aggregated flows associated with the "pig-biogas-fish" system, and takes one year as the time cycle for a 20-year designed operation scenario. Five free renewable resources inflowing to the "pig-biogas-fish" system are calculated in free renewable resources (RR) accounting, but to avoid double accounting, only the item with the highest value is adopted. And in this research, the earth cycle energy is the largest one compared with solar radiation energy, kinetic energy of wind, chemical energy of rain and gravitational potential energy of rain, so its value (6.48E+14 seJ/yr) is taken as RR inputs. For free nonrenewable resources (NR) accounting, 1.12E+14 seJ/yr, the main concern is nutrition from the natural topsoil losses and the soil degradation, which serves as the fundamental support for this ecological agriculture system.

Table 3.1.1   Emergy Accounting for the "Pig-biogas-fish" System

Class	Item	p	Unit	UEV (seJ/unit)	u (seJ/yr)
Renewable resources from free environment (RR)					
100.00%R	Solar radiation	2.51E+13 [a]	J/yr	1.00E+00	2.51E+13
100.00%R	Wind(kinetic)	2.85E+09 [b]	J/yr	2.41E+03 [c]	6.87E+12
100.00%R	Rain(chemical)	1.01E+10 [d]	J/yr	2.93E+04 [c]	2.96E+14
100.00%R	Rain(geopotential)	3.66E+08 [e]	J/yr	1.69E+04 [c]	6.18E+12
100.00%R	Earth cycle	1.17E+10 [f]	J/yr	5.54E+04 [c]	6.48E+14
Subtotal					6.48E+14
Nonrenewable resources from free environment (NR)					
0.00%R	Soil loss	9.39E+08 [g]	J/yr	1.19E+05 [c]	1.12E+14
Subtotal					1.12E+14

Continued

Class	Item	p	Unit	UEV (seJ/unit)	u (seJ/yr)
Purchased social renewable and nonrenewable inputs ($RP+NP$)					
34.65%R [h]	Labor and services(L&S)	5.08E+01 [i]	$/yr	9.45E+12 [j]	4.80E+14
Pigsty					
9.06%R [h]	Cement and bricks	1.90E+01	kg/yr	4.88E+11 [k]	9.27E+12
9.06%R [h]	Lime	1.25E+01	kg/yr	5.41E+12 [k]	6.76E+13
4.35%R [h]	Steel	2.63E+00	kg/yr	5.20E+12[k]	1.37E+13
85.10%R [h]	Feed	1.20E+03	kg/yr	2.16E+12 [k]	2.59E+15
29.33% R [h]	Drugs	4.80E-02	kg/yr	1.58E+14 [k]	7.58E+12
29.33%R [h]	Disinfectant	4.00E-01	kg/yr	1.02E+13 [k]	4.08E+12
75.70%R [h]	Water	5.66E+04	kg/yr	7.49E+08 [k]	4.24E+13
21.29%R [h]	Electricity	2.30E+08	J/yr	5.06E+05 [k]	1.16E+14
Biogas pool					
9.06%R [h]	Cement	4.50E+01	kg/yr	4.88E+11 [k]	2.20E+13
33.27%R [h]	Sand and pebble	5.00E+01	kg/yr	1.61E+09 [c]	8.05E+10
12.46%R [h]	Plastic pipe	4.00E+00	kg/yr	9.85E+12 [k]	3.94E+13
4.35%R [h]	Steel mold	1.25E+02	kg/yr	7.76E+12 [k]	9.70E+14
Fishpond					
9.06%R [h]	Lime	1.80E+02	kg/yr	5.41E+12[k]	9.74E+14
11.93%R [h]	Bleach	3.20E+00	kg/yr	1.02E+12 [k]	3.26E+13
23.80%R [h]	Aerator	5.00E-02	set/yr	3.45E+16[k]	1.72E+15
85.10%R[h]	Feed	1.95E+03	kg/yr	2.16E+12[k]	4.21E+15
13.80%R [h]	Nitrogen fertilizer	2.00E+02	kg/yr	5.23E+12 [k]	1.05E+15
13.80%R [h]	Phosphate fertilizer	1.00E+02	kg/yr	1.19E+13 [k]	1.19E+15
Subtotal					1.35E+16
System feedback (SF)					
	Swine manure	8.42E+09 [l]	J/yr	2.60E+04 [m]	2.19E+14
	Biogas residues (N)	5.52E+01 [n]	kg/yr	5.23E+12 [k]	2.89E+14
	Biogas residues (P)	6.72E+01 [n]	kg/yr	1.19E+12 [k]	7.97E+14
Subtotal					1.31E+15

121

Continued

Class	Item	p	Unit	UEV (seJ/unit)	u (seJ/yr)
Produced energy (Ep)					
	Pig	9. 80E+09[o]	J/yr		
	Biogas	1. 00E+10[p]	J/yr		
	Fish	9. 34E+10[q]	J/yr		
Subtotal		1. 13E+11	J/yr		
U (with L&S)		1. 43E+16	seJ/yr		
U (without L&S)		1. 38E+16	seJ/yr		

[a] Solar energy = (area) x (average insolation) x (1−albedo) = (5. 32E+3 m^2) x (5. 90E+9 $J/m^2/$ yr) x (1−20%) = 2. 51E+13 J/yr.

[b] Wind energy = (area) x (density of air) x (average annual wind velocity)^3 x (annual working time) x (drag coefficient) = (5. 32E+3 m^2) x (1. 23 kg/m^3) x (2. 40 m/s)^3 x (3. 15E+7 s/yr) x (0. 001) = 2. 85E+09 J/yr.

[c] Refer to Odum (1996) with the baseline of 9. 26E+24 seJ/yr. UEVs adopted from that study is multiplied by 1. 61 for conversion to the new baseline.

[d] Rain energy (chemical) = (area) x (evapotranspiration) x (rain density) x (Gibbs free energy) = (5. 32E+3 m^2) x (3. 86E−1 m/yr) x (1. 00E+3 kg/m^3) x (4. 94E+3 J/kg) = 1. 01E+10 J/yr.

[e] Rain energy (geopotential) = (area) x (rainfall) x (runoff rate) x (average elevation) x (rain density) x (gravity) = (5. 32E+3 m^2) x (1. 30E+0 m) x (20%) x (2. 70E+1 m) x (1. 00E+3 kg/m^3) x (9. 80m/s^2) = 3. 66E+8 J/yr.

[f] Energy of earth cycle = (area) x (heat flow) x (annual working time) = (5. 32E+3 m^2) x (7. 00E− 2 W/m^2) x (3. 15E+7 s/yr) = 1. 17E+10 J/yr.

[g] Lost energy = (area) x (total soil loss per year in China)/(National territory area) x (average organic content) x (energy content/g organic) = (5. 32E+3 m^2) x (5. 00E+15 g/yr)/(9. 60E+10 m^2) x (1. 5%) x (22. 63 J/g) = 9. 39E+08 J/yr.

[h] Refer to Chen and Chen (2010).

[i] Labor and services = (area) x (average wage) x (exchange rate between RMB and $ in 2004) = (5. 32E+3 m^2) x (7. 90E−2 $RMB/m^2/yr$) x (1. 21E−1 $/RMB) = 5. 08E+01 $/yr.

[j] Refer to Yang et al. (2010) with the baseline of 9. 26E+24 seJ/yr. UEVs adopted from that study is multiplied by 1. 61 for conversion to the new baseline.

[k] Refer to Zhou (2008) with the baseline of 9. 26E+24 seJ/yr. UEVs adopted from that study is multiplied by 1. 61 for conversion to the new baseline.

[l] Energy of swine manure = (manure per year) x (organic matter content) x (standard energy value) = (4. 16E+3 kg/yr) x (15%) x (1. 35E+7 J/kg) = 8. 42E+09 J/yr.

[m] Refer to Wei et al. (2009) with the baseline of 1. 58E+25 seJ/yr. UEVs adopted from that study is multiplied by 0. 96 for conversion to the new baseline.

[n] Refer to Lin et al. (2008).

[o] Energy of pig = (output) x (calorific value) = (1. 00E+3 kg/yr) x (2. 34E+3 Kcal/kg) x (4. 19E+ 3 J/Kcal) = 9. 80E+09 J/yr.

[p] Energy of biogas = (output) x (calorific value) = (4. 00E+2 m^3/yr) x (2. 50E+7 J/m^3) = 1. 00E+ 10 J/yr.

[q] Energy of fish = (output) x (calorific value) = (9. 60E+3 kg/yr) x (2. 33E+3 Kcal/kg) x (4. 19E +3 J/Kcal) = 9. 34E+10 J/yr.

Purchased social inputs ($RP+NP$) include those bought from the economy, such as electricity, fertilizer and human labor. And renewable percent of each item is listed in Column 1, Table 3. 1. 1 according to Chen and Chen (2010), which provides a detailed calculation of the renewable and nonrenewable emergy inputs of 135 sectors in China with an ecological input-output modeling. Swine manure in the pigsty system and biogas residues in the biogas pool system are counted as system feedback (SF), and they amount to 1. 31E+ 15 seJ per year, implying that 1. 31E+15 seJ of emergy is recycled in internal system every year and helps propel its self-organization. Produced energy (Ep), 1. 13E + 11 J/yr, mainly comprises three products, namely pig, biogas and fish, among which pig and fish are imported into the market directly, and biogas is used by the household and helps cut down the amount of coal bought from the market.

The results show that the total emergy inputs (U) of the "pig-biogas-fish" system are 1. 43E+16 seJ/yr (1. 38E+16 seJ/yr without L&S), and among them the major emergy inputs are ascribed to purchases ($RP+NP$), 1. 35E+16 seJ/yr with the largest percentage of 94. 69%. As shown in Figure 3. 1. 3, RR accounts for 4. 53% of the total emergy inputs, while NR takes up 0. 78%. Both RR and NR are supplied by the free environment and denote the direct support from the nature. The two parts are calculated as 7. 60E+14 seJ/yr altogether. Besides, the purchases can be divided into four parts: labor and services; the pigsty system; the biogas pool system and the fishpond system. Emergy inputs of the fishpond system are 9. 17E + 15 seJ/yr, taking the largest share (64. 16%) of the total emergy, and they are mainly caused by materials used in operation and maintenance phases because emergy associated with fish feed and fertilizer takes up 70. 24% of total emergy in fishpond system.

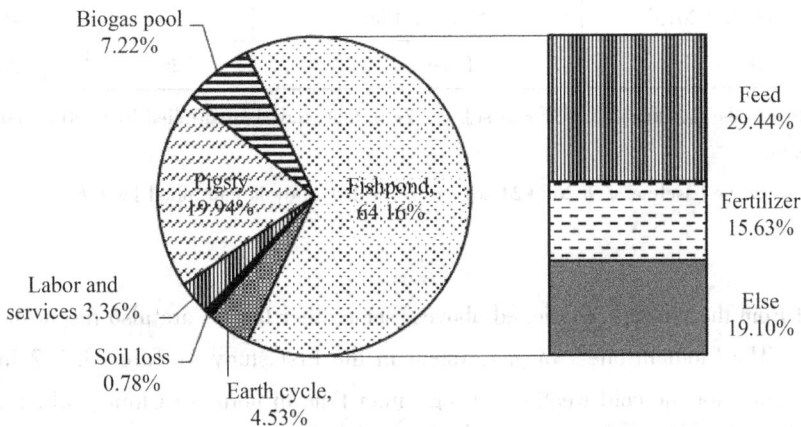

Figure 3. 1. 3   Fractions of Emergy Inputs for the "Pig-biogas-fish" System

The second largest contribution (19. 94%) to the total emergy is from the pigsty system for materials used in construction, operation and maintenance phases. But for the biogas pool system, only materials used to construct the biogas digester are counted here since raw materials for fermentation can be supplied by the pigsty system, and the biogas pool system takes up 7. 22%. Labor and services part, the part referring to construction manpower and labor for operation, accounts for a proportion of 3. 36%. In this part, human labor and society service are linked up to nature, and this part is an important part in the environmental accounting, although usually neglected in traditional energy analysis.

3. 1. 3. 2   Transformaty (Tr)

Tr is a crucial parameter, which denotes the overall efficiency of the system. Those with greater transformities demand more emergy to generate the same amount of products. For the "pig-biogas-fish" system, Tr is calculated as 1. 26E+05 seJ/J. Table 3. 1. 2 lists Trs of some typical biogas systems in previous studies. Given that the baseline adopted has a direct impact on the value of Tr, all Trs in Table 3. 1. 2 are converted to the common baseline of 1. 52E+25 seJ/yr to make them comparable. Some numerical variations can be seen in the table, and they are mainly attributed to the differences in production efficiency and the different values of UEVs adopted in emergy analysis.

Table 3. 1. 2   Comparison of Tr of Some Typical Biogas Systems

No.		Location	Lifetime (yr)	Tr (seJ/J)
1	Wei et al. (2009) [a]	Beijing, China	20	1. 98E+05
2	Ciotola et al. (2011) [b]	Earte University, Costa Rica	20	8. 73E+04
3	Chen and Chen (2012) [a]	Guangxi, China	20	3. 63E+05
4	Wu et al. (2013) [b]	Shanxi, China	20	2. 40E+06
5	This study	Hubei, China	20	1. 26E+05

[a] Relative to the baseline of 1. 58E+25 seJ/yr. Tr in that study is multiplied by 0. 96 for conversion to the new baseline.

[b] Relative to the baseline of 9. 26E+24 seJ/yr. Tr in that study is multiplied by 1. 61 for conversion to the new baseline.

Apart from the reasons mentioned above, some other factors are also responsible for the differences. The "four in one" biogas system in the first study in Table 3. 1. 2 included a solar greenhouse for the cold weather during winter time in northern China, which increased emergy inputs of this biogas system. This also reflects that the warm-wet climate in southern China can help improve the efficiency of biogas systems. The second research took the biogas digester as the research object rather than the integrated biogas-utilization system, and only the emergy investment associated with the digester was considered, so Tr in that study is smaller than that in our study. And it proves that the biogas energy utilization has a higher efficiency considering the lower Tr. The biogas-linked agricultural ecosystem introduced by the third study added the five free renewable emergy inputs, i. e. solar radiation, rain (chemical), rain (geopotential), wind (kinetic) and earth cycle together in RR accounting, which is different from the calculation in this study. Also, the fourth study used the sum of the five free renewable emergy inputs as RR inflow. Besides, the biogas was calculated as a kind of feedback rather than a product in that study. However, the differences between these researches can offer insight into the performance of the biogas technology from different perspectives.

3. 1. 3. 3 Emergy-based Indicators

Listed in Table 3. 1. 3 are emergy fluxes and indicators of the "pig-biogas-fish" system. Pr of the "pig-biogas-fish" system is 52.66%, while it is 25.00% for the conventional agriculture system in China (Jiang et al., 2007), implying that for the total inputs, the ratio of renewable inputs in the "pig-biogas-fish" system is larger than that in the conventional agriculture system and that the integrated biogas-utilization system can reduce consumption of nonrenewable energy by making full use of renewable energy. EYR of the "pig-biogas-fish" system is 1.06, which implies that 0.06 unit of free environmental resources can be exploited when one unit of purchased inputs is invested in this system. ELR of the "pig-biogas-fish" system is 0.90, indicating that nonrenewable emergy used in this biogas system is less than the renewable one.

Table 3. 1. 3 Emergy Fluxes and Indicators for the "Pig-biogas-fish" System

Flux	Value	Unit
Free renewable emergy (RR)	6.48E+14	seJ/yr
Free nonrenewable emergy (NR)	1.12E+14	seJ/yr
Purchased renewable emergy (RP)	6.88E+15	seJ/yr
Purchased nonrenewable emergy (NP)	6.65E+15	seJ/yr
Total emergy use (U)	1.43E+16	seJ/yr
Total feedback (F)	1.31E+15	seJ/yr
Indicator	Value	
Renewable percentage index (Pr)	52.66%	
Emergy yield ratio (EYR)	1.06	
Environmental loading ratio (ELR)	0.90	
Environmental sustainability index (ESI)	1.17	
Emergy feedback ratio (EFR)	9.64%	

Moreover, combining *EYR* with *ELR*, *ESI* gives a comprehensive analysis on the sustainability of this system, and it is calculated as 1.17, higher than that of the conventional agriculture system (0.74), demonstrating that the integrated biogas-utilization system has a higher sustainability. Last but not least, index *EFR* illustrates that the system feedback emergy of the "pig-biogas-fish" system is 9.64% of the purchased emergy, and it also manifests that recycled materials can decrease the purchased inputs by 9.64%.

3. 1. 3. 4   Impacts of Operation Time

The advantages of the "pig-biogas-fish" system are discussed above in the optimal scenario of 20-year stable operation. However, most of the biogas projects suffer from a high rate of obsolescence after 3 years of operation. And to determine the influence of lifespan on sustainability for this integrated biogas-utilization system, six other scenarios with different running times from 5 years to 10 years are shown in Figure 3.1.4 below.

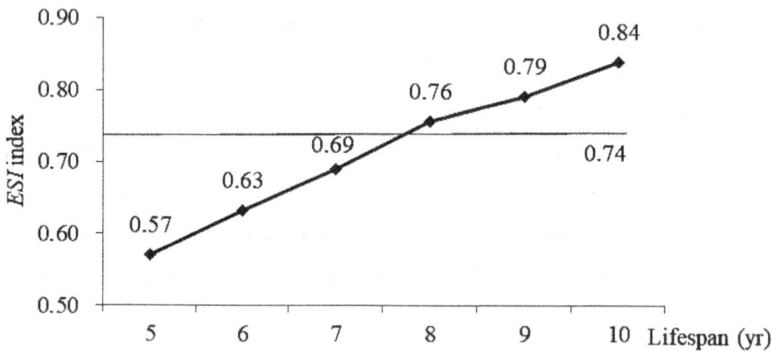

Figure 3. 1. 4   Sustainability of the Six Scenarios with Different Running Times

The sustainability of the six scenarios is presented with *ESI* index, which is calculated following the emergy accounting process introduced in Section 3.1.2. Since one year is chosen as the time span, for each scenario, the construction materials and machinery used in the whole biogas system are converted to annual flows according to its service life that ranges from 5 to 10 years. As pointed out in Equation (3.1.6), the higher the index of *ESI*, the higher the sustainability of the system is. It can be witnessed that sustainability of the biogas system is closely correlated with its lifespan that the longer the working time is, the higher the sustainability is. *ESI* of the "pig-biogas-fish" system with 5 years of operation life is 0.57, while it is 0.84 for the system with 10 years of working life, increasing by 47.37%.

There are two main reasons behind this dynamic trend. The first one is the higher index of *EYR* for the scenario with longer operation life (Figure 3.1.5). Regarding the construction materials invested in the construction process and the machinery bought at the

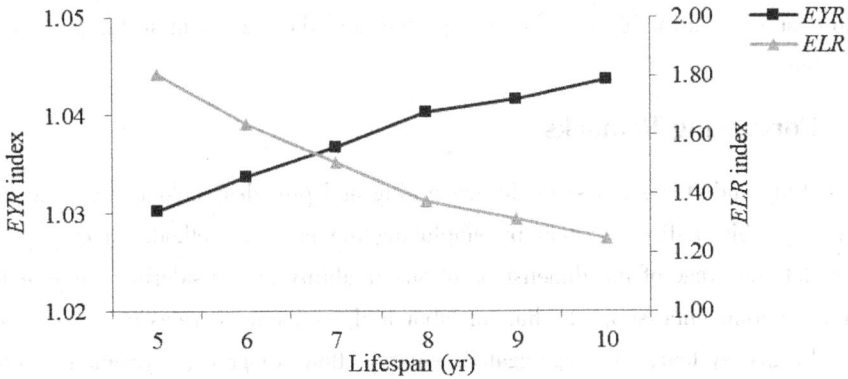

Figure 3. 1. 5   *EYR* and *ELR* for the Six Scenarios with Different Running Times

beginning of the operation process, the total amount of them is constant in all scenarios, but the annual amounts of them are different in six scenarios due to the different lifespans. As the lifespan of the biogas system enlarges, the annual flows associated with the construction materials and the machinery decrease in inverse proportion, leading to the same amount of reduction of both purchased emergy ($RP + NP$) and the total emergy inputs (U) and consequently the increase of *EYR*. The other one is the decline in *ELR*, also depicted in Figure 3. 1. 5. It is attributed to the small renewable percent of the construction materials and the machinery. When annual flows decrease in the above case, the nonrenewable part of purchased emergy (*NP*) declines faster than the renewable part (*RP*). In summary, the longer the operation time of the biogas system is, the greater the return is obtained per unit of emergy investment and the lower the pressure is caused on the environment. Since *ESI* is the ratio of *EYR* to *ELR*, the numerator increases while the denominator decreases, resulting in a rise in sustainability.

The line of 0. 74 standing for *ESI* of the conventional agriculture system is presented in Figure 3. 1. 4 to make a comparison. The "pig-biogas-fish" systems in two adjacent scenarios, i. e. the 7-year lifespan and the 8-year lifespan demonstrate a gain or loss on the contrary. The 7-year scenario has a lower sustainability than the conventional agriculture system, implying an adverse effect on the sustainable development of the agriculture, while the 8-year scenario has a favorable impact. It is therefore projected that the "pig-biogas-fish" system should work normally for at least 8 years to prove its benefit in sustainability.

In fact, only a small proportion of biogas systems can work for 8 years or more than 8 years to exhibit their advantages in sustainability. The high rate of obsolescence is mainly due to a lack of follow-up service and management of biogas digesters. In China, the development of household biogas projects mostly focuses on the construction and fails to take management into consideration. Therefore, an endeavor to provide follow-up service is urgent to ensure the favorable function of digesters and the maximum sustainable benefits of biogas systems.

3.1.4   Concluding Remarks

This study undertakes a systematic accounting and provides ecological indicators for an integrated "pig-biogas-fish" system by employing the emergy method. Emergy provides a more complete coverage of the dimensions of sustainability by considering different forms of materials, environmental support, human labor and economic services on a common basis. For this biogas system, the aggregated emergy flow diagram, systematic accounting tabulation and ecological indicator framework are exhibited separately. The results show that for the "pig-biogas-fish" system with a lifespan of 20 years, Tr is calculated as $1.26E+05$ seJ/J and the sustainability indicator, ESI is 1.17. When compared with the conventional agriculture system in China, the "pig-biogas-fish" system displays its superiority for the favorable ecological advantages.

Since most of the household biogas systems cannot work for 20 years before they are obsoleted, the impact of lifespan on sustainability for the "pig-biogas-fish" system is discussed in this study. It reveals that the "pig-biogas-fish" system should be well operated for 8 years to obtain a higher sustainability than the conventional agriculture system.

References

Brown, M.T., Ulgiati, S., 1997. Emergy-based Indices and Ratios to Evaluate Sustainability: Monitoring Economies and Technology Toward Environmentally Sound Innovation. *Ecological Engineering*, 9, 51-69.

Brown, M.T., Ulgiati, S., 2004. Energy Quality, Emergy, and Transformity: H. T. Odum's Contributions to Quantifying and Understanding Systems. *Ecological Modelling*, 178, 201-213.

Brown, M.T., Ulgiati, S., 2010. Updated Evaluation of Exergy and Emergy Driving the Geobiosphere: A Review and Refinement of the Emergy Baseline. *Ecological Modelling*, 221, 2501-2508.

Chen, G.Q., Chen, Z.M., 2010. Carbon Emissions and Resources use by Chinese Economy 2007: A 135-sector Inventory and Input-output Embodiment. *Communications in Nonlinear Science and Numerical Simulation*, 15, 3647-3732.

Chen, S.Q., Chen, B., 2012. Sustainability and Future Alternatives of Biogas-linked Agrosystem (BLAS) in China: An Emergy Synthesis. *Renewable and Sustainable Energy Reviews*, 16, 3948-3959.

Ciotola, R.J., Lansing, S., Martin, J.F., 2011. Emergy Analysis of Biogas

Production and Electricity Generation from Small-scale Agricultural Digesters. *Ecological Engineering*, 37, 1681-1691.

Jiang, M. M., Chen, B., Zhou, J. B., Tao, F. R., Li, Z., Yang, Z. F., Chen, G. Q., 2007. Emergy Account for Biomass Resource Exploitation by Agriculture in China. *Energy Policy*, 35, 4704-4719.

Lin, C., Wei, X. M., Jiang, W. T., 2008. Emergy Analysis of Biogas Project Ecological Model. Proceedings of International Semir on Rural Bimass Energy & ASEAN Plus Three Forum on Biomass Energy, 240-246.

Odum, H. T., 1996. Environmental Accounting: Emergy and Environmental Decision making. John Wiley and Sons, New York.

Wei, X. M., Chen, B., Qu, Y. H., Lin, C., Chen, G. Q., 2009. Emergy Analysis for "Four in One" Peach Production System in Beijing. *Communications in Nonlinear Science and Numerical Simulation*, 14, 946-958.

Yang, Z. F., Jiang, M. M., Chen, B., Zhou, J. B., Chen, G. Q., Li, S. C., 2010. Solar Emergy Evaluation for Chinese Economy. *Energy Policy*, 38, 875-886.

Zhou, J. B., 2008. Embodied Ecological Elements Accounting of National Economy, College of Engineering. Peking University, Beijing.

3. 2　Renewability and Sustainability of Biogas System: Cosmic Exergy Based Assessment for a Case in China[①]

3. 2. 1　Introduction

In the current context of energy shortage and climate change, the development of renewable and sustainable energy has become an important global strategy. By the end of early 2013, supporting policies for renewable energy have been established in 127 countries, drastically ascending from 45 countries in 2005. Biogas is a gaseous fuel produced by anaerobic digestion of biomass and waste, and biogas fermentation technology is considered a cost-effective way of renewable energy generation without increasing atmospheric CO_2 concentration. Some evidence shows that about 3,000 years ago, biogas was used for heating water by ancient Assyrian, which partly reflected that biogas was one of the earliest energy resources harnessed in human history. But this resource was not scientifically described until 1776, when the Italian physicist, A. Volta, proved CH_4 in biogas. Since then, continual efforts have been made to exploit and improve the biogas fermentation

---

① Published on *Renewable and Sustainable Energy Reviews*, Volume 51, pp. 1509-1524, with a few modifications due to space constraints. Reuse permission has been obtained from Elsevier.

technology. In the 1970s, because of the outbreak of oil crisis, people were forced to pursue alternative energy resources. Biogas, a traditional way of using biomass to ensure energy delivery, has therefore arrested extensive attention and found broad application worldwide.

Different from large and community-scale biogas plants that are primarily constructed in developed countries, small and domestic-scale biogas digesters are generally used in rural households in developing countries, such as China, India, and Nepal. By 2009, about 35 million household biogas digesters have been deployed in China, making China the country with the largest number of household biogas pools in the world. The agricultural production in China bases the family as a unit. This directly leads to the successful popularization of household biogas use throughout the country. In recent years, with the advance of ecological construction countryside, an integrated biogas engineering, which combines biogas technology with eco-agriculture technology, has dominated rural biogas market. In the integrated biogas engineering, agricultural and household wastes are collected into the biogas pool for anaerobic digestion; after fermentation, biogas is treated as clean fuel in households, while biogas residue is recycled in agricultural production as organic fertilizer. The integrated biogas engineering unveils great advantages in waste treatment, energy supply, environmental conservation and organic food production. As a result, its development and implementation are being highlighted by our government in the 2011-2015 Five-Year Plan. However, it must be noted that, similar with other artificial efforts, the integrated biogas engineering also requires resource inputs in its fabrication and operation processes, such as natural resources of sunlight and rain, and social resources of cement and steel that emit greenhouse gas (GHG) emission to the atmosphere. Hence, confronted with the continuous constructions and deployment of integrated biogas systems, it is crucial to probe into their overall performance of economic and ecological perspectives.

Extensive evaluations have been performed to quantify the biogas system's economic and ecological benefits, especially its renewability and sustainability. In the assessment of renewability and sustainability, two factors in terms of the utilization efficiency of resources (both natural and social resources) and environmental impact, are most frequently considered. As a consequence, different quantitative indices, like economic cost, land occupation, carbon emission, energy consumption and exergy depletion have been explored. In fact, a promising evaluation system is expected to take account of both the environmental values and the economic values on an equivalent basis. Given these, thermodynamic concepts, which can build a bridge between social economy and natural environment, have therefore arrested extensive attention. At first, energy seems suitable to act as a common metric for tradable commodities, human labor and free resources because energy is more or less rooted in everything. However, according to the first law of thermodynamics, energy is always in conservation and can never be consumed in any case. It is therefore meaningless to discuss the energy efficiency of an anthropic system since it will always be 100%. Exergy derives from a combination of the first two Laws of Thermodynamics. It is a measurement of the available energy, i. e., the maximal working capacity. In contrast to energy, exergy is not subject to a conservation law but is consumed or destroyed due to irreversibilities inherent in all physical processes. Since all real activities in society are irreversible, exergy is the "real resource" that is consumed to sustain the social-economic-ecological complex system of the world. As a consequence, it is the optimization of exergy utilization that should be essentially investigated in sustainable development. In this regard, exergy becomes a valid renewability and sustainability metric.

Exergy is defined as the maximum work that can be extracted from a system in the process of reaching equilibrium with its reference environment. Previous assessments of biogas systems concerning exergy can be classified into three groups. First is the traditional exergy model, which mainly focuses on the tradable resources in social economy. In these calculations, exergy of a resource mainly consists of the resource's physical and chemical exergy, and its magnitude depends on the temperature, pressure and chemical composition of both the resource and the ambient. It reveals the resource's current thermodynamic state in a chosen reference environment. For the first group, each resource associated with the biogas system is studied individually. The relationships between resources, and the relationships between the resource and the environment are ignored. The second group is conducted on the global scale of the terrestrial ecosystem, and the methods being used include the cumulative exergy, extended exergy and life cycle exergy analysis. In these models, not only the traditional exergy content, but also all exergy inputs in the economic system for producing the resource and all exergy costs for restoring potential contamination in the environmental system, are accounted as the total exergy of the resource. However, for free exergy inputs from the natural environment, such as sunlight and wind, the second group fails to take them into consideration. As a result, the third one expands the research scale by putting the research object into the solar-terrestrial ecosystem. Odum's solar emergy theory has been the most representative. Citing Odum's words: "Solar emergy is the available solar energy used up directly and indirectly to make a service or product" (Odum et al., 2000). All energy contributions of free environment investment, goods, services and information are measured in the unit of solar energy since solar energy had been considered as the only source of all the other energies on the earth. Then based on the concept of environmental philosophy and a systematic study of the exergy budget for the earth, in Chen's studies (Chen, 2005), the driving force of the earth system has been shown to be the cosmic exergy flux due to thermal difference between the solar radiation and cosmic background microwave, instead of the solar energy itself, and the scarcity of the cosmic exergy availability as the fundamental natural resource for the ecosystem and humankind was also revealed. Hence, a new method based on cosmic exergy has been developed associated with the universal scale of the cosmic-solar-terrestrial ecosystem, as shown in Figure 3.2.1.

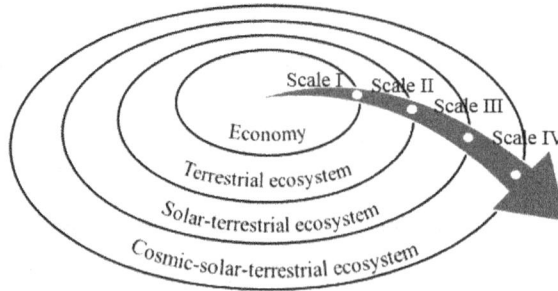

Figure 3.2.1   The Conceptual Framework of the System Scales for Exergy Evaluation

So far, the cosmic exergy method has been applied to numerous systems. For the global system, Chen and Chen (2011) investigated the cosmic exergy consumption within its economic system in the year of 2000 by exploiting an ecological input-output model. For a national system, Chen and Chen (2010) established a 135-sector database of embodied intensity regarding cosmic exergy for Chinese economy 2007. For an urban system, Jiang et al. (2010) illustrated a cosmic exergy based ecological economic evaluation of the Beijing urban ecosystem during the period 1978-2004. In addition, Chen et al. (2011) applied the cosmic exergy method to a regional project of constructed wetland, and presented a general assessment for the wetland. Grounded in these existing studies, this work aims to provide a detailed accounting in terms of resources, economics and pollution for a selected integrated biogas engineering in Hubei Province, China via the cosmic exergy method. A set of indices are also devised to reveal the renewability and sustainability of this system.

3.2.2   Materials and Methodology

3.2.2.1   The Integrated Biogas Engineering

Through realizing the maximization of recycling for organic wastes, the integrated biogas engineering declares its sound environmental and economic advantages over the conventional agricultural industry. And it has gained constant support from the government with policy preferences, subsidies, and technology guidance in China. Due to geographical and climatic reasons, the aquaculture industry is relatively developed in southern China. The integrated biogas model combining biogas technology with fish farming is therefore prevailing in the south. A typical southern system with biogas production capacity of 400 m^3/yr, is therefore chosen as a case study in this study.

The study site is located in Zhongzhouzi fishery, Jinzhou City, Hubei Province. In recent years, Jinzhou is committed to the development of green agriculture, and chooses Zhongzhouzi fishery as a pilot site for the integrated biogas engineering. Since the local economy is based primarily on pig breeding and fish culture, the integrated pig-biogas-fish engineering is vigorously promoted by the government. By the end of 2010, 80 household biogas digesters have been put into use and the current biogas users account for 78% of all families in Zhongzhouzi. The investigated system consists of a pigsty, an 8 m^3 hydraulic pressure biogas digester and a fishpond. The pigsty covers an area of 20 m^2, while the fishpond is 5,300 m^2. The workflow is as follows: through raising pigs, residents put the pig manure into the biogas digester to produce biogas for everyday lighting and cooking. Meanwhile, biogas residues are taken out as base fertilizer for the fishpond. This integrated biogas engineering was built in 2007 with the construction cost and annual operation/maintenance cost summing up to 6,626 CNY (abbreviation for China Yuan) and 18,300 CNY, respectively. Despite the fact price levels and exchange rates vary across time, constant values referring to the 2007 basis are applied in our study for simplicity.

3.2.2.2 Corresponding Conventional Production System

To make a distinction between pre- and post-construction of the biogas system, a model of conventional production system is composed versus the integrated biogas engineering. It just consists of a pigsty system with an area of 20 m^2 and a fishpond of 5,300 m^2. In the conventional system, coal is the major energy source for everyday lighting and cooking, and the amount of energy provided by the coal is equal to that provided by the biogas in the integrated biogas system. Without biogas residues, the quantity of the fertilizer applied to the fishpond in the conventional system should be increased to meet the demand of pond culture.

3.2.2.3 Cosmic Exergy

The word "exergy" was first proposed by Rant in 1953, but was not applied in the ecological contexts until the 1970s. Exergy (EX) for a given system can be briefly expressed as below:

$$E_X = T_0(S_{eq}^{tot} - S^{tot}) \qquad (3.2.1)$$

where T_0 is the thermodynamic temperature of the environment, S_{eq}^{tot} is the entropy of the total system as a combination of the given system and the local environment when the total system is in thermodynamic equilibrium, and S^{tot} is the entropy of the total system at the given deviation from equilibrium. Exergy of a system plays multiple roles as resource, buffering capacity and environmental impact, for observer, system and environment, respectively. For the observer that faces the system and local environment, exergy is a measurement of the real resource availability. For the system itself, exergy represents the aliveness and vitality of the system. For the local environment, exergy is a description of environmental impact, in terms of the potential to change the status of the environment. Particularly, exergy embodied in pollution expresses the minimum external work needed to be identified to eliminate the pollution.

Cosmic exergy is a special kind of exergy with cosmic background that is taken as the thermodynamic reference environment. The planet earth is just like a heat machine of radiation transformation that subjects to a hot thermal reservoir of solar radiation and a cold thermal reservoir of cosmic background microwave radiation. The earth system receives radiation from the hot reservoir and ejects radiation to the cold reservoir. Due to the irreversibility of the earth system, entropy of the leaving radiation is larger than that of the absorbed radiation, that is, exergy associated with the leaving radiation is less than that with the incoming radiation. And the exergy loss serves as the ultimate resources to revitalize the meteorological system, feed the hydrological cycle and sustain all other natural and anthropogenic phenomena on the earth. Accordingly, the fundamental resource sustaining the ecosphere can be conceptualized as the cosmic exergy obtained by the material earth. Everything on the earth has to be produced by work process that consumes cosmic exergy, either it is assisted by people or not. As pointed out by Szargut, one of the pioneers to set foot in exergy analysis, exergy consumption connected with the fabrication of particular products is their ecological cost (Szargut et al., 2002). Combining Szargut's framework of cumulative exergy with Odum's solar emergy, cosmic exergy of the product or service is defined as the cosmic exergy previously used up directly and indirectly to make the product or service. Thus, cosmic exergy can provide a systematic measurement by integrating natural investments, social goods, services and environmental impacts on a common unit of cosmic joule (abbreviated Jc).

As indicated in Chen (2006), anthropogenic cosmic exergy use could be compared with cosmic exergy consumption of some terrestrial processes occurring near the earth's surface, implying cosmic exergy is a kind of scarce and valuable resource on earth. It helps perceive the threat of human impacts on global sustainability. To be more specific, cosmic exergy raises a unified thermodynamic metric for evaluating resource depletion and environment degradation, and the cosmic exergy accounting can provide essential indicators for renewability and sustainability evaluation.

3. 2. 2. 4   Procedure for Cosmic Exergy Accounting

3. 2. 2. 4. 1   Overview of Cosmic Exergy Diagram

The procedure of cosmic exergy based assessment is similar to that of solar emergy analysis. The first step is to draw an overview cosmic exergy diagram to define the boundary of the given system and identify the inputs and outputs. For the integrated biogas system, the exergy systems language diagram is depicted in Figure 3. 2. 2. The input fluxes from free natural resources ($Ires$) are categorized into renewable resources ($Ires-r$) and nonrenewable resources ($Ires-n$). The inputs from economy ($Ieco$) denote social goods and services bought from external system into the biogas system, embracing electricity, cement, and so on. They can also be divided into renewable ($Ieco-r$) and nonrenewable ($Ieco-n$) ones. Therefore, the total inputs (I) are equal to the sum of cosmic exergy inflows ($Ires+Ieco$). Correspondingly, the system yield (Y) comprises three kinds of products (P) and the undesired by-products (environment impact, EI). All the processes mentioned above will inevitably lead to environmental impact, and because the impact is negative, EI is defined less than zero, i.e. $EI \leq 0$. In this study, only GHG emissions and pig manure are considered in the calculation of EI due to data limitation.

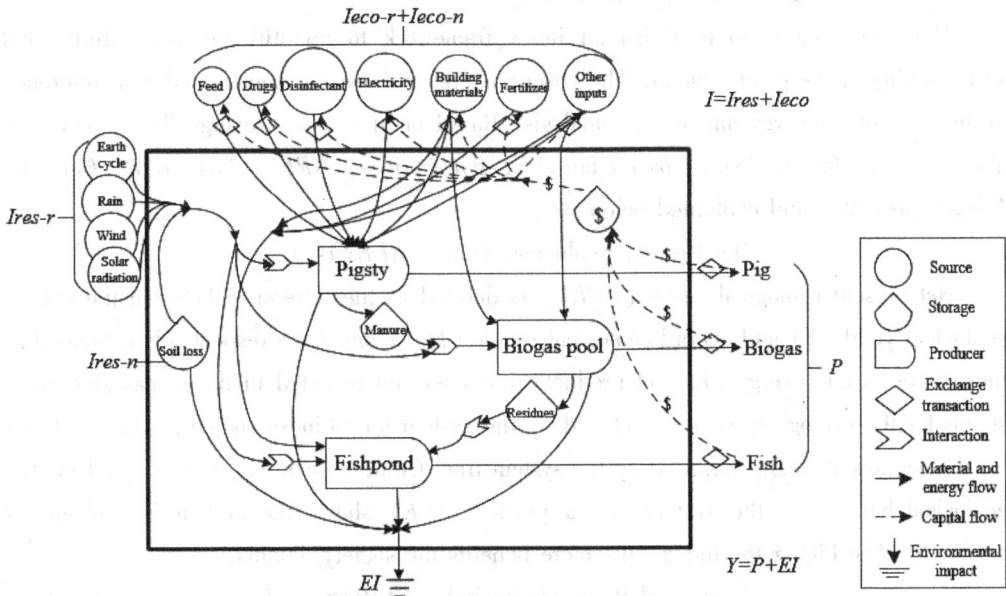

Figure 3.2.2 System Diagram of a Typical Integrated Biogas Engineering in Terms of Cosmic Exergy

3.2.2.4.2 Transformity of Cosmic Exergy

The second step is to obtain the cosmic exergy value of each item considered in the integrated biogas system. All inflows and outflows in Figure 3.2.2 with raw data such as joules, kilograms or dollars are converted into cosmic exergy with the unit of Jc. And for this conversion, cosmic exergy transformity (Tc) is defined as the cosmic exergy required to make per unit (joule or mass or money) of a product or service. Thus, for a given product (pr) invested or produced in the integrated biogas system, its cosmic exergy (Ec) can be calculated as

$$Ec = pr \cdot Tc \tag{3.2.2}$$

135

Chen (2006) calculated the global cosmic exergy baseline to be 45 TW (1.41E+21 Jc/yr) and updated Tcs for natural resources corresponding to solar emergy transformities that were previously given by Odum. Afterwards, Chen and Chen (2010) further detailed the calculation, and developed a systematic database of Tc for Chinese economy according to the average productivity in China, which is adopted in this study as the supporting data. Similar to the unit price of goods that acts as a reflection of socially average labor hours in traditional economics, Tc in the database is determined by the average ecological work done in making and sustaining the product, service and emission. Hence, Ec is equal to the amount of ecological work that is required if pr is produced upon the average productivity in Chinese economic system.

3.2.2.4.3   Cosmic Exergy Based Indices

The final step is to establish an index framework to quantify the renewability and sustainability of the given system. The cosmic exergy indices are constructed with reference to those of solar emergy and exergy analysis. Based on the cosmic exergy flows mentioned above ($Ires\text{-}r$, $Ires\text{-}n$, $Ieco\text{-}r$, $Ieco\text{-}n$ and Y), five indices, $NPEV$, ERI, EYR, ELR and ESI are presented and explained below:

$$\text{Net Present Ecological Value } (NPEV) = Y - I \qquad (3.2.3)$$

Net present ecological value ($NPEV$) is defined as the difference between the overall ecological yield (Y) and overall ecological inputs (I). Y and I are respectively estimated as the sum of cosmic exergy (Ec) of products produced and invested in the biogas system. Y stands for the ecological wealth produced by the system for Chinese society, while I stands for the ecological wealth required by the system from Chinese society. So $NPEV$ reflects the ecological balance of the system and a positive $NPEV$ shows the system is ecologically profitable. The higher the index, the more benefits the society obtains.

$$\text{Ecological Renewability Index } (ERI) = Ir/I \qquad (3.2.4)$$

As the ratio of all free or purchased renewable inputs ($Ir = Ires\text{-}r + Ieco\text{-}r$) to the total inputs ($I$), ecological renewability index (ERI) depicts the renewable resources' contribution in the total inputs of the given system. A system with higher ERI implies higher renewability.

$$\text{Ecological Yield Ratio } (EYR) = Y/Ieco \qquad (3.2.5)$$

As the overall yield (Y) divided by the total purchased inputs ($Ieco$), ecological yield ratio (EYR) reflects the efficacy of the concerned system utilizing the external investment. A system with higher EYR is more competitive in attracting external investment.

$$\text{Ecological Loading Ratio } (ELR) = In/Ir \qquad (3.2.6)$$

As the ratio of total nonrenewable inputs ($In = Ires\text{-}n + Ieco\text{-}n$) to total renewable ones (Ir), ecological loading ratio (ELR) indicates the stress that the system exerts on the environment. The lower the ratio, the lower the pressure is on local environment. Compared to EYR that quantifies the competitiveness in accordance with the quantity of resources, ELR evaluates the competitiveness according to their quality.

$$\text{Ecological Sustainability Index } (ESI) = EYR/ELR \qquad (3.2.7)$$

As EYR is divided by ELR, ecological sustainability index (ESI) implies the integration of ecological yield and load and thus can be applied to appraise the ecological sustainability. The higher the index, the higher the sustainability of the system is.

3. 2. 3 Results and Discussion

3. 2. 3. 1 Cosmic Exergy Accounting for the Integrated Biogas Engineering

Table 3. 2. 1 is the cosmic exergy evaluation sheet of the integrated biogas system and corresponding footnotes are shown in Appendix I. Only the cosmic exergy of the construction and operation stages is accounted for, with that of the demolition stage being ignored. One year is chosen as the time span in this research, so the infrastructure and machinery investment in the biogas system is converted to annual flows based on the service life (estimated 20 years).

Table 3. 2. 1　Cosmic Exergy Accounting for the Integrated Biogas Engineering[a]

Class	Item	pr	Unit	Tc (Jc/unit)	Ec (Jc/yr)
Renewable inputs of natural resources ($Ires\text{-}r$)					
100. 00%R	Solar radiation	2. 51E+13	J/yr	1. 02E−05	2. 56E+08
100. 00%R	Wind (kinetic)	2. 85E+09	J/yr	3. 21E−02	9. 15E+07
100. 00%R	Rain (chemical)	1. 01E+10	J/yr	6. 26E−01	6. 32E+09
100. 00%R	Rain (geopotential)	3. 66E+08	J/yr	3. 62E−01	1. 32E+08
100. 00%R	Geothermal	1. 17E+10	J/yr	7. 82E−03	9. 15E+07
Nonrenewable inputs of natural resources ($Ires\text{-}n$)					
0. 00%R	Topsoil loss	1. 14E+03	kg/yr	4. 33E+07	4. 94E+10
Renewable and nonrenewable inputs purchased from economic market ($Ieco$)					
6. 20%R	Labor and services	4. 55E+03	CNY/yr	5. 45E+07	2. 48E+11
Pigsty					
0. 79%R	Cement	1. 05E+01	CNY/yr	1. 56E+08	1. 64E+09
0. 79%R	Lime	1. 50E+01	CNY/yr	1. 56E+08	2. 34E+09

Continued

Class	Item	pr	Unit	Tc (Jc/unit)	Ec (Jc/yr)
0.73%R	Bricks	1.60E+01	CNY/yr	1.72E+08	2.76E+09
0.47%R	Steel	2.25E+01	CNY/yr	2.13E+08	4.79E+09
46.63%R	Feed	5.20E+03	CNY/yr	8.36E+07	4.35E+11
4.65%R	Drugs	2.40E+02	CNY/yr	8.16E+07	1.96E+10
1.17%R	Disinfectant	2.00E+01	CNY/yr	1.16E+08	2.33E+09
1.49%R	Water	5.66E+01	CNY/yr	6.72E+07	3.80E+09
1.17%R	Electricity	3.20E+02	CNY/yr	1.97E+08	6.31E+10
Biogas pool					
0.79%R	Cement	1.35E+01	CNY/yr	1.56E+08	2.11E+09
0.35%R	Sand and pebble	1.30E+01	CNY/yr	3.28E+08	4.27E+09
1.23%R	Plastic pipe	4.50E+00	CNY/yr	1.04E+08	4.69E+08
1.01%R	Steel mold	6.00E+01	CNY/yr	1.44E+08	8.67E+09
1.20%R	Cooker	1.55E+01	CNY/yr	1.02E+08	1.58E+09
Fishpond					
0.79%R	Lime	2.88E+01	CNY/yr	1.56E+08	4.50E+09
0.70%R	Bleach	3.20E+01	CNY/yr	1.78E+08	5.70E+09
0.88%R	Aerator	1.00E+02	CNY/yr	1.23E+08	1.23E+10
67.50%R	Feed	7.20E+03	CNY/yr	1.12E+08	8.04E+11
0.62%R	Nitrogen fertilizer	4.00E+02	CNY/yr	1.98E+08	7.93E+10
0.62%R	Phosphate fertilizer	2.75E+02	CNY/yr	1.98E+08	5.45E+10
Yield (Y)					
	Pig	8.00E+03	CNY/yr	1.95E+08	1.56E+12
	Biogas	5.72E+02	CNY/yr	9.30E+08	5.32E+11
	Fish	5.40E+04	CNY/yr	1.12E+08	6.03E+12
	GHG(direct)	-3.04E+03	kg/yr	5.42E+07	-1.65E+11
	GHG(indirect)	-4.72E+03	kg/yr	5.42E+07	-2.56E+11

^a Footnotes are presented in Appendix I.

Renewable natural resources inputs ($Ires\text{-}r$) and nonrenewable natural resources inputs ($Ires\text{-}n$) of the integrated biogas engineering are calculated as 6. 89E+09 Jc/yr and 4. 94E+10 Jc/yr, respectively. For $Ires\text{-}r$, five free renewable resources inflowing to the biogas system are considered, and the dominant item is the chemical energy of rain. And for $Ires\text{-}n$, the main concern is nutrition from natural topsoil losses and the soil degradation, which is the fundamental supporter for this ecological agricultural system. In purchased inputs ($Ieco$) accounting, renewable proportion of each item listed in the first Column of Table 3. 2. 1 is from Chen and Chen (2010), which provides a detailed calculation of the renewable and nonrenewable cosmic exergy inputs for 135 sectors in China. The results show that the system requires 1. 76E+12 Jc/yr of cosmic exergy inputs from external economic system to sustain its running. Furthermore, it should be noted that GHG emissions of the integrated engineering are treated as the output of the system, but the value is negative for its adverse effect on environment. Both direct and indirect GHG emissions are considered here. The direct ones (see Appendix K) mainly include three items: (1) CH_4 released by enteric fermentation of the pig; (2) N_2O produced by fermentation process in the biogas digester and CO_2 generated by the biogas combustion; (3) CO_2 and CH_4 emitted by the fishpond. The indirect emissions (see Appendix L) are the emissions caused by materials input since these materials are produced by other systems, and GHG is ejected during the production process.

In Figure 3. 2. 3 (a), a sketch reflecting the overall resources investment and yield status of the integrated biogas system is provided. For this biogas system, the total cosmic exergy investment (I) amounts to 1. 82E+12 Jc/yr, of which $Ires$ and $Ieco$ contribute 3. 10% and 96. 90%, respectively. And it exhibits the strong dependence of the biogas system on the external economic system. However, as shown in the figure, the renewable economic investment ($Ieco\text{-}r$) takes up nearly half of total economic inputs, featuring the distinct characteristic of ecological agricultural system. Besides, the total yield (Y) of the integrated biogas engineering, 7. 71E+12 Jc/yr, can be divided into four parts: pig, biogas, fish and environmental impact (EI). The yield of fish is 6. 03E+12 Jc/yr, and it occupies the largest share (78. 28%) of the total yield, followed by the pork product (20. 28%). Unlike the products of pig and fish, which enter the market directly, biogas is used by the household and helps cut down the amount of fuels bought from the market. The yield of biogas accounts for a proportion of 6. 90%. Because the pig manure is managed effectively by the biogas digester, additional treatment of pig manure pollution isn't needed in the integrated system. Only GHG emissions of the system are counted in EI, making a negative contribution of −5. 45% to the total yield.

3. 2. 3. 2   Comparison with the Conventional Production System

In order to analyze ecological performance and characteristic of the integrated biogas engineering, a comparison between the integrated biogas system and the corresponding conventional production system is conducted. The calculations of the conventional system follow the assessment scheme introduced above. Cosmic exergy flows from and to the conventional system are presented in Table 3. 2. 2 in detail.

Table 3. 2. 2   Cosmic Exergy Accounting for the Conventional Production System[a]

Class	Item	pr	Unit	Tc (Jc/unit)	Ec (Jc/yr)
Renewable inputs of natural resources (Ires-r)					
100. 00%R	Solar radiation	2. 51E+13	J/yr	1. 02E−05	2. 56E+08
100. 00%R	Wind (kinetic)	2. 85E+09	J/yr	3. 21E−02	9. 15E+07
100. 00%R	Rain (chemical)	1. 01E+10	J/yr	6. 26E−01	6. 32E+09
100. 00%R	Rain (geopotential)	3. 66E+08	J/yr	3. 62E−01	1. 32E+08
100. 00%R	Geothermal	1. 17E+10	J/yr	7. 82E−03	9. 15E+07
Nonrenewable inputs of natural resources (Ires-n)					
0. 00%R	Topsoil loss	1. 14E+03	kg/yr	4. 33E+07	4. 94E+10
Renewable and nonrenewable inputs purchased from economic market (Ieco)					
6. 20%R	Labor and services	4. 00E+03	CNY/yr	5. 45E+07	2. 48E+11
Pigsty					
0. 79%R	Cement	1. 05E+01	CNY/yr	1. 56E+08	1. 64E+09
0. 79%R	Lime	1. 50E+01	CNY/yr	1. 56E+08	2. 34E+09
0. 73%R	Bricks	1. 60E+01	CNY/yr	1. 72E+08	2. 76E+09
0. 47%R	Steel	2. 25E+01	CNY/yr	2. 13E+08	4. 79E+09
46. 63%R	Feed	5. 20E+03	CNY/yr	8. 36E+07	4. 35E+11
4. 65%R	Drugs	2. 40E+02	CNY/yr	8. 16E+07	1. 96E+10
1. 17%R	Disinfectant	2. 00E+01	CNY/yr	1. 16E+08	2. 33E+09
1. 49%R	Water	5. 66E+01	CNY/yr	6. 72E+07	3. 80E+09
1. 17%R	Electricity	3. 20E+02	CNY/yr	1. 97E+08	6. 31E+10
Farmer					
0. 18%R	Coal	5. 72E+02	CNY/yr	9. 30E+08	5. 32E+11

Continued

Class	Item	pr	Unit	Tc (Jc/unit)	Ec (Jc/yr)
Fishpond					
0. 79%R	Lime	2. 88E+01	CNY/yr	1. 56E+08	4. 50E+09
0. 70%R	Bleach	3. 20E+01	CNY/yr	1. 78E+08	5. 70E+09
0. 88%R	Aerator	1. 00E+02	CNY/yr	1. 23E+08	1. 23E+10
67. 50%R	Feed	7. 20E+03	CNY/yr	1. 12E+08	8. 04E+11
0. 62%R	Nitrogen fertilizer	4. 00E+03	CNY/yr	1. 98E+08	7. 93E+11
0. 62%R	Phosphate fertilizer	2. 75E+03	CNY/yr	1. 98E+08	5. 45E+11
Yield (Y)					
	Pig	8. 00E+03	CNY/yr	1. 95E+08	1. 56E+12
	Fish	5. 40E+04	CNY/yr	1. 12E+08	6. 03E+12
	GHG(direct)	−1. 85E+03	kg/yr	5. 42E+07	−1. 00E+11
	GHG(indirect)	−1. 41E+04	kg/yr	5. 42E+07	−7. 63E+11
	Pig manure	−3. 20E+03	kg/yr	3. 72E+05	−1. 19E+09

ᵃ Footnotes are presented in Appendix J.

The amount of free natural resource inputs ($Ires$) is correlated with the area of the system. Since the conventional production system shares the same area with the integrated biogas system, they have the same natural inputs of 5. 63E + 10 Jc/yr. The economic investment ($Ieco$) of the conventional system is calculated as 3. 45E+12 Jc/yr, 96. 02% larger than that of the integrated biogas system (1. 76E+12 Jc/yr). The conventional system has no biogas digesters, therefore the building material inputs and labor inputs associated with the biogas digester are excluded in $Ieco$. However, without biogas and biogas fertilizer, more coal and chemical fertilizer are used in the conventional system, giving rise to the increase of $Ieco$. Moreover, without biogas digester, pig manure is discharged directly, and causes environmental pollution (EI). Thus, for the system yield (Y), two products (pig and fish) and three by-products (direct GHG, indirect GHG and pig manure) are contained, and they total up to 6. 73E+12 Jc/yr.

As shown in Figure 3. 2. 3(b), the total inputs (I) for the conventional production system are 3. 51E + 12 Jc/yr. Amongst I, nonrenewable investment from economy system ($Ieco-n$) occupies the biggest fraction of 76. 42%, followed by $Ieco-r$, $Ires-n$ and $Ires-r$ with shares of 21. 97%, 1. 41% and 0. 20%, respectively. Pig and fish are the target products in the conventional system with positive contribution to the total yield of 23. 22% and 89. 64%, separately. And environmental impact (EI) is the undesirable by-product with a negative percentage of −12. 85% to the total yield.

(a)

(b)

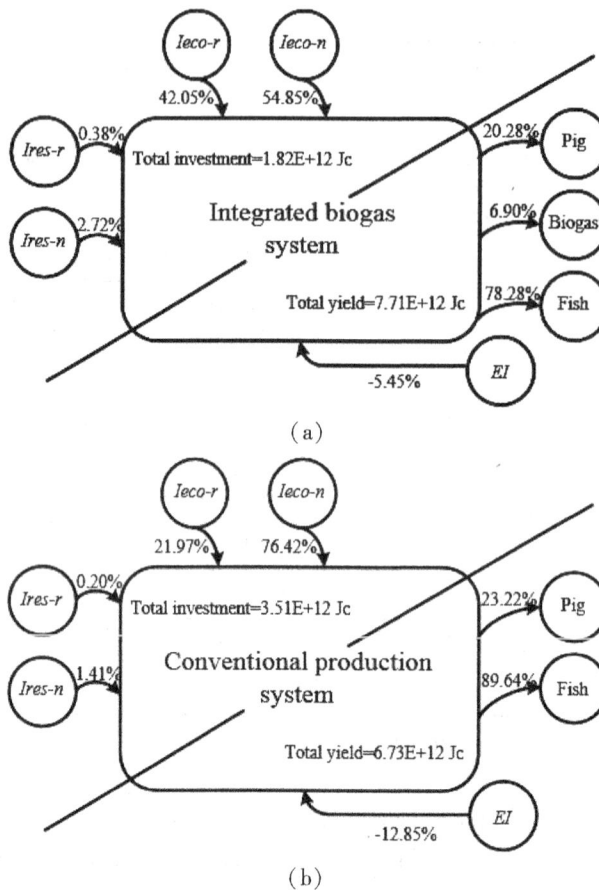

Figure 3. 2. 3   Overall Resources Investment and Yield for (a) the Integrated Biogas Engineering;
(b) the Conventional Production System

3. 2. 3. 3   Aggregated Indices Based on Cosmic Exergy

Fluxes and indices upon cosmic exergy are listed in Table 3. 2. 3 for the two systems. The cosmic exergy flux data are collected and calculated based on the results given in Table 3. 2. 1 and Table 3. 2. 2. And indices of the two systems are computed according to Equations (3. 2. 3)-(3. 2. 7). Net present ecological value of the integrated biogas engineering is 5. 89E+12 Jc/yr, implying that this biogas system can create a positive wealth of 5. 89E+12 Jc for Chinese society every year. For the conventional production system, it is 3. 22E+ 12 Jc/yr, revealing that both systems are ecologically profitable. However, the benefits brought by the integrated biogas system are almost twice that of the conventional system. Two main reasons may answer for this difference. The first one is the decline in investment for the integrated biogas engineering. In the integrated system, although the biogas pool requires material inputs of 1. 71E + 10 Jc/yr in its construction process, its products can cut down coal and chemical fertilizer consumption by 5. 31E + 11 Jc/yr and

142

1. 20E+12 Jc/yr, respectively. Thus, the total inputs in the integrated system are less than that in the conventional system. The other one is related to the by-products, *EI*. Pig manure is collected in the integrated system for recycling, while it is discharged directly and causes environmental pollution in the conventional system, so the integrated biogas system can alleviate 1. 19E+09 Jc/yr of pig manure pollution. What's more, both chemical fertilizer industry and coal industry are carbon-intensive emitters, the indirect GHG emissions of the integrated system are therefore abated with the reduced use of fertilizer and coal by 5. 08E+11 Jc/yr. In summary, compared with the conventional production system, the integrated biogas system produces less negative by-products and possesses a higher *Y*.

Table 3. 2. 3 Cosmic Exergy Based Fluxes and Indices for the Two Systems

		IBS [a]	CPS [b]
Flux			
Renewable inputs of natural resources (Jc/yr)	*Ires-r*	6. 89E+09	6. 89E+09
Nonrenewable inputs of natural resources (Jc/yr)	*Ires-n*	4. 49E+10	4. 49E+10
Renewable inputs purchased from economic market (Jc/yr)	*Ieco-r*	7. 64E+11	7. 70E+11
Nonrenewable inputs purchased from economic market (Jc/yr)	*Ieco-n*	9. 96E+11	2. 68E+12
Total renewable inputs (Jc/yr)	$Ir = Ires\text{-}r + Ieco\text{-}r$	7. 71E+11	7. 77E+11
Total nonrenewable inputs (Jc/yr)	$In = Ires\text{-}n + Ieco\text{-}n$	1. 05E+12	2. 73E+12
Total inputs (Jc/yr)	$I = Ir + In$	1. 82E+12	3. 51E+12
Total yield (Jc/yr)	*Y*	7. 71E+12	6. 73E+12
Index			
Net present ecological value (Jc/yr)	$NPEV = Y\text{-}I$	5. 89E+12	3. 22E+12
Ecological renewability index	$ERI = Ir/I$	42. 43%	22. 17%
Ecological yield ratio	$EYR = Y/Ieco$	4. 38	1. 95
Ecological loading ratio	$ELR = In/Ir$	1. 36	3. 51
Ecological sustainability index	$ESI = EYR/ELR$	3. 23	0. 56

[a] Integrated biogas system.

[b] Conventional production system.

The renewable proportion in total resource investments for the integrated biogas system approximately double that for the conventional system (42. 43% vs. 22. 17%). It implies that the integrated biogas system requires less nonrenewable resources in its production process, so it has a positive effect on nonrenewable resources conservation. Therefore, the integrated biogas system as an artificial ecological engineering achieves a higher renewability than the conventional system. And it is attributed to the small renewable portion of the fertilizer and coal, which are intensively consumed in the conventional agricultural system.

The integrated system obtains a much higher yield compared to the conventional system, which gives credit to the conclusion that the integrated system needs less external investment than the conventional system to obtain the same yield. The much smaller ecological loading ratio for the integrated system suggests that it imposes much smaller pressure on local environment than the conventional one. As a result, the ecological sustainability index shows that the sustainability of the integrated biogas system is five times larger than that of the conventional system (3.23 vs. 0.56). The positive results for the concerned integrated biogas system indicate that the biogas-linked ecological systems are consistent with the requirement of sustainable development, which is fully supportive for policy makers in their action towards further development of such ecological agricultural system.

3.2.4   Concluding Remarks

This study focuses on quantifying the renewability and sustainability of a typical integrated biogas engineering in Hubei Province, China in context of cosmic-solar-terrestrial ecosystem.

As endowed with properties of both usefulness and scarcity, cosmic exergy can provide an essential measure of "real wealth" for not only products and services in economic system, but also free resources in environmental system. With the help of the cosmic exergy method, systematic diagram, detailed inventory and aggregated indices of the chosen biogas system are presented in this study.

Results reveal that in a 20-year designed lifetime scenario, almost half of the total cosmic exergy inputs for the integrated biogas system are attributed to renewable resources free or purchased. Both desirable products and undesirable by-products produced by the system are taken consideration into system's total yields. In addition, a comparison between the integrated biogas system and a conventional production system is conducted to shed light on their differences in economic and ecological aspects. Based on the indices introduced here, the integrated biogas engineering turns out with a positive net ecological benefit, nearly double that of the conventional production system. What's more, the renewability and sustainability of the integrated biogas system is calculated respectively twofold and six fold of the conventional system.

Due to the delicate design in accordance with local conditions of southern China, local agricultural wastes are effectively used by the integrated biogas system. Besides, the utilization of biogas and biogas residue helps release the pressure of fossil fuels and chemical fertilizer on the environment. The present work of cosmic exergy analysis of the biogas engineering could have essential implications for comprehensive environmental planning and policy-making.

References

Chen, G. Q., 2005. Exergy Consumption of the Earth. *Ecological Modelling*, 184, 363-380.

Chen, G. Q., 2006. Scarcity of Exergy and Ecological Evaluation Based on Embodied Exergy. *Communications in Nonlinear Science and Numerical Simulation*, 11, 531-552.

Chen, G. Q., Chen, Z. M., 2010. Carbon Emissions and Resources Use by Chinese Economy 2007: A 135-sector Inventory and Input-output Embodiment. *Communications in Nonlinear Science and Numerical Simulation* , 15, 3647-3732.

Chen, G. Q., Chen, Z. M., 2011. Greenhouse Gas Emissions and Natural Resources Use by the World Economy: Ecological Input-output Modeling. *Ecological Modelling*, 222, 2362-2376.

Chen, Z. M., Chen, B., Chen, G. Q., 2011. Cosmic Exergy Based Ecological Assessment for a Wetland in Beijing. *Ecological Modelling*, 222, 322-329.

Jiang, M. M., Chen, Z. M., Zhang, B., Li, S. C., Xia, X. H., Zhou, S. Y., Zhou, J. B., 2010. Ecological Economic Evaluation Based on Emergy as Embodied Cosmic Exergy: A Historical Study for the Beijing Urban Ecosystem 1978-2004. *Entropy*, 12, 1696-1720.

Odum, H. T., Brown, M. T., Brandt-Williams, S., 2000. Handbook of Emergy Evaluation. Folio #1: Introduction and Global Budget. Center for Environmental Policy, University of Florida.

Szargut, J., Ziębik, A., Stanek, W., 2002. Depletion of the Non-renewable Natural Exergy Resources as a Measure of the Ecological Cost. *Energy Conversion and Management*, 43, 1149-1163.

3. 3　Estimating Green Net National Product for Puerto Rico: An Economic Measure of Sustainability[①]

3. 3. 1　Introduction

Located in the Caribbean Sea, Puerto Rico, an archipelago, is an unincorporated territory of the United States. The island of Puerto Rico has an area of about 3, 500 square

---

①　Published on *Environmental Management*, Volume 57, pp. 822-835, with a few modifications due to space constraints. Reuse permission has been obtained from Springer.

miles and a population around 3.8 million. The island is 99% dependent on fossil fuels for transportation and electricity and has one of the world's highest per capita car ownership with approximately 3 million vehicles. Emissions per capita are 230% that of the average per capita of the rest of the world and 333% that of Latin America. Since the 1940s, the island has experienced rapid changes in human activities, population distribution, and environmental systems due to industrialization and urbanization (Martinuzzi et al., 2009). For example, prior to industrialization, the majority (80%) of the population lived in rural areas. Now, approximately 50% of the land is classified as urban with the majority (94%) of the population living in urban areas. The past human activity also altered the original proportion of mangrove species (Martinuzzi et al., 2009) and solid waste management is becoming one of the biggest challenges in Puerto Rico (Miranda and Hale, 2005). All these changes and subsequent impacts reveal an urgency for sustainability research in Puerto Rico.

This study presents the data sources and methodology used to estimate GNNP for Puerto Rico. We acknowledge up front that many data gaps exist for calculating Puerto Rico's GNNP. Therefore, we focus on two research questions: (1) Can we estimate GNNP for Puerto Rico given the existing data? and (2) If so, is Puerto Rico moving toward or away from sustainability? Regardless, interpreting the results must be made with care (i.e., measurement errors in all variables, even those components that are typically included like the depreciation of man-made capital; Mota and Domingos 2013, p.196). Therefore, we consider this an interim estimate of GNNP for Puerto Rico. The study makes the following contributions. First, we estimate GNNP with the value of time and without business cycles for Puerto Rico in order to provide insights for the island's strategy for sustainable development. Second, we also add to the limited number of sustainability studies for Puerto Rico as part of a larger sustainability research project. Finally, we highlight the limitations of this research in order to improve future calculations.

Some economists define sustainability as non-declining utility over generations and have developed metrics that measure weak sustainability (e.g., Pezzey et al, 2006). Weak sustainability assumes ecological functions and/or resources (i.e., natural capital) can be replaced by technological or man-made surrogates to prevent the decline of the total stock of capital. GNNP and Genuine Savings (an aggregate measure of net investment) are two of the primary economic metrics related to sustainability found in the literature (e.g., Mota et al., 2010; Pezzey et al., 2006). Both metrics can help identify whether utility is non-declining (Pezzey et al., 2006). In theory, the change in GNNP should equal the real interest on Genuine Savings (Pezzey et al., 2006). When both metrics are augmented, time is incorporated into the variables such that it leads to changes in production possibilities (Pezzey et al., 2006). In this way, time is a productive stock that results in changes in production for reasons outside of the model. Conventional economic accounts, like Gross Domestic Product (GDP) and Gross National Product (GNP) are not good measures of sustainability because they exclude the value of leisure time, depreciation, pollution, and services produced by nature (Mota et al., 2010). The depreciation of all capital stocks, consumption of ecosystem services, and damages from pollution flows should be included in the calculation of GNNP. Net National Product (NNP) is the first step to calculate GNNP. The NNP can be adapted to include not only the depreciation of man-made capital but also the variation of other forms of capital (natural capital, human capital, social capital, etc.). The depreciation of natural capital can include both non-renewable and renewable resources. In fact, some accounting systems have been developed to serve as a platform for this type of analysis.

Previous studies have estimated GNNP for countries. For example, Mota et al. (2010) calculated Portugal's GNNP; and Pezzey et al. (2006) estimated GNNP for Scotland; all used a model for a small open economy.[①] Mota et al. (2010), Mota and Domingos (2013), and Pezzey et al. (2006) also included technological change in their models.

Besides national estimates, a few regional studies have been published. More recently, Heberling et al. (2012) calculated Green Net Regional Product, similar to GNNP but with a regionally-based focus on the San Luis Basin in south-central Colorado. Given the limited number of regional studies, this study contributes to the literature by adding new insights for evaluating sustainability in the Caribbean.

Our GNNP analysis for Puerto Rico is a new study built on Pezzey et al. (2006), Mota et al. (2010), and Heberling et al. (2012). We attempt to include the major issues of sustainability that Puerto Rico may face at present within our GNNP analysis. The issues included here are: municipal solid waste (Miranda and Hale, 2005), air emissions, mangrove area (Martinuzzi et al., 2009), and crushed stone mining. Finally, business cycles can obscure the interpretation of GNNP because the interpretation depends on full use of the production factors (Pezzey et al., 2006). Therefore, we analyze the results for the cycles.

3.3.2   Model

We define GNNP as the sum of real value of consumption and the real value of net investments:

$$\text{GNNP}(t) = \boldsymbol{P}(t)\boldsymbol{C}(t) + \boldsymbol{Q}^{\psi}(t)\dot{\boldsymbol{K}}^{\psi}(t) \tag{3.3.1}$$

where $\boldsymbol{C}(t)$ is consumption including both market and non-market goods as well as amenities

---

① A small open economy participates in international trade and exhibits price-taking behavior (Vincent et al. 1997).

(bold text represents vectors; Pezzey et al., 2006). Consumption determines the representative agent's utility $U(C(t))$. We have $Q^{\psi}(t) = (Q, Q^t)$ and $K^{\psi}(t) = (K, t)$ where Pezzey (2004) and Pezzey et al. (2006) refer to any variable corresponding to time as a stock as augmented, denoted by $^{\psi}$. $K^{\psi}(t)$ is the vector of the economy's productive stocks of environmental resources, man-made, and foreign capital; it includes time, t, which leads to exogenous changes in production possibilities such as exogenous technological progress (dot notation represents the rate of change over time; Pezzey et al., 2006). $P(t)$ and $Q^{\psi}(t)$ are the vectors of real prices for consumption and capital, respectively. The value of time, $Q^t(t)$ is the accounting price for t, the stock of time (Pezzey et al., 2006). Using a Divisia consumer price index to estimate real prices allows changes in GNNP to be interpreted as welfare changes (Mota et al., 2010; Pezzey et al., 2004).

Based on the general models in Pezzey et al. (2006), and Mota et al. (2010), we develop an empirical estimation for Puerto Rico. To estimate GNNP, the representative agent chooses the paths of consumption $C(t)$ and net investment $\dot{K}$ subject to the economy's production possibilities set to maximize welfare. Mathematically,

$$\underset{C,\,\dot{K}}{Max}\int_{0}^{\infty} U(C(t))e^{-\rho t}dt$$

$$\text{s. t. } [C(t),\ \dot{K}(t)] \in \Pi(K^{\psi}(t)) \tag{3.3.2}$$

where welfare is defined as the present value of utility using constant positive utility discount rate ρ and Π is the economy's attainable production possibilities set. The solution to the maximization problem in Equation (3.3.2) using real Divisia prices. Building on this, Pezzey et al. (2006) establishes the one-sided unsustainability test and demonstrates its application. Essentially, when GNNP is non-rising through time, the economy is said to be unsustainable. The test is one-sided because growth in GNNP is not enough to show the economy is necessarily sustainable (Pezzey et al., 2006).

To develop an estimation specific to Puerto Rico, we need to describe the capital and consumption bundles. We define the vector of capital stocks as

$$K = (K,\ K^f,\ S) \tag{3.3.3}$$

where K is the stock of man-made capital, which grows at a rate of investment (net of depreciation), K^f represents the stock of net foreign capital, and S is the vector of domestic stocks of renewable and nonrenewable resources. Following Mota et al. (2010), K^f grows as follows:

$$\dot{K}^f = rK^f + X - M + Q^R(R^x - R^m) \tag{3.3.4}$$

where r is the constant world interest rate, $X-M$ is net exports of the consumption/investment good, and $Q^R(R^x - R^m)$ is net resource exports, at world resource prices, $Q^R(t)$.

The stock of domestic resource i changes as

$$S^i = D^i + G^i(S^i) - R^{di} - R^{xi} + R^{mi}, \quad i = 1, \cdots, n \qquad (3.3.5)$$

where D are new discoveries of the resource, $G(S)$ is stock dependent natural growth, R^d is domestic use, R^x is exports, and R^m is imports.

Like Pezzey et al. (2006), Mota et al. (2010), and Heberling et al. (2012), we incorporate technological progress in production of the consumption/investment goods. Production of the consumption/investment goods, $F(K, \boldsymbol{R}^d + \boldsymbol{R}^m, t)$, is a function of man-made capital K, domestic and imported natural resources $\boldsymbol{R}^d$ and $\boldsymbol{R}^m$, and technological progress t (Pezzey et al., 2006). Production with net imports $(M - X)$ is used for consumption $C(t)$, net investment $\dot{K}(t)$, firms' total abatement expenditure $\boldsymbol{a}(t)$ for all pollutants, government spending $J(t)$ on mangrove protection, firms' resource discovery costs $V(\boldsymbol{D}, \boldsymbol{S})$ and firms' extraction costs $f(\boldsymbol{R}^d + \boldsymbol{R}^x - \boldsymbol{R}^m, \boldsymbol{S})$. Hence, $F(K, \boldsymbol{R}^d + \boldsymbol{R}^m, t) + M - X = C + \dot{K} + a + J + V(D, S) + f(\boldsymbol{R}^d + \boldsymbol{R}^x - \boldsymbol{R}^m, \boldsymbol{S})$ or rearranging,

$$\dot{K} = F(K, \boldsymbol{R}^d + \boldsymbol{R}^m, t) + M - X - C - a - J - V(D, S) - f(\boldsymbol{R}^d + \boldsymbol{R}^x - \boldsymbol{R}^m, \boldsymbol{S}) \qquad (3.3.6)$$

Notice that we do not include human capital in Equation (3.3.6), which is explained below.

We define $NNP(t) = C + J + \dot{K} + \dot{K}^f$, but this is not an appropriate measure of sustainability. As stated earlier, welfare is a measure of the present value of utility and utility is a function of consumption, but $NNP(t)$ does not incorporate the consumption of all commodities (e. g., amenities) needed to estimate GNNP. For Puerto Rico, we define utility as $U(\boldsymbol{C}) = U(C, \boldsymbol{E}, B)$ where $C(t)$ is consumption, $\boldsymbol{E}(t)$ is a vector of net emission flows which depend on production and abatement costs, and $B(J)$ is the flow of storm protection that results from government spending $J(t)$ on protecting and enhancing mangroves (Pezzey et al., 2006). The marginal cost of abating pollutant i is $e^i(t) = 1/-(\partial E^i/\partial a^i)$ (Mota et al., 2010; Pezzey et al., 2006). For our model, the emission vector includes the effect of energy consumption on climate change for future generations through CO_2 emissions following from Pezzey et al. (2006). The vector also includes other air emissions and solid waste.[1] We define $b(t) = 1/B'(J)$ as the marginal cost of increasing storm protection. With the appropriate assumptions and given the control variables, $C(t)$, $\boldsymbol{R}^d(t)$, $\boldsymbol{R}^x(t)$, $\boldsymbol{R}^m(t)$, $\boldsymbol{a}(t)$, $J(t)$, $M(t) - X(t)$, we can maximize welfare subject to $\dot{K}^f$, $\dot{S}$, $\dot{K}$ (Equations (3.3.4), (3.3.5), and (3.3.6)). Based on the maximization problem, and following Pezzey et al. (2006), we derive our GNNP model for Puerto Rico:

$$GNRP(t) = NNP(t) - \boldsymbol{e}\boldsymbol{E} + (bB - J) + (Q^R - f_R)\dot{S} + Q^t \qquad (3.3.7)$$

Once we estimate NNP, we subtract the costs of emissions $\boldsymbol{e}\boldsymbol{E}$, add the net benefit $(bB\text{-}J)$ of storm protection, subtract the value of crushed stone rents $(Q^R - f_R)\dot{S}$ and add the value of time Q^t. Following Mota et al. (2010), we estimate the value of time as

---

[1] Import-associated emissions are excluded from this vector.

$$Q'(t) = \int_t^\infty F_s e^{-R(s-t)} ds \approx \sum_{s=t+1}^{t+T} \frac{\Delta TFP_s}{TFP_s} \times GDP_s \times e^{-R(s-t)} \qquad (3.3.8)$$

where F_s represents future exogenous technical change, and R is the real interest rate. We set T at 15 years.

We did not explicitly include the depreciation of human capital in our estimate of GNNP as it can be considered part of aggregate consumption in NNP (i. e., education expenditures). If education expenditures are the best proxy for investment in human capital, then they are already included in the calculation (see Pezzey et al., 2006, for discussion). However, we are aware that these expenditures are typically considered a poor proxy for human capital depreciation (e. g., Ferreira and Vincent, 2005).

Based on the model, real prices should be adjusted using a Divisia consumer price index. We use consumer price index (CPI) as the best proxy (Mota et al., 2010). Finally, due to lack of marginal damage cost data through time, we assume e, the marginal cost of emissions, is constant, which allows us to set the price of consumption equal to one simplifying the GNNP calculation (Pezzey et al., 2006).

3.3.3   Data and Sources

Data collection in Puerto Rico required extensive collaborations with the Puerto Rico government and several federal and local agencies. As a result, our data come from a number of sources, and for each component of GNNP, we describe our data sources separately.

The calculation of NNP requires adjusting Gross National Product (GNP) by the depreciation of man-made capital stock. This nominal estimate is then converted into real NNP using the CPI. The data we used to estimate real NNP, including GNP and the depreciation of man-made capital stock, were available from the Puerto Rico Planning Board (e. g., Puerto Rico Planning Board (2009)). CPI was available from the Instituto de Estadisticas de Puerto Rico.[1]

To account for the depreciation of natural capital in GNNP, we need monetary values for each component. This requires an estimate of the change in the stock of natural capital and a real price. However, including real prices is difficult or impossible and requires some approximation (Pezzey et al., 2006; Mota et al., 2010). The literature discussed that incorporating the depreciation of non-market goods and services is difficult because of the lack of data and because these goods and services are not measured in standard, well-defined units like market goods. For environmental spillovers or externalities, such as air

---

[1]   Accessed at http://www. estadisticas. gobierno. pr/iepr/Estadisticas/InventariodeEstadisticas. aspx on August 20, 2015.

emissions, the shadow price is measured in terms of marginal damage cost of air emissions. One issue is that certain air emissions (e. g., carbon dioxide emissions) cause damages that extend beyond the local economy, and carbon emissions are therefore counted as an environmental cost equal to the global social cost of carbon.

We have three components of natural capital depreciation in the model (Equation (3.3.7)). They are total damage cost of pollution, value of mangroves for storm protection, and value of rent from crushed stone. Next, we describe data needed to estimate these components. For the first component, we combine air emissions and solid waste in our vector of emissions. Puerto Rico's Environmental Quality Board (EQB) provided air emission data for particulate matter (PM_{10}), sulfur dioxide (SO_2), nitrogen oxides (NO_x), and volatile organic compounds (VOC), which directly cause damages in Puerto Rico. The air emission data are available from 1992-2009, which limits our time series analysis. We obtained data for carbon dioxide emissions (CO_2) from 1980-2009 from Energy Information Administration.

Annual solid waste generation is a growing concern for Puerto Rico. According to Miranda and Hale (2005), landfilling has long been the dominant form of waste disposal on Puerto Rico, and landfills typically generate environmental costs through air and water emissions. Annual municipal solid waste (MSW) data is not specifically collected for Puerto Rico; instead, we estimated total solid waste per year using waste per capita per day multiplied by total population. We have two points of waste per capita per day: Miranda and Hale (2005) provided a data point of 3. 1lb MSW per person per day in 1988, and the other data point of 3. 91lb MSW per person per day was collected from a final report of waste characterization study prepared by the Solid Waste Management Authority of Puerto Rico. The Puerto Rico Planning Board provided estimates of population. The second component of natural capital depreciation is the value of mangroves. Mangroves provide hurricane and storm protection services and a loss in mangrove area may increase the damage cost of hurricanes or storms (Barbier, 2007). A study by Martinuzzi et al. (2009) provided 11 data points of mangrove area (hectare) in Puerto Rico over a period of 1800-2002 and we interpolated estimates of mangrove area for missing years. The sources for hurricane data were EM-DAT and the Puerto Rico Hurricane Center.[1] Assessing the quality of data from the Puerto Rico Hurricane Center was difficult, however.

The third component of natural capital depreciation is the value of crushed stones. Crushed stone is one of the leading mineral commodities in Puerto Rico. A series of Mineral

---

[1] EM-DAT: The OFDA/CRED International Disaster Database—www.emdat.be—Université catholique de Louvain-Brussels-Belgium. Accessed on August 20, 2015. Puerto Rico Hurricane Center was accessed at http://huracanado1.tripod.com/ on August 20, 2015.

Yearbooks (1933-2010) published by USGS provided nonfuel raw mineral production in Puerto Rico, in which the production (depletion) of crushed stone was available in both quantity and value on an annual basis.

The last adjustment to GNP is the value of time, Q', which requires estimates of both total factor productivity (TFP) growth and Gross National Product (GNP). We used TFP growth data from Collins et al. (2006) for Puerto Rico as our estimate of $\Delta TFPs/TFPs$, the long-term average TFP growth rate, which was 0.5% (1990-2004).

3.3.4　Calculation Methodology

Having described available data, we now present the approach to conducting economic valuation on each component and incorporating them in the GNNP model (Equation (3.3.7)). Our estimate of GNNP is converted into 2010 dollars using the CPI. Real NNP is presented in Column 3 of Table 3.3.1. The next step is to estimate the economic value of the depreciation of natural capital. We provide more detail here on how we combined shadow price and the change in natural capital stock.

For the majority of these components (except for the change in mangrove area and the value of time), we used benefit transfer, an alternative to collecting primary economic data, to estimate the economic value of the change in the natural capital. Benefit transfer applies economic value (e.g., willingness to pay for a change in environmental quality) from one study to another location or context. The accuracy depends on the existence and quality of applicable studies. This means the values estimated for the new study will depend on differences in the resources being valued and the relevant populations.

Air emissions include four pollutants that cause damages within the local economy (i.e. PM_{10}, NO_x, SO_2 and VOC), and one pollutant that causes global damages beyond the local economy (i.e., CO_2). To calculate total damage cost of air emissions (eE in Equation (3.3.7)), we need an estimate of each pollutant's marginal damage cost (e), which is associated with emitting an additional ton of pollution. We used the average values of rural and urban (2000 $): $350/ton of PM_{10}, $300/ton of NO_x, $1200/ton of SO_2 and $400/ton of VOC. We used a value approximately equal to $20/ton of CO_2 (2005 $). This was based on the Fisher-Tippett kernel density with the discount rate of 3%. Combining emissions and marginal damage cost, total damage cost of air emissions over the period 1993-2009 is presented in Column 4 of Table 3.3.1.

The annual environmental cost for solid waste ranged from $13.80-$73.40/ton of waste ($1997), which has taken account of the externality of landfill air emissions and costs due to leachate impacts on local soils and groundwater (Miranda and Hale 2005). We used $43.60/ton, the midpoint of the range, as the environmental cost of MSW. Total solid waste damage over the period 1993-2009 is presented in Column 5 of Table 3.3.1.

Table 3.3.1 Estimates of All Components of Green Net National Product (GNNP)[*]

(1)	(2) Real GNP	(3) Real NNP	(4) Air emission damage eE (air)	(5) Solid waste damage eE (solid waste)	(6) Mangroves bB-J	(7) Crushed stone $(Q^R - f_R)\dot{S}$	(8) Value of time Q^t	(9) GNNP, no Q^t	(10) Augmented GNNP
1993	$ 37,240.92	$ 33,551.78	$ (918.52)	$ (152.51)	$ 240.19	$ (24.61)	$ 5,135.39	$ 32,696.33	$ 37,831.72
1994	$ 38,916.92	$ 34,988.69	$ (931.00)	$ (153.65)	$ 241.24	$ (37.22)	$ 5,322.52	$ 34,108.07	$ 39,430.59
1995	$ 40,781.14	$ 36,829.63	$ (902.96)	$ (154.84)	$ 242.30	$ (49.84)	$ 5,469.01	$ 35,964.28	$ 41,433.29
1996	$ 42,117.81	$ 37,999.27	$ (922.54)	$ (156.09)	$ 243.35	$ (23.67)	$ 5,523.97	$ 37,140.31	$ 42,664.29
1997	$ 44,037.73	$ 39,807.79	$ (950.08)	$ (157.40)	$ 244.41	$ (31.55)	$ 5,638.05	$ 38,913.16	$ 44,551.21
1998	$ 47,783.08	$ 42,864.14	$ (1,048.85)	$ (158.78)	$ 245.47	$ (25.92)	$ 5,837.97	$ 41,876.06	$ 47,714.04
1999	$ 51,747.30	$ 45,858.19	$ (928.72)	$ (160.22)	$ 246.52	$ (24.95)	$ 5,983.46	$ 44,990.82	$ 50,974.28
2000	$ 54,320.12	$ 48,465.76	$ (955.00)	$ (161.34)	$ 247.58	$ (21.74)	$ 5,968.62	$ 47,575.26	$ 53,543.87
2001	$ 57,432.65	$ 51,172.72	$ (1,132.57)	$ (162.66)	$ 248.63	$ (16.10)	$ 6,084.12	$ 50,110.02	$ 56,194.15
2002	$ 58,651.09	$ 52,174.80	$ (1,179.13)	$ (163.47)	$ 249.69	$ (17.17)	$ 6,219.39	$ 51,064.72	$ 57,284.11
2003	$ 60,944.86	$ 54,520.67	$ (1,336.55)	$ (164.30)	$ 250.73	$ (25.03)	$ 6,269.45	$ 53,245.51	$ 59,514.96
2004	$ 63,474.93	$ 56,778.16	$ (1,323.57)	$ (164.99)	$ 251.77	$ (23.43)	$ 6,229.66	$ 55,517.93	$ 61,747.59
2005	$ 63,711.67	$ 56,906.74	$ (1,376.84)	$ (165.72)	$ 252.81	$ (21.38)	$ 5,994.87	$ 55,595.60	$ 61,590.47
2006	$ 63,930.89	$ 57,102.97	$ (1,440.89)	$ (166.39)	$ 253.85	$ (29.19)	$ 5,778.32	$ 55,720.34	$ 61,498.66
2007	$ 64,349.01	$ 57,571.98	$ (1,222.77)	$ (167.01)	$ 254.88	$ (35.14)	$ 5,608.28	$ 56,401.95	$ 62,010.23
2008	$ 63,368.72	$ 56,567.49	$ (1,198.61)	$ (167.50)	$ 255.92	$ (31.96)	$ 5,384.99	$ 55,425.33	$ 60,810.33
2009	$ 64,230.07	$ 57,277.64	$ (1,150.85)	$ (166.91)	$ 256.96	$ (24.06)	$ 5,422.59	$ 56,192.78	$ 61,615.37

[*] 2010 $ millions

The next component is the value of mangroves. We estimated the value of mangroves based on the marginal damage cost of a hurricane caused by a one hectare loss of mangrove area. We followed Barbier (2007) and used the expected damage function (EDF) approach to estimate the marginal damage cost. The EDF approach assumes that, "the value of an asset that yields a benefit in terms of reducing the probability and severity of some economic damage is measured by the reduction in the expected damage" (Barbier, 2007). The approach estimates how changes in the asset affect the probability of the damaging event occurring. For this study, the asset is a mangrove ecosystem and the damaging event is a hurricane. Using data of hurricane occurrence and mangrove area from 1800-2010, we estimated the increased probability of a damaging hurricane occurring associated with a one hectare loss of mangrove area. It is the resulting damage affected by the mangrove loss. We calculated the marginal damage cost using the estimated probability and annual average damage cost caused by hurricanes. The final estimate of marginal damage cost was rounded to \$ 30,000 per hectare (see Appendix N for our model estimating marginal damage cost). When mangrove area increases over time, this value implies a marginal benefit. Given our estimate of mangrove area and the marginal benefit (b), we can calculate total benefit generated by mangroves (bB). In addition, government spending on protecting mangroves (J) needs to be subtracted from total benefit of mangroves to avoid double-counting. However, for Puerto Rico, government spending on mangrove protection and enhancement was not itemized, so we assume it to be zero. Net benefit of mangroves (bB-J) over the period 1993-2009 is presented in Column 6 of Table 3.3.1.

The last component counted in the depreciation of natural capital is the value of crushed stone, $(Q^R - f_R)\dot{S}$ in Equation (3.3.7). The extraction quantity of crushed stone (S) was available from the Minerals Yearbook (USGS, 2012; see Section 3.3.3). The term ($Q^R - f_R$) corresponds to the marginal unit rent of crushed stone, where Q^R is the unit value of the extracted crushed stone also available from the Minerals Yearbook (USGS, 2012). For f_R, the marginal cost of exploiting crushed stone, we used the average cost as the marginal cost. Average cost was estimated to be 67.5% of the price in the US and we assumed this ratio remained constant. Using this ratio and the unit value of crushed stone from the *Minerals Yearbook*, we were able to estimate the average cost of exploiting crushed stone in Puerto Rico. The final value of crushed stone depletion over the period 1993-2009 is presented in Column 7 of Table 3.3.1.

As stated previously, for the value of time, we used the estimate of average TFP growth rate of 0.5% for Puerto Rico over the period 1990-2004 (Collins et al., 2006) as our estimate of $\Delta TFPs/TFPs$ and used T as 15 years. We used a 3% discount rate. The value of time (Column 8 of Table 3. 3. 1) ranged on average 8%-14% of real GNP.

3.3.5　Results

3. 3. 5. 1　Main Results

Following the methodology presented in the previous section and using the 17 years (1993-2009) of data, we estimated the GNNP for Puerto Rico, with no Q' (Column 9 of Table 3. 3. 1), and augmented GNNP (Column 10 of Table 3. 3. 1). The NNP, GNNP no Q', and augmented GNNP are all displayed in Figure 3. 3. 1; components of natural capital depreciation are displayed in Figure 3. 3. 2.

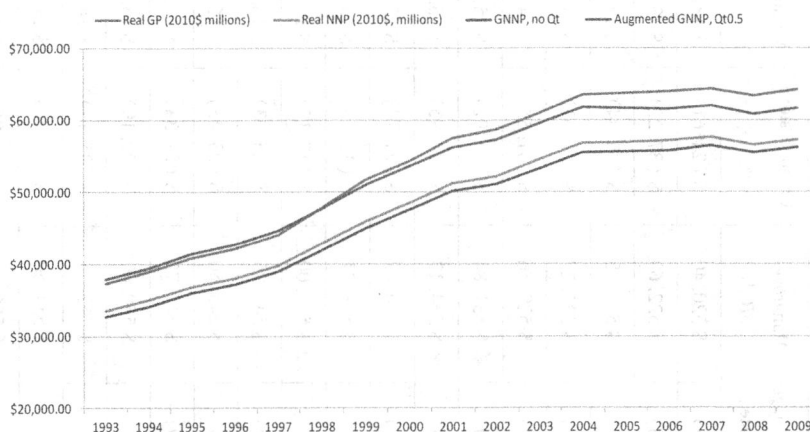

Figure 3. 3. 1　Real Net National Product (Real NNP), Green Net National Product (GNNP) with no Q', Augmented Green Net National Product (2010 $, millions)

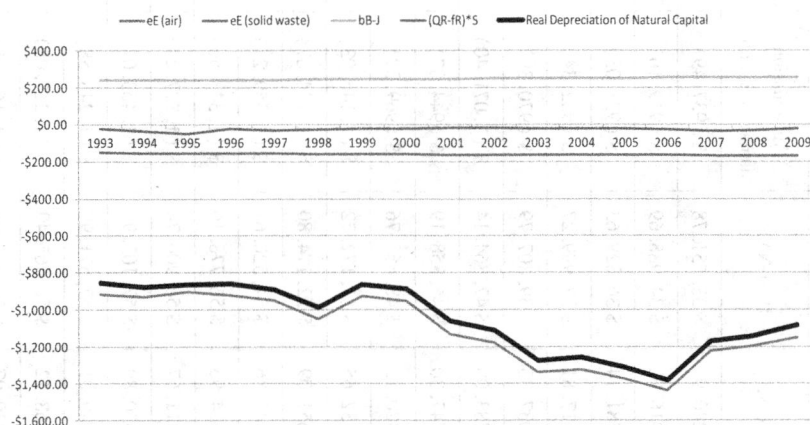

Figure 3. 3. 2　Components of Natural Capital Depreciation Including Air Emissions (eE), Solid Waste (eE), Mangrove Area ($bB-J$), Crushed Stone $[(Q^R-f_R)\dot{S}]$ (2010 $, Millions)

155

Table 3.3.2　Sensitivity Analysis [a]

(1)	(2) Real GNP	(3) Real NNP	(4) Air emission damage eE (air)	(5) Solid waste damage eE (solid waste)	(6) Mangroves $bB-J$	(7) Crushed stone $(Q^R - f_R)\dot{S}$	(8) Value of time Q^t	(9) GNNP, no Q^t	(10) Augmented GNNP
1993	$ 37,240.92	$ 33,551.78	$ (937.49)	$ (256.75)	$ 520.40	$ (24.61)	$ 13,352.03	$ 32,853.33	$ 46,205.36
1994	$ 38,916.92	$ 34,988.69	$ (949.16)	$ (258.66)	$ 522.69	$ (37.22)	$ 13,838.56	$ 34,266.34	$ 48,104.90
1995	$ 40,781.14	$ 36,829.63	$ (921.03)	$ (260.67)	$ 524.98	$ (49.84)	$ 14,219.42	$ 36,123.06	$ 50,342.48
1996	$ 42,117.81	$ 37,999.27	$ (942.34)	$ (262.78)	$ 527.27	$ (23.67)	$ 14,362.33	$ 37,297.74	$ 51,660.07
1997	$ 44,037.73	$ 39,807.79	$ (970.39)	$ (264.99)	$ 529.56	$ (31.55)	$ 14,658.93	$ 39,070.41	$ 53,729.34
1998	$ 47,783.08	$ 42,864.14	$ (1,071.40)	$ (267.30)	$ 531.84	$ (25.92)	$ 15,178.73	$ 42,031.37	$ 57,210.10
1999	$ 51,747.30	$ 45,858.19	$ (944.07)	$ (269.73)	$ 534.13	$ (24.95)	$ 15,556.99	$ 45,153.58	$ 60,710.57
2000	$ 54,320.12	$ 48,465.76	$ (969.39)	$ (271.61)	$ 536.42	$ (21.74)	$ 15,518.40	$ 47,739.43	$ 63,257.84
2001	$ 57,432.65	$ 51,172.72	$ (1,146.03)	$ (273.84)	$ 538.71	$ (16.10)	$ 15,818.72	$ 50,275.46	$ 66,094.18
2002	$ 58,651.09	$ 52,174.80	$ (1,194.67)	$ (275.19)	$ 541.00	$ (17.17)	$ 16,170.40	$ 51,228.76	$ 67,399.16
2003	$ 60,944.86	$ 54,520.67	$ (1,359.24)	$ (276.60)	$ 543.25	$ (25.03)	$ 16,300.58	$ 53,403.04	$ 69,703.62
2004	$ 63,474.93	$ 56,778.16	$ (1,343.56)	$ (277.76)	$ 545.50	$ (23.43)	$ 16,197.11	$ 55,678.90	$ 71,876.01
2005	$ 63,711.67	$ 56,906.74	$ (1,397.24)	$ (278.99)	$ 547.75	$ (21.38)	$ 15,586.66	$ 55,756.88	$ 71,343.54
2006	$ 63,930.89	$ 57,102.97	$ (1,463.07)	$ (280.11)	$ 550.00	$ (29.19)	$ 15,023.63	$ 55,880.59	$ 70,904.23
2007	$ 64,349.01	$ 57,571.98	$ (1,243.58)	$ (281.15)	$ 552.25	$ (35.14)	$ 14,581.52	$ 56,564.36	$ 71,145.88
2008	$ 63,368.72	$ 56,567.49	$ (1,217.08)	$ (281.98)	$ 554.50	$ (31.96)	$ 14,000.98	$ 55,590.96	$ 69,591.94
2009	$ 64,230.07	$ 57,277.64	$ (1,167.95)	$ (280.99)	$ 556.75	$ (24.06)	$ 14,098.73	$ 56,361.40	$ 70,460.12

[a] 2010 $ millions

Both NNP and GNNP no Q^t had upward trends and after 2004, they remained constant. The only negative range through the study period was 2007-2008. Augmented GNNP generally had an upward trend similar to GNNP no Q^t, but there was a second negative period 2004-2006. Following Pezzey et al. (2006), who suggested the change in GNNP is a one-sided test of weak sustainability (i. e., positive growth in GNNP is not enough to show the economy is sustainable), the calculation reveals Puerto Rico was moving away from sustainability during these years.

The small difference between NNP and GNNP no Q_t suggests the components of natural capital depreciation have a minimal effect. Natural capital depreciation ranges from 1.8%-2.5% of real NNP (however, caution should be taken in interpreting the actual values because we did not have data for all natural capital stocks or we dropped components that were assumed not to vary through time). Solid waste, mangroves, and crushed stones all have fairly constant and small estimates of depreciation over time; air emissions have relatively big estimates of depreciation, which account for the largest percent of total natural capital depreciation (Figure 3.3.2). Total natural capital depreciation had a downward trend over the period 1993-2009; however, because it is relatively small, natural capital depreciation resulted in no significant shift down from NNP to GNNP no Q_t (Figure 3.3.1).

3.3.5.2 Sensitivity Analysis

To test sensitivity, we focused on the components of natural capital depreciation and value of time. For air emissions, we applied alternative estimates: \$400/ton of PM_{10}, \$300/ton of NO_x, \$1300/ton of SO_2 and \$700/ton of VOC. The sensitivity estimates of total damage cost of air emissions are in Column 4 of Table 3.3.2. For the shadow price of solid waste, we used the upper bound estimate in Miranda and Hale (2005), \$73.4/ton. The sensitivity estimates of total environmental cost of solid waste are in Column 5 of Table 3.3.2. For the value of mangroves, we used \$65,000 per hectare (see Appendix N). We presented the sensitivity estimates of net benefit from protecting mangroves in Column 6 of Table 3.3.2. Unfortunately, we found no upper bound estimate for the marginal unit rent of crushed stone, thus, this component remains constant. We admit this approach still requires further studies. Finally, for the sensitivity of the value of time, the average TFP growth rate, $\Delta TFPs/TFPs$, was changed to 1.3% (Collins et al., 2006). We presented sensitivity estimates of value of time in Column 8 of Table 3.3.2.

In general, total natural capital depreciation based on the sensitivity analysis, is still a small portion of real NNP, ranging from 1.5% to 2.1%. When compared to the estimates in the main results (Figure 3.3.3), total natural capital depreciation using sensitivity estimates had slight changes, which caused only a minor effect on the estimates of GNNP no Q^t.

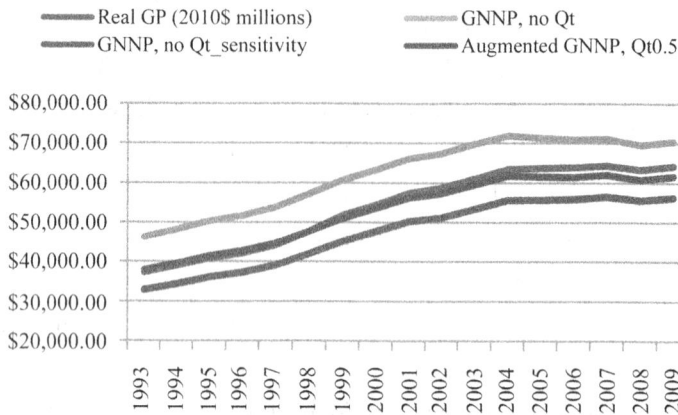

Figure 3. 3. 3   Sensitivity Analysis for Natural Capital Depreciation and Value of Time (2010 $, Millions)

3. 3. 6   Discussion

We estimated and presented the calculations for GNNP as well as the sensitivity estimates for Puerto Rico over a 17-year period. The data and methodology are not perfect. This section discusses the assumptions needed in order to estimate GNNP of Puerto Rico and some of the limitations we encountered. We focus on those assumptions and limitations related to our specific calculations of the GNNP for Puerto Rico and not those related to the theoretical foundation of this method and weak sustainability.

Assumptions related to calculating the shadow price of each component of natural capital depreciation can be found in the literature as discussed in Section 3. 3. 4. Because of the concerns over the assumptions, we conducted a sensitivity analysis using upper bounds of the shadow price for each component where data existed. We found minor differences for estimates on total value of natural capital depreciation.

In general, the accuracy of the estimates using our methodology depends on the availability of data. This issue includes both the problem of time lags in data releases and the availability of data needed for calculating sustainability metrics. Time lags can affect how early sustainability metrics can be calculated which impacts how useful metrics are for decision-making. On the other hand, depending on the availability data we cannot include all components of natural capital depreciation. If these components impact the slope of GNNP, then data availability can affect decision-making. For example, fisheries, coral reefs, water quality and quantity, invasive species, habitat loss (e. g., forest area) and soil erosion were all identified by stakeholders as important issues for Puerto Rico. However, due to data availability, we could not include these components in our calculation.

Although data for these types of natural capital were not sufficient for the GNNP calculations, limited information from literature may assist us with understanding what is happening to these natural capital now in Puerto Rico. For example, forest area in Puerto Rico is increasing due to natural regeneration on abandoned agricultural land. According to this report, forest cover grew from 32 percent in 1990 to 57 percent in 2003 for the island of Puerto Rico. For coral reef fishes in Puerto Rico, of the 25 reef fish species assessed, 16 species were below 30% spawning potential ratio (SPR①), 6 species were above 30% SPR, and 3 species could not be reliably determined due to low sample sizes. The findings indicate that a majority of snapper-grouper reef species in Puerto Rico are currently fished at unsustainable levels. With the shift from an agricultural economy to an industrial based economy, there has been a decrease in agricultural lands and increases in the area of secondary forest, urban lands, and construction sites. As a consequence, the net effect has been a reduction in soil erosion on the island; however, erosion and sedimentation of water supply reservoirs continue to be major environmental problems. For example, the Guadiana watershed supplies water to approximately 36% of the San Juan metropolitan population, but it has lost nearly 30% of its storage capacity due to sediment since it was built in 1974. With the limited information gleaned from these studies, there is an unknown effect on natural capital depreciation (some improvements and some degradation through time). However, natural capital depreciation is a relatively small component of GNNP and unlikely to lead to changes in the trend of GNNP.

Emissions of a flow pollutant and of a stock pollutant are supposed to be distinguished from each other. The flow pollutant has an immediate impact whereas the stock pollutant has future impacts after accumulation. In this study, PM_{10}, NO_x, SO_2 and VOC are flow pollutants and CO_2 is a stock pollutant. We used carbon flows (i. e. emissions) to estimate the annual social cost of carbon emissions, but global temperature is influenced by the absolute concentration of CO_2 in the atmosphere and CO_2 emissions remain in the atmosphere for many years. Therefore, Pezzey et al. (2006) noted the social cost of carbon emission estimates should incorporate the atmospheric lifetime cost of emissions. Our estimate of the marginal damage cost of carbon emissions included the lifetime cost of carbon emissions.

Solid waste is also a type of stock pollutant. We used data of municipal solid waste generation to calculate damage cost of solid waste; however, net increment of waste should be measured by generation subtracted by waste decomposition in the ground. We only had one observation for solid waste per capita per day from 1993-2009 (from a final report of waste characterization study, SWMA, 2003). The change for the total solid waste

---

① SPR is a management benchmark that measures a stock's potential to produce yields on a sustainable basis. 30% SPR is defined as the threshold below which a stock is no longer sustainable at current exploitation levels.

generation is therefore driven by the change in the population of Puerto Rico. Again, the absence of relevant studies and lack of data limited our calculation method.

The mangrove analysis faces a number of limitations. First, when calculating the net benefit of mangroves, government spending on mangrove protection was supposed to be subtracted from total benefit generated by mangroves; however, this spending was not available and we assume it to be zero. If not zero, natural capital depreciation would be slightly larger in absolute terms. In addition, we only had one data point for mangrove area in 2002 from Martinuzzi et al. (2009). Estimates of mangrove area for the remaining years were estimated based on linear interpolation. Although interpolated values may not be exact, they show the real increasing trend of mangrove area over time in Puerto Rico. Mangrove ecosystems provide two principal services, nursery and breeding habitats for offshore fisheries and natural "storm barriers" to periodic coastal storm events, but depending on the region, other products might include fuel wood, timber, raw materials, and crabs and shellfish (Barbier, 2007). In this study, we only considered the storm protection services and thus our estimate of mangrove value was limited. Compared to our confidence in estimating the value of the other components, we have the least confidence in the estimates from the expected damage function model due to the stability of the results.

For the value of crushed stones, we used average cost of exploitation instead of marginal cost to calculate the marginal unit rent of crushed stones. This implies the value of crushed stone depletion will be overestimated when incorporated in the GNNP for Puerto Rico (Davis and Moore, 2000). Davis and Moore (2000) derived an "unrestricted valuation principle" for valuing mineral resources in the ground and calculated correcting factors to use average instead of marginal costs when estimating Hotelling rent for different resources in the USA. They showed that in the absence of more specific data these correcting factors should be used for empirically correcting resource valuation for oil and minerals in other countries. They were confident in proposing a correcting factor of 0.7 for hard rock minerals in general (Davis and Moore, 2000). Crushed stone is not considered hard rock in the literature; therefore, we did not use a correction factor. This issue needs more discussion and additional research to improve the calculation of crushed stone values for Puerto Rico. We also have questions about the quality of quantity data on crushed stone based on anecdotal evidence. This needs further study and discussions with Puerto Rico experts.

The value of technological progress or the value of time (Equation (3.3.8)) clearly effects the results of our estimate of GNNP, more so than natural capital depreciation. For the sensitivity analysis, we used the long-term TFP growth rate of 1.3%. In Figure 3.3.3, GNNP no Q' and GNNP no Q' sensitivity almost overlap due to minor differences in the estimates of natural capital depreciation. Comparing the conventional economic account (GNP) and the GNNP no Q', we see GNNP no Q' is less than the conventional economic account. When the value of time using short-term and long-term TFP growth rate was separately added to these two estimates of GNNP, we see the augmented GNNP Q^t 1. 3 is well above the augmented GNNP Q^t 0. 5. The GNNP Q^t 1. 3 became greater than the Real GNP while the GNNP Q^t 0. 5 was slightly less than the Real GNP. Therefore, the difference between the calculations for Puerto Rico depends on the value of time (i. e., TFP growth rate). Mota et al. (2010) stated that both TFP growth and GNP growth can have significant impacts on the value of time, so these estimates are extremely important to the interpretation of changes in GNNP.

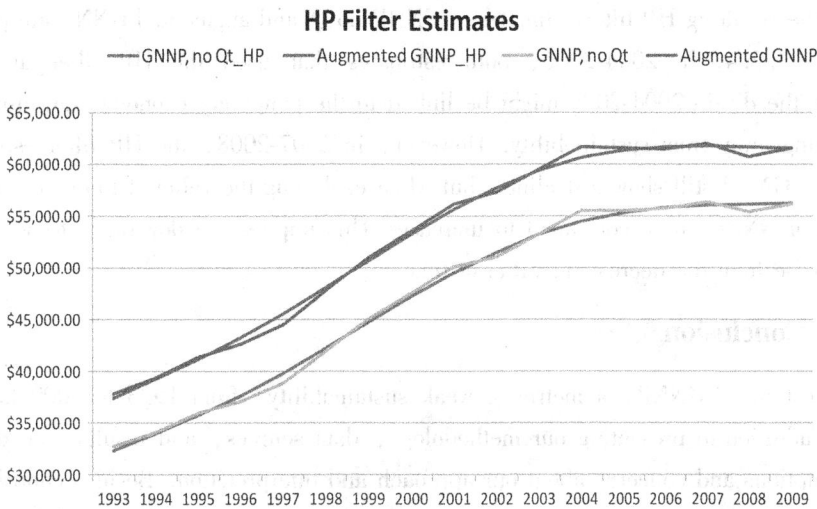

HP Filter Estimates

——GNNP, no Qt_HP   ——Augmented GNNP_HP   ——GNNP, no Qt   ——Augmented GNNP

Figure 3. 3. 4   Hodrick-Prescott Filter Estimates (Business Cycle Analysis) (2010 $, Millions)

Having identified the limitations and assumptions for each component in the GNNP, we now focus on the final estimate of the augmented GNNP Q^t 0. 5. Business cycles complicate the use of GNNP to analyze sustainability. Sustainability is concerned with the long-term and thus short-term business cycles may obscure the interpretation of the metric. The theoretical literature on GNNP assumes the economy is achieving its potential output. GNNP calculated with actual data reflects economic recessions that prevent GNNP from reaching its potential output. Temporary dips in GNNP due to the business cycle may not represent movement away from sustainability if potential GNNP is steadily increasing. The Puerto Rico Planning Board, in an April 19, 2012 press release, identified a deep recession beginning with the government shutdown in May 2006.[1] Thus, it is probably reasonable to expect some impact

---

[1]   Accessed at http://www. gdb-pur. com/documents/2012-04-19-JC-CP-Proyecciones-revFJC1-EngtrsFINALFINA L.pdf on August 20, 2015.

during the two periods 2004-2006 and 2007-2008. Augmented GNNP follows the declines in 2004-2006 and 2007-2008. This introduces some doubt as to whether the declines indicate movement away from sustainability or simply reflects the temporary economic downturn.

There is generally no accepted method of controlling for the business cycle in sustainability analysis, but Mota et al. (2010) were able to filter out the short-term cycles using a Hodrick-Prescott (HP) filter. This method was based on the assumption that a time series can be decomposed linearly in a trend and a cyclic component. Their results suggested indications for unsustainability in Portugal were related to a business cycle. Following Mota et al. (2010), we used a HP filter and obtained the trend of GNNP without business cycles. The resulting HP filter estimates of GNNP no Q^t and augmented GNNP are presented in Figure 3.3.4. In 2004-2006, both estimates that used the HP filter are rising, indicating the dip in 2004-2006 might be linked to the temporary economic downturn rather than moving away from sustainability. However, in 2007-2008, the HP filter estimates of augmented GNNP still show a decline, but when excluding the value of time, the HP filter estimates of GNNP no Q^t continued to increase. This implies the downward trend in 2007-2008 may be from the decreasing value of time.

3.3.7   Conclusion

We estimated GNNP, a metric of weak sustainability, from 1993 to 2009 for Puerto Rico. In addition to presenting our methodology, data sources, and results, we discussed the assumptions and concerns about our approach and interpretation. Besides contributing to limited sustainability studies for Caribbean regions, we included value of time (following relatively new literature recommendations) and addressed the issue of business cycles.

The results show that GNNP has an increasing trend over the 17 years studied with two periods of negative growth. Our analysis suggests that the negative growth in 2007-2008 was based on the decline in the value of time, suggesting movement away from sustainability. However, the negative growth in 2004-2006 was most likely caused by an economic downturn.

Before this metric can support decisions in Puerto Rico, we recommend continuing the research and data collection because of a number of limitations. We recognize that many important types of capital and ecosystem services are not included in the metric due to a lack of data. Ongoing research in Puerto Rico on these components may, at some point, lead to their inclusion. However, an important point is that calculating sustainability metrics like GNNP helps to identify the data and their appropriate form that is needed for including in the calculations. Future calculations then can be improved as empirical applications increase.

References

Barbier, E. B., 2007. Valuing Ecosystem Services as Productive Inputs. *Economic Policy*, 177-229.

Collins, S. M., Bosworth, B. P., Soto-Class, M. A., 2006. The Economy of Puerto Rico. Brookings Institution Press, Washington D. C.

Costanza, R., Hart, M., Posner, S., Talberth, J., 2009. Beyond GDP: The Need for New Measures of Progress. The Pardee Papers No. 4, Boston University.

Davis, G. A., Moore, D. J., 2000. Valuing Mineral Stocks and Depletion in Green National Income Accounts. *Environment and Development Economics*, 5, 109-127.

Ferreira, S., Vincent, J., 2005. Genuine Savings: Leading Indicator of Sustainable Development? *Economic Development and Cultural Change*, 53, 737-754.

Heberling, M. T., Templeton, J. J., Wu, S. S., 2012. Green Net Regional Product for the San Luis Basin, Colorado: An Economic Measure of Regional Sustainability. *Journal of Environmental Management*, 111, 287-297.

Martinuzzi, S., Grould, W. A., Lugo, A. E., Medina, E., 2009. Conversion and Recovery of Puerto Rican Mangroves: 200 Years of Change. *Forest Ecology and Management*, 257, 75-84.

Miranda, M. L., Hale, B., 2005. Paradise Recovered: Energy Production and Waste Management in Island Environments. *Energy Policy*, 33, 1691-1702.

Mota, R., Domingos, T., Martins, V., 2010. Analysis of Genuine Saving and Potential Green Net National Income: Portugal, 1990-2005. *Ecological Economics*, 69, 1934-1942.

Pezzey, J., Hanley, N., Turner, K., Tinch, D., 2006. Comparing Augmented Sustainability Measures for Scotland: Is There a Mismatch? *Ecological Economics*, 57, 60-74.

Appendixes

Appendix A Relationship Between Energy Exploitation and Embodied Energy Use

For clarity, the symbols defined in Section 1.1.2.3 are used here to explore the relationship between EED (energy exploited directly) and EEF (embodied energy in final use). Equation (1.1.1) in the body text describes the physical balance of embodied energy flows for Sector i in Region r. It should be noted that the final use provided by the sector is for both local region and foreign regions, that is, $\sum_{s=1}^{186} f_i^{rs} = f_i^{rr} + \sum_{s=1(s \neq r)}^{186} f_i^{rs}$. By substitution of the decomposition for final use into Equation (1.1.1) results,

$$e_i^r + \sum_{s=1}^{186} \sum_{j=1}^{26} (\varepsilon_j^s z_{ji}^{sr}) = \sum_{s=1}^{186} \sum_{j=1}^{26} (\varepsilon_i^r z_{ij}^{rs}) + \varepsilon_i^r f_i^{rr} + \sum_{s=1(s \neq r)}^{186} (\varepsilon_i^r f_i^{rs}) \tag{A1}$$

There are 26 sectors in Region r, and each sector has a balance equation like Equation (A1). By adding these 26 equations together, a physical balance of embodied energy flows for Region r can be obtained as

$$\sum_{i=1}^{26} e_i^r + \sum_{i=1}^{26} \sum_{s=1}^{186} \sum_{j=1}^{26} (\varepsilon_j^s z_{ji}^{sr}) = \sum_{i=1}^{26} \sum_{s=1}^{186} \sum_{j=1}^{26} (\varepsilon_i^r z_{ij}^{rs}) + \sum_{i=1}^{26} \varepsilon_i^r f_i^{rr} + \sum_{i=1}^{26} \sum_{s=1(s \neq r)}^{186} (\varepsilon_i^r f_i^{rs}) \tag{A2}$$

where the first term $\sum_{i=1}^{26} e_i^r$ indeed represents the total energy exploited directly in Region r (EED^r); the second term $\sum_{i=1}^{26} \sum_{s=1}^{186} \sum_{j=1}^{26} (\varepsilon_j^s z_{ji}^{sr})$ can be regarded as the sum of $\sum_{i=1}^{26} \varepsilon_i^r z_{ii}^{rr}$, $\sum_{i=1}^{26} \sum_{j=1(j \neq i)}^{26} (\varepsilon_j^r z_{ji}^{rr})$ and $\sum_{i=1}^{26} \sum_{s=1(s \neq r)}^{186} \sum_{j=1}^{26} (\varepsilon_j^s z_{ji}^{sr})$, respectively standing for the intermediate inputs from the sector itself, from the other 25 sectors in Region r, and from foreign regions; the third term can also be decomposed as $\sum_{i=1}^{26} \varepsilon_i^r z_{ii}^{rr}$, $\sum_{i=1}^{26} \sum_{j=1(j \neq i)}^{26} (\varepsilon_i^r z_{ij}^{rr})$ and $\sum_{i=1}^{26} \sum_{s=1(s \neq r)}^{186} \sum_{j=1}^{26} (\varepsilon_i^r z_{ij}^{rs})$, representing the intermediate outputs to the sector itself, to the other 25 sectors in Region r, and to foreign regions, distinctively. Moreover, an intermediate input to a sector is also recorded as an intermediate output from another sector.

So for Region r with all 26 sectors that are taken account of, there is $\sum\limits_{i=1}^{26}\sum\limits_{j=1(j\neq i)}^{26}(\varepsilon_j^r z_{ji}^{rr})=$

$\sum\limits_{i=1}^{26}\sum\limits_{j=1(j\neq i)}^{26}(\varepsilon_i^r z_{ij}^{rr})$. *Equation* $(A2)$ can therefore be expressed as

$$EED^r + \sum_{i=1}^{26}\sum_{s=1(s\neq r)}^{186}\sum_{j=1}^{26}(\varepsilon_j^s z_{ji}^{sr}) = \sum_{i=1}^{26}\sum_{s=1(s\neq r)}^{186}\sum_{j=1}^{26}(\varepsilon_i^r z_{ij}^{rs}) + \sum_{i=1}^{26}(\varepsilon_i^r f_i^{rr}) + \sum_{i=1}^{26}\sum_{s=1(s\neq r)}^{186}(\varepsilon_i^r f_i^{rs})$$

$$(A3)$$

Because the final demand of a region can be met by the goods and services produced in local area and foreign areas, the energy embodied in Region r's final use (EEF^r) defined by Equation (1.1.4) in the text can be decomposed as

$$EEF^r = \sum_{s=1}^{186}\sum_{j=1}^{26}(\varepsilon_j^s f_j^{sr}) = \sum_{i=1}^{26}(\varepsilon_i^r f_i^{rr}) + \sum_{s=1(s\neq r)}^{186}\sum_{j=1}^{26}(\varepsilon_j^s f_j^{sr}) \qquad (A4)$$

As a result, $\sum\limits_{i=1}^{26}(\varepsilon_i^r f_i^{rr})=EEF^r - \sum\limits_{s=1(s\neq r)}^{186}\sum\limits_{j=1}^{26}(\varepsilon_j^s f_j^{sr})$, and this allows Equation $(A3)$ to be expressed as

$$EED^r + \Big(\sum_{i=1}^{26}\sum_{s=1(s\neq r)}^{186}\sum_{j=1}^{26}(\varepsilon_j^s z_{ji}^{sr}) + \sum_{s=1(s\neq r)}^{186}\sum_{j=1}^{26}(\varepsilon_j^s f_j^{sr})\Big) = EEF^r$$

$$+ \Big(\sum_{i=1}^{26}\sum_{s=1(s\neq r)}^{186}\sum_{j=1}^{26}(\varepsilon_i^r z_{ij}^{rs}) + \sum_{i=1}^{26}\sum_{s=1(s\neq r)}^{186}(\varepsilon_i^r f_i^{rs})\Big) \qquad (A5)$$

where the term in the left parenthesis is EEI^r (energy embodied in Region r's imports) according to Equation (1.1.5) in the text, and that in the right parenthesis is EEX^r (energy embodied in Region r's exports) in line with Equation (1.1.6) in the text. Consequently, Equation (A5) can be finally presented as

$$EED^r + EEB^r = EEF^r \qquad (A6)$$

That is to say, for each region, the energy use for meeting the final demand is equal to the territorial energy exploitation plus energy use embodied in its net imports.

Appendix B Embodied Energy Inventories for the 186 Regions of 2010 (Unit: TJ)

| | Region | Abbr. | Embodied energy in final use | | Embodied energy in trades | | |
			EEF	Per-capita EEF	EEI	EEX	EEB
1	Afghanistan	AFG	1. 93E+05	6. 14E−03	2. 02E+05	9. 68E+03	1. 93E+05
2	Albania	ALB	1. 83E+05	5. 72E−02	1. 50E+05	3. 48E+04	1. 15E+05
3	Algeria	DZA	5. 40E+05	1. 52E−02	7. 21E+05	6. 48E+06	−5. 76E+06
4	Andorra	AND	3. 04E+04	3. 58E−01	3. 77E+04	7. 27E+03	3. 04E+04
5	Angola	AGO	5. 90E+05	3. 09E−02	2. 76E+05	3. 83E+06	−3. 55E+06
6	Antigua	ATG	2. 10E+04	2. 37E−01	2. 84E+04	7. 42E+03	2. 10E+04
7	Argentina	ARG	2. 35E+06	5. 83E−02	1. 26E+06	2. 23E+06	−9. 73E+05
8	Armenia	ARM	8. 78E+04	2. 84E−02	8. 72E+04	3. 61E+04	5. 11E+04
9	Aruba	ABW	2. 71E+04	2. 52E−01	4. 72E+04	2. 01E+04	2. 71E+04
10	Australia	AUS	6. 83E+06	3. 07E−01	2. 29E+06	8. 37E+06	−6. 08E+06
11	Austria	AUT	2. 20E+06	2. 62E−01	4. 08E+06	2. 38E+06	1. 69E+06
12	Azerbaijan	AZE	1. 76E+05	1. 92E−02	1. 66E+05	2. 73E+06	−2. 57E+06
13	Bahamas	BHS	7. 49E+04	2. 18E−01	1. 01E+05	2. 59E+04	7. 49E+04
14	Bahrain	BHR	2. 82E+05	2. 23E−01	2. 52E+05	7. 12E+05	−4. 60E+05
15	Bangladesh	BGD	1. 14E+06	7. 64E−03	3. 77E+05	3. 19E+05	5. 76E+04
16	Barbados	BRB	3. 90E+04	1. 43E−01	5. 03E+04	1. 13E+04	3. 90E+04
17	Belarus	BLR	2. 27E+02	3. 36E−03	2. 74E+04	2. 00E+05	−1. 73E+05
18	Belgium	BEL	2. 11E+06	1. 97E−01	1. 02E+07	8. 75E+06	1. 45E+06
19	Belize	BLZ	1. 98E+04	6. 34E−02	2. 92E+04	9. 44E+03	1. 98E+04
20	Benin	BEN	8. 03E+04	9. 08E−03	3. 05E+04	3. 62E+04	−5. 70E+03
21	Bermuda	BMU	1. 02E+05	1. 57E+00	1. 12E+05	1. 03E+04	1. 02E+05
22	Bhutan	BTN	2. 43E+04	3. 35E−02	3. 58E+04	1. 15E+04	2. 43E+04
23	Bolivia	BOL	1. 74E+05	1. 75E−02	1. 17E+05	6. 43E+05	−5. 27E+05

Continued

	Region	Abbr.	Embodied energy in final use		Embodied energy in trades		
			EEF	Per-capita EEF	EEI	EEX	EEB
24	Bosnia and Herzegovina	BIH	1.85E+05	4.91E−02	1.03E+05	1.01E+05	1.67E+03
25	Botswana	BWA	2.34E+05	1.17E−01	2.08E+05	1.98E+04	1.88E+05
26	Brazil	BRA	1.39E+07	7.11E−02	6.79E+06	3.26E+06	3.54E+06
27	British Virgin Islands	VGB	1.50E+04	6.47E−01	2.61E+04	1.10E+04	1.50E+04
28	Brunei	BRN	5.54E+04	1.39E−01	8.11E+04	8.03E+05	−7.22E+05
29	Bulgaria	BGR	4.59E+05	6.13E−02	6.50E+05	6.31E+05	1.83E+04
30	Burkina Faso	BFA	4.68E+04	2.84E−03	5.55E+04	8.76E+03	4.68E+04
31	Burundi	BDI	3.32E+04	3.96E−03	4.05E+04	7.36E+03	3.32E+04
32	Cambodia	KHM	1.70E+05	1.20E−02	1.33E+05	1.15E+05	1.82E+04
33	Cameroon	CMR	2.00E+05	1.02E−02	1.03E+05	2.55E+05	−1.52E+05
34	Canada	CAN	1.30E+07	3.82E−01	1.10E+07	1.47E+07	−3.64E+06
35	Cape Verde	CPV	2.16E+04	4.35E−02	2.63E+04	4.75E+03	2.16E+04
36	Cayman Islands	CYM	2.91E+04	5.18E−01	3.67E+04	7.61E+03	2.91E+04
37	Central African Republic	CAF	2.46E+04	5.59E−03	2.96E+04	5.06E+03	2.46E+04
38	Chad	TCD	2.32E+05	2.07E−02	4.75E+04	8.36E+04	−3.61E+04
39	Chile	CHL	1.31E+06	7.66E−02	1.73E+06	8.02E+05	9.25E+05
40	Chinese Mainland	CHN	8.46E+07	6.42E−02	2.56E+07	3.57E+07	−1.01E+07
41	Colombia	COL	3.07E+06	6.64E−02	8.14E+05	2.16E+06	−1.34E+06
42	Congo	COG	1.17E+05	2.89E−02	1.10E+05	7.21E+05	−6.10E+05
43	Costa Rica	CRI	2.49E+05	5.35E−02	2.68E+05	1.21E+05	1.47E+05
44	Croatia	HRV	4.37E+05	9.93E−02	5.07E+05	2.46E+05	2.61E+05
45	Cuba	CUB	3.75E+05	3.33E−02	2.20E+05	6.61E+04	1.54E+05
46	Cyprus	CYP	1.88E+05	2.32E−01	2.18E+05	3.41E+04	1.84E+05
47	Czech Republic	CZE	3.06E+06	2.91E−01	5.44E+06	3.71E+06	1.73E+06
48	Cote Divoire	CIV	1.27E+05	6.04E−03	1.70E+05	4.24E+04	1.27E+05

Continued

	Region	Abbr.	Embodied energy in final use		Embodied energy in trades		
			EEF	Per-capita *EEF*	*EEI*	*EEX*	*EEB*
49	DR Congo	COD	1.06E+06	1.61E−02	2.32E+05	1.80E+05	5.26E+04
50	Denmark	DNK	1.42E+06	2.56E−01	2.25E+06	1.80E+06	4.48E+05
51	Djibouti	DJI	2.51E+04	2.82E−02	3.46E+04	9.49E+03	2.51E+04
52	Dominican Republic	DOM	3.05E+05	3.07E−02	3.39E+05	6.73E+04	2.72E+05
53	Ecuador	ECU	9.92E+05	6.86E−02	2.82E+05	4.35E+05	−1.53E+05
54	Egypt	EGY	3.19E+06	3.94E−02	1.27E+06	1.78E+06	−5.09E+05
55	El Salvador	SLV	2.11E+05	3.40E−02	1.60E+05	4.40E+04	1.16E+05
56	Eritrea	ERI	4.14E+04	7.88E−03	2.48E+04	7.68E+03	1.71E+04
57	Estonia	EST	3.10E+05	2.31E−01	4.08E+05	3.05E+05	1.04E+05
58	Ethiopia	ETH	4.22E+05	5.09E−03	8.02E+04	9.74E+05	−8.94E+05
59	Fiji	FJI	3.07E+04	3.57E−02	4.04E+04	9.64E+03	3.07E+04
60	Finland	FIN	2.39E+06	4.46E−01	5.70E+06	4.03E+06	1.67E+06
61	France	FRA	1.53E+07	2.37E−01	2.61E+07	1.64E+07	9.68E+06
62	French Polynesia	PYF	4.55E+04	1.68E−01	5.16E+04	6.11E+03	4.55E+04
63	Gabon	GAB	7.66E+04	5.09E−02	7.59E+04	5.99E+05	−5.23E+05
64	Gambia	GMB	5.35E+03	3.09E−03	6.25E+03	9.03E+02	5.35E+03
65	Gaza Strip	PSE	1.05E+05	2.68E−02	1.11E+05	6.34E+03	1.05E+05
66	Georgia	GEO	2.74E+05	6.29E−02	2.66E+05	4.73E+04	2.19E+05
67	Germany	DEU	1.68E+07	2.04E−01	3.52E+07	2.40E+07	1.12E+07
68	Ghana	GHA	2.73E+05	1.12E−02	2.28E+05	2.37E+05	−8.89E+03
69	Greece	GRC	3.94E+06	3.47E−01	4.77E+06	1.23E+06	3.54E+06
70	Greenland	GRL	1.36E+04	2.38E−01	1.76E+04	3.98E+03	1.36E+04
71	Guatemala	GTM	2.99E+05	2.08E−02	2.49E+05	2.66E+05	−1.69E+04
72	Guinea	GIN	4.14E+04	4.14E−03	2.74E+04	5.55E+05	−5.28E+05
73	Guyana	GUY	5.40E+05	7.16E−01	5.43E+05	2.98E+03	5.40E+05

Continued

	Region	Abbr.	Embodied energy in final use		Embodied energy in trades		
			EEF	Per-capita EEF	EEI	EEX	EEB
74	Haiti	HTI	1.23E+05	1.23E−02	7.23E+04	2.23E+04	5.00E+04
75	Honduras	HND	1.48E+05	1.95E−02	1.51E+05	9.55E+04	5.54E+04
76	Hong Kong, China	HKG	5.01E+06	7.10E−01	6.84E+06	1.83E+06	5.00E+06
77	Hungary	HUN	1.62E+06	1.63E−01	3.09E+06	1.93E+06	1.16E+06
78	Iceland	ISL	2.08E+05	6.50E−01	1.14E+05	9.11E+04	2.27E+04
79	India	IND	2.00E+07	1.63E−02	6.03E+06	8.32E+06	−2.29E+06
80	Indonesia	IDN	1.12E+07	4.67E−02	3.24E+06	8.00E+06	−4.76E+06
81	Iran	IRN	9.20E+06	1.24E−01	1.34E+06	6.79E+06	−5.45E+06
82	Iraq	IRQ	3.10E+06	9.79E−02	1.12E+06	3.30E+06	−2.18E+06
83	Ireland	IRL	7.50E+05	1.68E−01	1.63E+06	9.65E+05	6.69E+05
84	Israel	ISR	1.16E+06	1.56E−01	1.85E+06	8.50E+05	9.95E+05
85	Italy	ITA	1.22E+07	2.02E−01	1.89E+07	7.95E+06	1.10E+07
86	Jamaica	JAM	9.10E+04	3.32E−02	9.99E+04	2.83E+04	7.16E+04
87	Japan	JPN	3.56E+07	2.82E−01	4.20E+07	1.05E+07	3.15E+07
88	Jordan	JOR	2.76E+05	4.47E−02	3.55E+05	9.04E+04	2.65E+05
89	Kazakhstan	KAZ	2.48E+06	1.55E−01	1.26E+06	5.34E+06	−4.09E+06
90	Kenya	KEN	7.46E+05	1.84E−02	2.58E+05	1.72E+05	8.59E+04
91	Kuwait	KWT	1.70E+06	6.20E−01	5.39E+05	4.48E+06	−3.94E+06
92	Kyrgyzstan	KGZ	2.73E+05	5.11E−02	3.31E+05	1.12E+05	2.19E+05
93	Laos	LAO	4.18E+04	6.75E−03	5.33E+04	1.15E+04	4.18E+04
94	Latvia	LVA	3.78E+05	1.68E−01	4.57E+05	1.68E+05	2.89E+05
95	Lebanon	LBN	3.16E+05	7.46E−02	3.85E+05	7.86E+04	3.07E+05
96	Lesotho	LSO	6.13E+04	2.82E−02	7.30E+04	1.17E+04	6.13E+04
97	Liberia	LBR	1.83E+04	4.59E−03	3.93E+04	2.10E+04	1.83E+04
98	Libya	LBY	1.58E+05	2.49E−02	1.87E+05	3.96E+06	−3.77E+06

Continued

	Region	Abbr.	Embodied energy in final use		Embodied energy in trades		
			EEF	Per-capita EEF	EEI	EEX	EEB
99	Liechtenstein	LIE	2.97E+04	8.25E−01	3.96E+04	9.87E+03	2.97E+04
100	Lithuania	LTU	1.09E+06	3.29E−01	2.43E+06	1.39E+06	1.04E+06
101	Luxembourg	LUX	4.50E+05	8.86E−01	9.79E+05	5.34E+05	4.45E+05
102	Macao, China	MAC	9.56E+04	1.73E−01	1.34E+05	3.83E+04	9.56E+04
103	Madagascar	MDG	4.70E+04	2.27E−03	5.53E+04	8.33E+03	4.70E+04
104	Malawi	MWI	7.98E+04	5.35E−03	9.53E+04	1.55E+04	7.98E+04
105	Malaysia	MYS	3.46E+06	1.22E−01	3.66E+06	3.79E+06	−1.35E+05
106	Maldives	MDV	3.57E+04	1.13E−01	4.56E+04	9.93E+03	3.57E+04
107	Mali	MLI	3.13E+04	2.04E−03	3.43E+04	3.04E+03	3.13E+04
108	Malta	MLT	6.24E+04	1.50E−01	8.77E+04	2.54E+04	6.23E+04
109	Mauritania	MRT	3.80E+04	1.10E−02	5.05E+04	1.24E+04	3.80E+04
110	Mauritius	MUS	1.03E+05	7.95E−02	1.37E+05	3.36E+04	1.03E+05
111	Mexico	MEX	8.68E+06	7.65E−02	5.05E+06	5.91E+06	−8.62E+05
112	Moldova	MDA	4.66E+02	3.40E−03	1.01E+03	5.98E+03	−4.97E+03
113	Monaco	MCO	2.98E+04	8.42E−01	4.08E+04	1.10E+04	2.98E+04
114	Mongolia	MNG	8.30E+04	3.01E−02	8.37E+04	6.16E+05	−5.32E+05
115	Montenegro	MNE	1.20E+05	1.91E−01	1.03E+05	2.03E+04	8.32E+04
116	Morocco	MAR	5.22E+05	1.63E−02	6.55E+05	1.70E+05	4.85E+05
117	Mozambique	MOZ	3.40E+05	1.45E−02	9.61E+04	2.62E+05	−1.65E+05
118	Myanmar	MMR	1.71E+05	3.57E−03	1.35E+03	7.73E+05	−7.72E+05
119	Namibia	NAM	1.39E+05	6.08E−02	1.73E+05	4.77E+04	1.26E+05
120	Nepal	NPL	3.07E+05	1.03E−02	1.05E+05	1.70E+05	−6.44E+04
121	Netherlands	NLD	3.60E+06	2.17E−01	1.37E+07	1.31E+07	6.79E+05
122	Netherlands Antilles	ANT	7.15E+04	3.56E−01	9.06E+04	1.91E+04	7.15E+04
123	New Caledonia	NCL	6.96E+04	2.77E−01	8.62E+04	1.66E+04	6.96E+04

Continued

	Region	Abbr.	Embodied energy in final use		Embodied energy in trades		
			EEF	Per-capita *EEF*	*EEI*	*EEX*	*EEB*
124	New Zealand	NZL	1. 02E+06	2. 34E−01	7. 52E+05	4. 35E+05	3. 16E+05
125	Nicaragua	NIC	1. 05E+05	1. 82E−02	7. 86E+04	3. 75E+04	4. 11E+04
126	Niger	NER	5. 43E+04	3. 50E−03	6. 08E+04	6. 49E+03	5. 43E+04
127	Nigeria	NGA	3. 91E+06	2. 47E−02	7. 64E+05	7. 52E+06	−6. 76E+06
128	North Korea	PRK	2. 12E+05	8. 68E−03	6. 84E+04	7. 25E+05	−6. 56E+05
129	Norway	NOR	3. 10E+06	6. 36E−01	1. 61E+06	7. 02E+06	−5. 41E+06
130	Oman	OMN	2. 59E+05	9. 30E−02	4. 33E+05	3. 19E+06	−2. 76E+06
131	Pakistan	PAK	2. 43E+06	1. 40E−02	5. 67E+05	8. 32E+05	−2. 65E+05
132	Panama	PAN	2. 32E+05	6. 59E−02	2. 80E+05	8. 38E+04	1. 96E+05
133	Papua New Guinea	PNG	1. 23E+05	1. 80E−02	1. 68E+05	4. 49E+04	1. 23E+05
134	Paraguay	PRY	3. 30E+05	5. 11E−02	1. 78E+05	1. 45E+05	3. 26E+04
135	Peru	PER	8. 52E+05	2. 93E−02	4. 66E+05	4. 25E+05	4. 08E+04
136	Philippines	PHL	1. 79E+06	1. 92E−02	1. 68E+06	8. 72E+05	8. 10E+05
137	Poland	POL	4. 50E+06	1. 18E−01	3. 68E+06	2. 00E+06	1. 68E+06
138	Portugal	PRT	2. 15E+06	2. 01E−01	2. 57E+06	6. 58E+05	1. 91E+06
139	Qatar	QAT	1. 96E+06	1. 11E+00	2. 89E+05	5. 80E+06	−5. 51E+06
140	Romania	ROU	2. 98E+06	1. 39E−01	3. 64E+06	1. 81E+06	1. 83E+06
141	Russia	RUS	5. 00E+06	3. 50E−02	4. 55E+06	5. 37E+07	−4. 91E+07
142	Rwanda	RWA	3. 38E+04	3. 18E−03	3. 82E+04	4. 37E+03	3. 38E+04
143	Samoa	WSM	1. 44E+04	7. 86E−02	2. 33E+04	8. 89E+03	1. 44E+04
144	San Marino	SMR	1. 48E+04	4. 70E−01	2. 11E+04	6. 28E+03	1. 48E+04
145	Sao Tome and Principe	STP	1. 52E+04	9. 19E−02	1. 99E+04	4. 69E+03	1. 52E+04
146	Saudi Arabia	SAU	3. 15E+06	1. 15E−01	2. 84E+06	2. 22E+07	−1. 94E+07
147	Senegal	SEN	1. 15E+05	9. 27E−03	9. 32E+04	4. 51E+04	4. 81E+04
148	Serbia	SRB	8. 41E+05	1. 14E−01	4. 38E+05	3. 84E+04	3. 99E+05

Continued

	Region	Abbr.	Embodied energy in final use		Embodied energy in trades		
			EEF	Per-capita EEF	EEI	EEX	EEB
149	Seychelles	SYC	2. 74E+04	3. 17E−01	3. 65E+04	9. 02E+03	2. 74E+04
150	Sierra Leone	SLE	2. 37E+04	4. 04E−03	2. 97E+04	5. 97E+03	2. 37E+04
151	Singapore	SGP	2. 44E+06	4. 80E−01	5. 26E+06	2. 85E+06	2. 41E+06
152	Slovakia	SVK	3. 27E+06	5. 99E−01	6. 13E+06	3. 12E+06	3. 01E+06
153	Slovenia	SVN	4. 33E+05	2. 13E−01	6. 62E+05	3. 85E+05	2. 77E+05
154	Somalia	SOM	1. 49E+04	1. 60E−03	1. 83E+04	3. 38E+03	1. 49E+04
155	South Africa	ZAF	3. 74E+06	7. 45E−02	1. 69E+06	4. 79E+06	−3. 10E+06
156	South Korea	KOR	1. 51E+07	3. 13E−01	2. 70E+07	1. 38E+07	1. 32E+07
157	Spain	ESP	9. 97E+06	2. 16E−01	1. 71E+07	8. 59E+06	8. 54E+06
158	Sri Lanka	LKA	2. 39E+05	1. 14E−02	2. 65E+05	2. 58E+05	6. 55E+03
159	Suriname	SUR	3. 47E+04	6. 62E−02	4. 55E+04	1. 08E+04	3. 47E+04
160	Swaziland	SWZ	8. 32E+04	7. 01E−02	1. 18E+05	3. 49E+04	8. 32E+04
161	Sweden	SWE	2. 48E+06	2. 65E−01	3. 72E+06	2. 63E+06	1. 09E+06
162	Switzerland	CHE	2. 04E+06	2. 66E−01	2. 77E+06	1. 26E+06	1. 51E+06
163	Syria	SYR	3. 85E+05	1. 89E−02	3. 90E+05	1. 16E+06	−7. 73E+05
164	Taiwan, China	TWN	1. 40E+06	6. 04E−02	2. 74E+06	1. 89E+06	8. 54E+05
165	Tajikistan	TJK	1. 18E+05	1. 72E−02	1. 11E+05	5. 63E+04	5. 51E+04
166	Tanzania	TZA	1. 13E+05	2. 60E−03	1. 33E+05	1. 98E+04	1. 13E+05
167	Thailand	THA	4. 66E+06	6. 73E−02	5. 18E+06	3. 48E+06	1. 70E+06
168	TFYR Macedonia	MKD	2. 71E+05	1. 33E−01	3. 27E+05	1. 24E+05	2. 03E+05
169	Togo	TGO	8. 24E+04	1. 37E−02	4. 46E+04	5. 56E+04	−1. 10E+04
170	Trinidad and Tobago	TTO	1. 03E+05	7. 67E−02	1. 78E+05	1. 92E+06	−1. 75E+06
171	Tunisia	TUN	4. 71E+05	4. 49E−02	4. 66E+05	3. 35E+05	1. 31E+05
172	Turkey	TUR	7. 49E+06	1. 03E−01	8. 50E+06	2. 36E+06	6. 14E+06
173	Turkmenistan	TKM	3. 38E+05	6. 71E−02	2. 96E+05	1. 94E+06	−1. 64E+06

Continued

	Region	Abbr.	Embodied energy in final use		Embodied energy in trades		
			EEF	Per-capita *EEF*	*EEI*	*EEX*	*EEB*
174	Uganda	UGA	1. 09E+05	3. 25E−03	1. 16E+05	7. 70E+03	1. 09E+05
175	Ukraine	UKR	2. 29E+06	5. 04E−02	2. 82E+06	3. 82E+06	−1. 00E+06
176	UAE	ARE	2. 49E+06	3. 32E−01	2. 85E+06	7. 74E+06	−4. 89E+06
177	United Kingdom	GBR	1. 27E+07	2. 04E−01	1. 49E+07	8. 48E+06	6. 45E+06
178	United States	USA	1. 01E+08	3. 26E−01	6. 44E+07	3. 54E+07	2. 90E+07
179	Uruguay	URY	2. 39E+05	7. 10E−02	2. 27E+05	7. 40E+04	1. 53E+05
180	Uzbekistan	UZB	1. 36E+06	4. 95E−02	2. 49E+05	1. 20E+06	−9. 47E+05
181	Vanuatu	VUT	1. 22E+04	5. 11E−02	1. 87E+04	6. 41E+03	1. 22E+04
182	Venezuela	VEN	5. 03E+06	1. 74E−01	9. 10E+05	4. 19E+06	−3. 28E+06
183	Viet Nam	VNM	1. 69E+06	1. 93E−02	1. 05E+06	2. 13E+06	−1. 09E+06
184	Yemen	YEM	2. 56E+05	1. 06E−02	2. 35E+05	7. 91E+05	−5. 55E+05
185	Zambia	ZMB	2. 47E+05	1. 89E−02	1. 42E+05	2. 08E+05	−6. 63E+04
186	Zimbabwe	ZWE	1. 73E+05	1. 38E−02	1. 57E+05	3. 33E+05	−1. 76E+05

Appendix C   Sectors Included in the World Economic Input-output Table

Sector code	Sector content	Sector grouping
1	Agriculture	Agriculture
2	Fishing	Agriculture
3	Mining and quarrying	Mining
4	Food and beverages	Light manufacturing
5	Textiles and wearing apparel	Light manufacturing
6	Wood and paper	Light manufacturing
7	Petroleum, chemical and non-metallic mineral products	Heavy manufacturing
8	Metal products	Heavy manufacturing
9	Electrical and machinery	Heavy manufacturing
10	Transport equipment	Heavy manufacturing
11	Other manufacturing	Light manufacturing
12	Recycling	Light manufacturing
13	Electricity, gas and water	Electricity
14	Construction	Service
15	Maintenance and repair	Service
16	Wholesale trade	Service
17	Retail trade	Service
18	Hotels and restaurants	Service
19	Transport	Transport
20	Post and telecommunications	Service
21	Financial intermediation and business activities	Service
22	Public administration	Service
23	Education, health and other services	Service
24	Private households	Service
25	Others	Others
26	Re-export and re-import	Others

Appendix D 188 Regions Included in World Economic Input-output Table

	Region	Abbr.	Region grouping	Income group
1	Afghanistan	AFG	Europe & Eurasia	Low income
2	Albania	ALB	Europe & Eurasia	Upper middle income
3	Algeria	DZA	Africa	Upper middle income
4	Andorra	AND	Europe & Eurasia	High income
5	Angola	AGO	Africa	Lower middle income
6	Antigua	ATG	South & Central America	High income
7	Argentina	ARG	South & Central America	Upper middle income
8	Armenia	ARM	Europe & Eurasia	Lower middle income
9	Aruba	ABW	South & Central America	High income
10	Australia	AUS	Asia Pacific	High income
11	Austria	AUT	Europe & Eurasia	High income
12	Azerbaijan	AZE	Europe & Eurasia	Upper middle income
13	Bahamas	BHS	South & Central America	High income
14	Bahrain	BHR	Middle East	High income
15	Bangladesh	BGD	Asia Pacific	Lower middle income
16	Barbados	BRB	South & Central America	High income
17	Belarus	BLR	Europe & Eurasia	Upper middle income
18	Belgium	BEL	Europe & Eurasia	High income
19	Belize	BLZ	South & Central America	Upper middle income
20	Benin	BEN	Africa	Low income
21	Bermuda	BMU	Europe & Eurasia	High income
22	Bhutan	BTN	Europe & Eurasia	Lower middle income
23	Bolivia	BOL	South & Central America	Lower middle income
24	Bosnia and Herzegovina	BIH	Europe & Eurasia	Upper middle income
25	Botswana	BWA	Africa	Upper middle income
26	Brazil	BRA	South & Central America	Upper middle income
27	British Virgin Islands	VGB	Europe & Eurasia	High income

Continued

	Region	Abbr.	Region grouping	Income group
28	Brunei	BRN	Asia Pacific	High income
29	Bulgaria	BGR	Europe & Eurasia	Upper middle income
30	Burkina Faso	BFA	Africa	Low income
31	Burundi	BDI	Africa	Low income
32	Cambodia	KHM	Asia Pacific	Lower middle income
33	Cameroon	CMR	Africa	Lower middle income
34	Canada	CAN	North America	High income
35	Cape Verde	CPV	Africa	Lower middle income
36	Cayman Islands	CYM	South & Central America	High income
37	Central African Republic	CAF	Africa	Low income
38	Chad	TCD	Africa	Low income
39	Chile	CHL	South & Central America	High income
40	Chinese Mainland	CHN	Asia Pacific	Upper middle income
41	Colombia	COL	South & Central America	Upper middle income
42	Congo	COG	Africa	Lower middle income
43	Costa Rica	CRI	South & Central America	Upper middle income
44	Croatia	HRV	Europe & Eurasia	Upper middle income
45	Cuba	CUB	South & Central America	Upper middle income
46	Cyprus	CYP	Middle East	High income
47	Czech Republic	CZE	Europe & Eurasia	High income
48	Cote Divoire	CIV	Africa	Lower middle income
49	DR Congo	COD	Africa	Low income
50	Denmark	DNK	Europe & Eurasia	High income
51	Djibouti	DJI	Africa	Lower middle income
52	Dominican Republic	DOM	South & Central America	Upper middle income
53	Ecuador	ECU	South & Central America	Upper middle income
54	Egypt	EGY	Africa	Lower middle income
55	El Salvador	SLV	South & Central America	Lower middle income
56	Eritrea	ERI	Africa	Low income
57	Estonia	EST	Europe & Eurasia	High income

Continued

	Region	Abbr.	Region grouping	Income group
58	Ethiopia	ETH	Africa	Low income
59	Fiji	FJI	Asia Pacific	Upper middle income
60	Finland	FIN	Europe & Eurasia	High income
61	France	FRA	Europe & Eurasia	High income
62	French Polynesia	PYF	Europe & Eurasia	High income
63	Gabon	GAB	Africa	Upper middle income
64	Gambia	GMB	Africa	Low income
65	Gaza Strip	PSE	Middle East	Lower middle income
66	Georgia	GEO	Europe & Eurasia	Lower middle income
67	Germany	DEU	Europe & Eurasia	High income
68	Ghana	GHA	Africa	Lower middle income
69	Greece	GRC	Europe & Eurasia	High income
70	Greenland	GRL	North America	High income
71	Guatemala	GTM	South & Central America	Lower middle income
72	Guinea	GIN	Africa	Low income
73	Guyana	GUY	South & Central America	Upper middle income
74	Haiti	HTI	South & Central America	Low income
75	Honduras	HND	South & Central America	Lower middle income
76	Hong Kong, China	HKG	Asia Pacific	High income
77	Hungary	HUN	Europe & Eurasia	High income
78	Iceland	ISL	Europe & Eurasia	High income
79	India	IND	Europe & Eurasia	Lower middle income
80	Indonesia	IDN	Asia Pacific	Lower middle income
81	Iran	IRN	Middle East	Upper middle income
82	Iraq	IRQ	Middle East	Upper middle income
83	Ireland	IRL	Europe & Eurasia	High income
84	Israel	ISR	Middle East	High income
85	Italy	ITA	Europe & Eurasia	High income
86	Jamaica	JAM	South & Central America	Upper middle income
87	Japan	JPN	Asia Pacific	High income

Continued

	Region	Abbr.	Region grouping	Income group
88	Jordan	JOR	Middle East	Lower middle income
89	Kazakhstan	KAZ	Europe & Eurasia	Upper middle income
90	Kenya	KEN	Africa	Lower middle income
91	Kuwait	KWT	Middle East	High income
92	Kyrgyzstan	KGZ	Europe & Eurasia	Lower middle income
93	Laos	LAO	Asia Pacific	Lower middle income
94	Latvia	LVA	Europe & Eurasia	High income
95	Lebanon	LBN	Middle East	Upper middle income
96	Lesotho	LSO	Africa	Lower middle income
97	Liberia	LBR	Africa	Low income
98	Libya	LBY	Africa	Upper middle income
99	Liechtenstein	LIE	Europe & Eurasia	High income
100	Lithuania	LTU	Europe & Eurasia	High income
101	Luxembourg	LUX	Europe & Eurasia	High income
102	Macao, China	MAC	Asia Pacific	High income
103	Madagascar	MDG	Africa	Low income
104	Malawi	MWI	Africa	Low income
105	Malaysia	MYS	Asia Pacific	Upper middle income
106	Maldives	MDV	Europe & Eurasia	Upper middle income
107	Mali	MLI	Africa	Low income
108	Malta	MLT	Europe & Eurasia	High income
109	Mauritania	MRT	Africa	Lower middle income
110	Mauritius	MUS	Africa	Upper middle income
111	Mexico	MEX	North America	Upper middle income
112	Moldova	MDA	Europe & Eurasia	Lower middle income
113	Monaco	MCO	Europe & Eurasia	High income
114	Mongolia	MNG	Europe & Eurasia	Lower middle income
115	Montenegro	MNE	Europe & Eurasia	Upper middle income
116	Morocco	MAR	Africa	Lower middle income

Continued

	Region	Abbr.	Region grouping	Income group
117	Mozambique	MOZ	Africa	Low income
118	Myanmar	MMR	Asia Pacific	Lower middle income
119	Namibia	NAM	Africa	Upper middle income
120	Nepal	NPL	Europe & Eurasia	Low income
121	Netherlands	NLD	Europe & Eurasia	High income
122	Netherlands Antilles	ANT	Europe & Eurasia	High income
123	New Caledonia	NCL	Asia Pacific	High income
124	New Zealand	NZL	Asia Pacific	High income
125	Nicaragua	NIC	South & Central America	Lower middle income
126	Niger	NER	Africa	Low income
127	Nigeria	NGA	Africa	Lower middle income
128	North Korea	PRK	Asia Pacific	Low income
129	Norway	NOR	Europe & Eurasia	High income
130	Oman	OMN	Middle East	High income
131	Pakistan	PAK	Middle East	Lower middle income
132	Panama	PAN	South & Central America	Upper middle income
133	Papua New Guinea	PNG	Asia Pacific	Lower middle income
134	Paraguay	PRY	South & Central America	Upper middle income
135	Peru	PER	South & Central America	Upper middle income
136	Philippines	PHL	Asia Pacific	Lower middle income
137	Poland	POL	Europe & Eurasia	High income
138	Portugal	PRT	Europe & Eurasia	High income
139	Qatar	QAT	Middle East	High income
140	Romania	ROU	Europe & Eurasia	Upper middle income
141	Russia	RUS	Europe & Eurasia	Upper middle income
142	Rwanda	RWA	Africa	Low income
143	Samoa	WSM	Asia Pacific	Upper middle income
144	San Marino	SMR	Europe & Eurasia	High income
145	Sao Tome and Principe	STP	Africa	Lower middle income

Continued

	Region	Abbr.	Region grouping	Income group
146	Saudi Arabia	SAU	Middle East	High income
147	Senegal	SEN	Africa	Low income
148	Serbia	SRB	Europe & Eurasia	Upper middle income
149	Seychelles	SYC	Africa	High income
150	Sierra Leone	SLE	Africa	Low income
151	Singapore	SGP	Asia Pacific	High income
152	Slovakia	SVK	Europe & Eurasia	High income
153	Slovenia	SVN	Europe & Eurasia	High income
154	Somalia	SOM	Africa	Low income
155	South Africa	ZAF	Africa	Upper middle income
156	South Korea	KOR	Asia Pacific	High income
157	South Sudan	SDS	Africa	Low income
158	Spain	ESP	Europe & Eurasia	High income
159	Sri Lanka	LKA	Europe & Eurasia	Lower middle income
160	Sudan	SUD	Africa	Low income
161	Suriname	SUR	South & Central America	Upper middle income
162	Swaziland	SWZ	Africa	Lower middle income
163	Sweden	SWE	Europe & Eurasia	High income
164	Switzerland	CHE	Europe & Eurasia	High income
165	Syria	SYR	Middle East	Lower middle income
166	Taiwan, China	TWN	Asia Pacific	High income
167	Tajikistan	TJK	Europe & Eurasia	Lower middle income
168	Tanzania	TZA	Africa	High income
169	Thailand	THA	Asia Pacific	Upper middle income
170	TFYR Macedonia	MKD	Europe & Eurasia	Upper middle income
171	Togo	TGO	Africa	Low income
172	Trinidad and Tobago	TTO	South & Central America	High income
173	Tunisia	TUN	Africa	Lower middle income
174	Turkey	TUR	Europe & Eurasia	Upper middle income

Continued

	Region	Abbr.	Region grouping	Income group
175	Turkmenistan	TKM	Europe & Eurasia	Upper middle income
176	Uganda	UGA	Africa	Low income
177	Ukraine	UKR	Europe & Eurasia	Lower income
178	UAE	ARE	Middle East	High income
179	UK	GBR	Europe & Eurasia	Low income
180	USA	USA	North America	High income
181	Uruguay	URY	South & Central America	High income
182	Uzbekistan	UZB	Europe & Eurasia	Lower middle income
183	Vanuatu	VUT	Asia Pacific	Lower middle income
184	Venezuela	VEN	South & Central America	Upper middle income
185	Viet Nam	VNM	Asia Pacific	Lower middle income
186	Yemen	YEM	Middle East	Lower middle income
187	Zambia	ZMB	Africa	Lower middle income
188	Zimbabwe	ZWE	Africa	Low income

Appendix E Energy Use Inventories for the 188 Regions of 2013 (Unit: TJ)

Region	Exploitation, production and consumption associated energy use			Energy use embodied in imports			Energy use embodied in exports		
	EED	EEP	EEC	EEI_p	EEI_c	EEI	EEX_p	EEX_c	EEX
Afghanistan	0.00E+00	2.95E+04	4.93E+04	2.96E+04	2.02E+04	4.97E+04	6.18E+02	3.99E+02	1.02E+03
Albania	8.52E+04	1.35E+05	1.68E+05	6.82E+04	3.92E+04	1.07E+05	1.81E+04	6.24E+03	2.44E+04
Algeria	5.76E+06	3.37E+05	5.19E+05	4.21E+05	2.18E+05	6.39E+05	5.86E+06	3.57E+04	5.89E+06
Andorra	0.00E+00	1.07E+04	1.62E+04	1.20E+04	6.13E+03	1.81E+04	1.55E+03	6.43E+02	2.19E+03
Angola	4.10E+06	4.94E+05	5.29E+05	1.47E+05	6.80E+04	2.15E+05	3.76E+06	3.29E+04	3.79E+06
Antigua	0.00E+00	5.43E+03	8.13E+03	6.39E+03	3.09E+03	9.48E+03	1.00E+03	3.88E+02	1.39E+03
Argentina	2.99E+06	2.27E+06	2.50E+06	1.11E+06	5.27E+05	1.64E+06	1.83E+06	2.99E+05	2.13E+06
Armenia	3.39E+04	4.37E+04	5.60E+04	2.58E+04	1.51E+04	4.09E+04	1.58E+04	2.87E+03	1.86E+04
Aruba	0.00E+00	1.26E+04	2.03E+04	2.56E+04	9.96E+03	3.56E+04	1.29E+04	2.28E+03	1.52E+04
Australia	1.44E+07	6.31E+06	6.68E+06	1.38E+06	1.02E+06	2.41E+06	9.68E+06	6.60E+05	1.03E+07
Austria	5.07E+05	2.25E+06	2.45E+06	3.84E+06	9.20E+05	4.76E+06	2.13E+06	7.16E+05	2.84E+06
Azerbaijan	2.49E+06	2.90E+05	2.54E+05	1.26E+05	3.87E+04	1.65E+05	2.29E+06	7.46E+04	2.37E+06
Bahamas	0.00E+00	4.59E+04	5.84E+04	5.40E+04	1.70E+04	7.10E+04	9.10E+03	4.49E+03	1.36E+04
Bahrain	9.23E+05	3.29E+05	2.78E+05	5.31E+04	3.54E+04	8.85E+04	6.50E+05	8.69E+04	7.37E+05
Bangladesh	1.20E+06	1.23E+06	1.19E+06	2.29E+05	1.45E+05	3.74E+05	1.86E+05	1.83E+05	3.69E+05
Barbados	0.00E+00	1.49E+04	2.32E+04	1.75E+04	1.02E+04	2.78E+04	3.33E+03	1.92E+03	5.25E+03

Continued

Region	Exploitation, production and consumption associated energy use			Energy use embodied in imports			Energy use embodied in exports		
	EED	EEP	EEC	EEI_p	EEI_c	EEI	EEX_p	EEX_c	EEX
Belarus	1.67E+05	1.32E+03	8.33E+02	5.62E+04	7.80E+02	5.70E+04	2.27E+05	1.27E+03	2.28E+05
Belgium	6.17E+05	3.40E+06	2.08E+06	9.89E+06	7.43E+05	1.06E+07	7.13E+06	2.06E+06	9.19E+06
Belize	0.00E+00	6.05E+03	9.03E+03	7.66E+03	3.87E+03	1.15E+04	1.76E+03	8.84E+02	2.65E+03
Benin	9.34E+04	9.29E+04	9.41E+04	1.43E+04	8.31E+03	2.26E+04	1.47E+04	7.14E+03	2.18E+04
Bermuda	0.00E+00	2.03E+04	2.84E+04	2.08E+04	8.46E+03	2.92E+04	1.08E+03	3.82E+02	1.46E+03
Bhutan	0.00E+00	7.47E+03	1.19E+04	1.05E+04	5.10E+03	1.56E+04	3.02E+03	6.20E+02	3.64E+03
Bolivia	9.18E+05	1.10E+05	1.41E+05	5.97E+04	4.17E+04	1.01E+05	8.54E+05	1.04E+04	8.64E+05
Bosnia and Herzegovina	1.93E+05	1.72E+05	1.91E+05	5.25E+04	3.25E+04	8.51E+04	7.44E+04	1.34E+04	8.78E+04
Botswana	5.59E+04	1.86E+05	2.22E+05	1.41E+05	4.12E+04	1.82E+05	1.12E+04	5.23E+03	1.65E+04
Brazil	1.06E+07	1.37E+07	1.41E+07	5.74E+06	1.11E+06	6.86E+06	2.56E+06	7.40E+05	3.30E+06
British Virgin Islands	0.00E+00	4.75E+03	6.54E+03	6.74E+03	2.81E+03	9.55E+03	1.83E+03	1.02E+03	2.85E+03
Brunei	7.11E+05	2.05E+04	3.43E+04	3.42E+04	1.72E+04	5.14E+04	7.25E+05	3.35E+03	7.28E+05
Bulgaria	4.43E+05	4.59E+05	5.11E+05	3.96E+05	1.67E+05	5.63E+05	3.79E+05	1.15E+05	4.94E+05
Burkina Faso	0.00E+00	2.30E+04	4.06E+04	2.41E+04	1.80E+04	4.21E+04	1.06E+03	4.31E+02	1.49E+03
Burundi	0.00E+00	6.10E+03	8.35E+03	6.44E+03	2.46E+03	8.90E+03	7.82E+02	2.22E+02	1.00E+03
Cambodia	1.71E+05	1.55E+05	1.50E+05	5.55E+04	3.49E+04	9.04E+04	7.14E+04	3.99E+04	1.11E+05
Cameroon	3.76E+05	1.79E+05	1.79E+05	4.75E+04	2.49E+04	7.24E+04	2.45E+05	2.49E+04	2.70E+05
Canada	1.82E+07	1.39E+07	1.35E+07	1.11E+07	2.04E+06	1.32E+07	1.55E+07	2.43E+06	1.79E+07

Continued

Region	Exploitation, production and consumption associated energy use			Energy use embodied in imports			Energy use embodied in exports		
	EED	EEP	EEC	EEI_p	EEI_c	EEI	EEX_p	EEX_c	EEX
Cape Verde	0.00E+00	6.59E+03	1.05E+04	7.33E+03	4.25E+03	1.16E+04	7.65E+02	3.27E+02	1.09E+03
Cayman Islands	0.00E+00	7.86E+03	1.08E+04	8.52E+03	3.48E+03	1.20E+04	8.84E+02	5.79E+02	1.46E+03
Central African Republic	0.00E+00	4.34E+03	6.22E+03	4.62E+03	2.03E+03	6.65E+03	6.01E+02	1.53E+02	7.54E+02
Chad	1.84E+05	1.65E+05	1.62E+05	7.52E+03	3.50E+03	1.10E+04	2.14E+04	6.58E+03	2.79E+04
Chile	6.26E+05	1.53E+06	1.54E+06	1.72E+06	2.90E+05	2.01E+06	8.43E+05	2.77E+05	1.12E+06
Chinese Mainland	1.07E+08	1.22E+08	1.12E+08	4.09E+07	3.38E+06	4.42E+07	2.66E+07	1.32E+07	3.98E+07
Hong Kong, China	4.10E+03	3.34E+06	5.64E+06	4.93E+06	3.16E+06	8.09E+06	1.54E+06	8.56E+05	2.39E+06
Macao, China	0.00E+00	6.39E+04	9.95E+04	8.17E+04	5.25E+04	1.34E+05	1.12E+04	1.68E+04	2.80E+04
Taiwan, China	5.66E+05	1.45E+06	1.21E+06	1.80E+06	3.51E+05	2.16E+06	9.20E+05	5.90E+05	1.51E+06
Colombia	5.26E+06	2.35E+06	2.63E+06	4.89E+05	4.29E+05	9.18E+05	3.45E+06	1.55E+05	3.61E+06
Congo	6.27E+05	7.07E+04	7.54E+04	2.97E+04	1.37E+04	4.34E+04	5.88E+05	9.02E+03	5.97E+05
Costa Rica	1.03E+05	1.99E+05	2.34E+05	1.51E+05	7.53E+04	2.26E+05	5.85E+04	4.07E+04	9.93E+04
Croatia	1.52E+05	3.35E+05	4.21E+05	3.16E+05	1.39E+05	4.55E+05	1.32E+05	5.24E+04	1.84E+05
Cuba	2.45E+05	3.35E+05	3.87E+05	1.20E+05	7.70E+04	1.97E+05	2.82E+04	2.47E+04	5.29E+04
Cyprus	4.56E+03	1.08E+05	1.62E+05	1.17E+05	6.27E+04	1.80E+05	1.36E+04	8.77E+03	2.23E+04
Czech Republic	1.26E+06	3.69E+06	3.28E+06	6.10E+06	5.44E+05	6.64E+06	3.68E+06	9.52E+05	4.63E+06
Cote Divoire	0.00E+00	3.00E+04	4.57E+04	3.88E+04	1.99E+04	5.87E+04	9.46E+03	4.22E+03	1.37E+04

Continued

Region	Exploitation, production and consumption associated energy use			Energy use embodied in imports			Energy use embodied in exports		
	EED	EEP	EEC	EEI_p	EEI_c	EEI	EEX_p	EEX_c	EEX
DR Congo	9.05E+05	8.37E+05	8.60E+05	9.40E+04	4.42E+04	1.38E+05	1.58E+05	2.08E+04	1.79E+05
Denmark	7.05E+05	1.24E+06	1.26E+06	1.81E+06	4.78E+05	2.29E+06	1.32E+06	4.61E+05	1.78E+06
Djibouti	0.00E+00	4.21E+03	6.42E+03	4.92E+03	2.52E+03	7.43E+03	7.63E+02	3.07E+02	1.07E+03
Dominican Republic	4.28E+04	2.22E+05	2.76E+05	2.14E+05	8.78E+04	3.02E+05	3.25E+04	3.38E+04	6.62E+04
Ecuador	1.24E+06	9.03E+05	9.38E+05	1.76E+05	1.07E+05	2.83E+05	5.09E+05	7.21E+04	5.82E+05
Egypt	3.49E+06	1.91E+06	2.03E+06	5.61E+05	2.16E+05	7.77E+05	2.12E+06	9.94E+04	2.22E+06
El Salvador	9.52E+04	1.72E+05	1.93E+05	9.85E+04	5.03E+04	1.49E+05	2.32E+04	2.87E+04	5.18E+04
Eritrea	2.68E+04	2.63E+04	2.69E+04	3.76E+03	1.76E+03	5.52E+03	3.55E+03	1.16E+03	4.71E+03
Estonia	2.37E+05	3.55E+05	3.42E+05	3.66E+05	7.17E+04	4.38E+05	2.44E+05	8.43E+04	3.28E+05
Ethiopia	1.90E+06	2.17E+05	4.09E+04	1.29E+04	4.08E+04	5.37E+04	1.68E+06	2.16E+05	1.90E+06
Fiji	0.00E+00	1.13E+04	1.85E+04	1.36E+04	8.65E+03	2.23E+04	2.21E+03	1.54E+03	3.76E+03
Finland	7.55E+05	2.71E+06	2.25E+06	5.31E+06	2.83E+05	5.60E+06	3.33E+06	7.47E+05	4.07E+06
France	5.70E+06	1.48E+07	1.43E+07	2.16E+07	3.14E+06	2.48E+07	1.26E+07	3.60E+06	1.62E+07
French Polynesia	0.00E+00	1.82E+04	3.07E+04	1.96E+04	1.36E+04	3.32E+04	1.46E+03	1.11E+03	2.57E+03
Gabon	5.73E+05	6.33E+04	7.58E+04	3.49E+04	1.92E+04	5.40E+04	5.43E+05	6.67E+03	5.49E+05
Gambia	0.00E+00	3.67E+03	5.59E+03	3.95E+03	2.03E+03	5.98E+03	3.85E+02	1.10E+02	4.95E+02
Gaza Strip	0.00E+00	2.57E+04	4.43E+04	2.69E+04	1.88E+04	4.57E+04	6.32E+02	1.95E+02	8.28E+02

Continued

Region	Exploitation, production and consumption associated energy use			Energy use embodied in imports			Energy use embodied in exports		
	EED	EEP	EEC	EEI_p	EEI_c	EEI	EEX_p	EEX_c	EEX
Georgia	5.98E+04	1.73E+05	2.28E+05	1.64E+05	7.08E+04	2.35E+05	4.93E+04	1.52E+04	6.45E+04
Germany	5.04E+06	1.69E+07	1.57E+07	3.41E+07	5.83E+06	3.99E+07	2.27E+07	7.01E+06	2.97E+07
Ghana	4.03E+05	2.76E+05	2.82E+05	5.85E+04	4.46E+04	1.03E+05	1.83E+05	3.89E+04	2.22E+05
Greece	3.90E+05	3.45E+06	3.68E+06	4.19E+06	5.30E+05	4.72E+06	1.07E+06	2.93E+05	1.37E+06
Greenland	0.00E+00	4.66E+03	8.74E+03	6.03E+03	4.66E+03	1.07E+04	1.59E+03	5.75E+02	2.16E+03
Guatemala	3.64E+05	3.19E+05	2.79E+05	1.41E+05	7.05E+04	2.12E+05	1.88E+05	1.10E+05	2.97E+05
Guinea	0.00E+00	1.13E+04	1.94E+04	1.33E+04	8.46E+03	2.18E+04	2.43E+03	4.06E+02	2.84E+03
Guyana	0.00E+00	5.25E+05	8.75E+05	5.34E+05	3.51E+05	8.84E+05	1.60E+03	6.18E+02	2.22E+03
Haiti	1.40E+05	1.32E+05	1.24E+05	1.45E+04	7.00E+03	2.15E+04	2.38E+04	1.51E+04	3.88E+04
Honduras	1.06E+05	1.29E+05	1.29E+05	7.28E+04	3.89E+04	1.12E+05	5.04E+04	3.88E+04	8.92E+04
Hungary	4.27E+05	1.89E+06	1.62E+06	3.06E+06	3.27E+05	3.39E+06	1.59E+06	5.94E+05	2.19E+06
Iceland	2.21E+05	2.31E+05	2.23E+05	8.30E+04	3.32E+04	1.16E+05	7.27E+04	4.09E+04	1.14E+05
India	2.19E+07	2.15E+07	2.13E+07	5.74E+06	1.82E+06	7.55E+06	6.31E+06	2.03E+06	8.34E+06
Indonesia	1.93E+07	1.25E+07	1.25E+07	3.01E+06	8.82E+05	3.89E+06	9.76E+06	8.86E+05	1.06E+07
Iran	1.25E+07	4.58E+06	4.97E+06	1.05E+06	5.20E+05	1.57E+06	8.90E+06	1.34E+05	9.04E+06
Iraq	6.60E+06	6.47E+05	7.30E+05	2.14E+05	8.81E+04	3.02E+05	6.13E+06	4.90E+03	6.13E+06
Ireland	9.50E+04	7.93E+05	6.90E+05	1.32E+06	2.99E+05	1.62E+06	6.21E+05	4.02E+05	1.02E+06

Continued

Region	Exploitation, production and consumption associated energy use			Energy use embodied in imports			Energy use embodied in exports		
	EED	EEP	EEC	EEI_p	EEI_c	EEI	EEX_p	EEX_c	EEX
Israel	2.70E+05	1.39E+06	1.30E+06	1.60E+06	2.37E+05	1.84E+06	5.31E+05	3.29E+05	8.61E+05
Italy	1.54E+06	1.25E+07	1.17E+07	1.73E+07	2.13E+06	1.94E+07	6.37E+06	2.99E+06	9.36E+06
Jamaica	2.15E+04	6.12E+04	8.31E+04	5.05E+04	3.04E+04	8.09E+04	1.22E+04	8.52E+03	2.08E+04
Japan	1.17E+06	3.24E+07	3.36E+07	3.92E+07	4.11E+06	4.33E+07	8.70E+06	2.95E+06	1.16E+07
Jordan	1.12E+04	1.35E+05	2.11E+05	1.68E+05	9.27E+04	2.61E+05	4.48E+04	1.72E+04	6.20E+04
Kazakhstan	7.08E+06	2.28E+06	2.42E+06	9.01E+05	3.27E+05	1.23E+06	5.66E+06	-1.85E+05	5.84E+06
Kenya	7.36E+05	7.38E+05	7.36E+05	1.29E+05	5.70E+04	1.86E+05	1.27E+05	5.88E+04	1.85E+05
Kuwait	7.14E+06	2.15E+06	2.05E+06	1.76E+05	3.40E+05	5.16E+05	5.17E+06	4.36E+05	5.61E+06
Kyrgyzstan	7.36E+04	1.58E+05	3.21E+05	1.66E+05	1.87E+05	3.53E+05	7.96E+04	2.48E+04	1.04E+05
Laos	0.00E+00	1.36E+05	2.26E+04	1.54E+04	9.89E+03	2.53E+04	2.47E+03	8.45E+02	3.32E+03
Latvia	8.97E+04	3.28E+05	4.13E+05	3.50E+05	1.31E+05	4.81E+05	1.09E+05	4.64E+04	1.55E+05
Lebanon	1.03E+04	2.09E+05	2.87E+05	2.30E+05	1.02E+05	3.31E+05	3.17E+04	2.33E+04	5.50E+04
Lesotho	0.00E+00	1.54E+04	2.77E+04	1.75E+04	1.33E+04	3.08E+04	1.52E+03	1.02E+03	2.54E+03
Liberia	0.00E+00	2.72E+03	3.58E+03	4.39E+03	1.43E+03	5.82E+03	1.78E+03	5.66E+02	2.35E+03
Libya	2.58E+06	1.02E+05	1.04E+05	8.41E+04	3.36E+04	1.18E+05	2.59E+06	3.20E+04	2.62E+06
Liechtenstein	0.00E+00	3.77E+03	4.68E+03	3.45E+03	1.03E+03	4.48E+03	4.05E+02	1.18E+02	5.23E+02
Lithuania	5.93E+04	1.48E+06	1.23E+06	2.80E+06	1.42E+05	2.94E+06	1.35E+06	3.89E+05	1.74E+06

Continued

Region	Exploitation, production and consumption associated energy use			Energy use embodied in imports			Energy use embodied in exports		
	EED	EEP	EEC	EEI_p	EEI_c	EEI	EEX_p	EEX_c	EEX
Luxembourg	5.85E+03	3.12E+05	4.79E+05	6.34E+05	2.57E+05	8.91E+05	3.08E+05	8.90E+04	3.97E+05
Madagascar	0.00E+00	2.34E+04	4.15E+04	2.64E+04	2.05E+04	4.68E+04	3.65E+03	2.32E+03	5.96E+03
Malawi	0.00E+00	2.15E+04	3.09E+04	2.39E+04	1.11E+04	3.50E+04	2.60E+03	1.65E+03	4.25E+03
Malaysia	3.96E+06	4.02E+06	3.80E+06	3.80E+06	5.65E+05	4.36E+06	3.78E+06	7.84E+05	4.56E+06
Maldives	0.00E+00	1.02E+04	1.58E+04	1.14E+04	6.08E+03	1.74E+04	1.16E+03	4.99E+02	1.66E+03
Mali	0.00E+00	1.55E+04	2.59E+04	1.58E+04	1.09E+04	2.67E+04	8.02E+02	4.19E+02	1.22E+03
Malta	3.90E+02	3.41E+04	5.74E+04	4.94E+04	2.89E+04	7.83E+04	1.64E+04	5.68E+03	2.21E+04
Mauritania	0.00E+00	1.72E+04	2.89E+04	2.10E+04	1.38E+04	3.48E+04	4.28E+03	2.15E+03	6.43E+03
Mauritius	9.36E+03	5.95E+04	8.35E+04	5.99E+04	3.70E+04	9.70E+04	1.06E+04	1.30E+04	2.35E+04
Mexico	9.07E+06	8.50E+06	8.30E+06	4.69E+06	1.28E+06	5.98E+06	5.29E+06	1.49E+06	6.78E+06
Moldova	1.28E+04	2.36E+04	2.17E+03	1.64E+03	6.68E+02	2.30E+03	1.09E+04	8.58E+02	1.18E+04
Monaco	0.00E+00	4.68E+03	5.55E+03	4.21E+03	1.11E+03	5.32E+03	5.46E+02	2.39E+02	7.85E+02
Mongolia	6.84E+05	7.61E+04	8.72E+04	4.26E+04	2.24E+04	6.50E+04	6.51E+05	1.12E+04	6.63E+05
Montenegro	3.20E+04	5.45E+04	6.70E+04	3.21E+04	1.44E+04	4.65E+04	5.81E+03	1.89E+03	7.70E+03
Morocco	7.83E+04	2.76E+05	4.02E+05	2.96E+05	1.77E+05	4.73E+05	9.47E+04	5.09E+04	1.46E+05
Mozambique	6.96E+05	5.52E+05	5.04E+05	2.63E+04	1.35E+04	3.98E+04	1.70E+05	6.16E+04	2.32E+05
Myanmar	9.71E+05	2.80E+05	2.24E+05	1.27E+03	3.37E+02	1.61E+03	6.97E+05	5.67E+04	7.53E+05

Continued

Region	Exploitation, production and consumption associated energy use			Energy use embodied in imports			Energy use embodied in exports		
	EED	EEP	EEC	EEI_p	EEI_c	EEI	EEX_p	EEX_c	EEX
Namibia	1.85E+04	7.71E+04	1.02E+05	7.48E+04	3.61E+04	1.11E+05	1.73E+04	1.16E+04	2.89E+04
Nepal	3.61E+05	3.35E+05	2.66E+05	4.58E+04	3.45E+04	8.03E+04	7.42E+04	1.04E+05	1.78E+05
Netherlands	2.91E+06	5.68E+06	4.08E+06	1.52E+07	1.34E+06	1.66E+07	1.25E+07	2.94E+06	1.55E+07
Netherlands Antilles	0.00E+00	1.09E+04	3.27E+04	1.44E+04	2.53E+04	3.97E+04	4.53E+03	3.46E+03	7.99E+03
New Caledonia	0.00E+00	1.67E+04	2.69E+04	1.95E+04	1.06E+04	3.00E+04	3.87E+03	3.63E+02	4.23E+03
New Zealand	6.78E+05	9.68E+05	9.71E+05	6.17E+05	1.80E+05	7.97E+05	3.46E+05	1.78E+05	5.23E+05
Nicaragua	8.91E+04	8.92E+04	8.85E+04	3.12E+04	1.61E+04	4.73E+04	3.35E+04	1.68E+04	5.02E+04
Niger	1.26E+05	1.32E+05	1.39E+05	2.40E+04	1.25E+04	3.64E+04	1.98E+04	5.10E+03	2.49E+04
Nigeria	1.07E+07	3.99E+06	3.73E+06	3.50E+05	2.23E+05	5.73E+05	6.94E+06	4.79E+05	7.42E+06
North Korea	1.01E+06	1.32E+05	1.15E+05	2.08E+04	7.60E+03	2.84E+04	8.99E+05	2.41E+04	9.24E+05
Norway	8.02E+06	2.67E+06	2.81E+06	1.12E+06	5.24E+05	1.64E+06	6.40E+06	3.85E+05	6.79E+06
Oman	3.17E+06	2.02E+05	2.43E+05	3.83E+05	8.16E+04	4.65E+05	3.35E+06	4.04E+04	3.39E+06
Pakistan	2.73E+06	2.40E+06	2.24E+06	2.23E+05	1.32E+05	3.56E+05	5.56E+05	2.97E+05	8.53E+05
Panama	4.14E+04	1.58E+05	2.03E+05	1.43E+05	7.11E+04	2.14E+05	3.08E+04	2.69E+04	5.78E+04
Papua New Guinea	0.00E+00	3.43E+05	5.14E+04	3.76E+04	2.08E+04	5.84E+04	8.10E+03	3.69E+03	1.18E+04
Paraguay	3.12E+05	2.18E+05	2.83E+05	5.60E+04	7.71E+04	1.33E+05	1.52E+05	1.15E+04	1.64E+05
Peru	9.08E+05	8.28E+05	9.74E+05	3.60E+05	1.82E+05	5.42E+05	4.36E+05	3.57E+04	4.72E+05

189

Continued

Region	Exploitation, production and consumption associated energy use			Energy use embodied in imports			Energy use embodied in exports		
	EED	EEP	EEC	EEI_p	EEI_c	EEI	EEX_p	EEX_c	EEX
Philippines	1.03E+06	1.98E+06	2.05E+06	1.79E+06	3.00E+05	2.09E+06	8.47E+05	2.32E+05	1.08E+06
Poland	2.97E+06	4.39E+06	4.90E+06	3.30E+06	1.06E+06	4.36E+06	1.87E+06	5.48E+05	2.42E+06
Portugal	2.41E+05	1.41E+06	1.77E+06	1.63E+06	5.80E+05	2.21E+06	4.86E+05	2.16E+05	7.02E+05
Qatar	9.38E+06	1.97E+05	2.51E+05	2.35E+05	7.02E+04	3.05E+05	9.34E+06	1.56E+04	9.36E+06
Romania	1.09E+06	3.49E+06	3.32E+06	3.96E+06	2.68E+05	4.23E+06	1.52E+06	4.32E+05	1.96E+06
Russia	5.61E+07	5.59E+06	6.18E+06	4.60E+06	1.37E+06	5.97E+06	5.54E+07	7.80E+05	5.62E+07
Rwanda	0.00E+00	1.40E+04	2.34E+04	1.51E+04	9.60E+03	2.47E+04	8.57E+02	2.17E+02	1.07E+03
Samoa	0.00E+00	2.66E+03	3.57E+03	3.38E+03	1.24E+03	4.62E+03	7.76E+02	3.38E+02	1.11E+03
San Marino	0.00E+00	9.02E+03	1.33E+04	1.21E+04	4.73E+03	1.68E+04	1.26E+03	4.71E+02	1.73E+03
Sao Tome and Principe	0.00E+00	2.25E+03	3.11E+03	3.19E+03	1.10E+03	4.29E+03	9.21E+02	2.41E+02	1.16E+03
Saudi Arabia	2.57E+07	1.54E+06	2.26E+06	1.67E+06	8.77E+05	2.55E+06	2.49E+07	1.60E+05	2.51E+07
Senegal	7.52E+04	8.52E+04	9.13E+04	3.89E+04	2.28E+04	6.18E+04	2.97E+04	1.67E+04	4.64E+04
Serbia	4.76E+05	5.45E+05	6.34E+05	1.29E+05	9.14E+04	2.20E+05	7.05E+03	1.74E+03	8.80E+03
Seychelles	0.00E+00	6.52E+03	9.44E+03	7.73E+03	3.65E+03	1.14E+04	1.65E+03	7.31E+02	2.38E+03
Sierra Leone	0.00E+00	9.14E+03	1.38E+04	1.01E+04	5.11E+03	1.52E+04	1.27E+03	4.72E+02	1.74E+03
Singapore	2.69E+04	2.90E+06	2.74E+06	5.81E+06	1.04E+06	6.85E+06	2.95E+06	1.20E+06	4.15E+06
Slovakia	2.79E+05	4.17E+06	3.67E+06	6.59E+06	2.73E+05	6.86E+06	2.66E+06	7.75E+05	3.43E+06

Continued

Region	Exploitation, production and consumption associated energy use			Energy use embodied in imports			Energy use embodied in exports		
	EED	EEP	EEC	EEI_p	EEI_c	EEI	EEX_p	EEX_c	EEX
Slovenia	1.49E+05	3.72E+05	4.31E+05	5.24E+05	1.69E+05	6.93E+05	3.05E+05	1.10E+05	4.16E+05
Somalia	0.00E+00	2.16E+03	2.65E+03	1.96E+03	5.36E+02	2.49E+03	1.98E+02	4.49E+01	2.43E+02
South Africa	6.94E+06	3.23E+06	3.32E+06	1.15E+06	5.35E+05	1.68E+06	4.80E+06	4.50E+05	5.25E+06
South Korea	1.82E+06	1.56E+07	1.44E+07	2.66E+07	1.59E+06	2.82E+07	1.32E+07	2.80E+06	1.60E+07
South Sudan	2.19E+05	1.97E+05	1.92E+05	1.94E+03	5.49E+02	2.49E+03	2.46E+04	5.66E+03	3.02E+04
Spain	1.44E+06	1.23E+07	1.17E+07	1.66E+07	1.79E+06	1.84E+07	5.85E+06	2.40E+06	8.25E+06
Sri Lanka	2.27E+05	2.16E+05	2.36E+05	1.37E+05	8.58E+04	2.23E+05	1.50E+05	6.61E+04	2.16E+05
Sudan	6.55E+05	6.46E+05	6.46E+05	1.78E+03	5.32E+02	2.32E+03	4.29E+03	4.83E+02	4.77E+03
Suriname	0.00E+00	1.12E+04	2.01E+04	1.47E+04	9.80E+03	2.45E+04	3.11E+03	8.65E+02	3.98E+03
Swaziland	0.00E+00	4.40E+04	5.76E+04	5.33E+04	1.94E+04	7.27E+04	9.11E+03	5.76E+03	1.49E+04
Sweden	1.46E+06	2.57E+06	2.56E+06	3.32E+06	7.14E+05	4.04E+06	2.21E+06	7.21E+05	2.93E+06
Switzerland	5.42E+05	1.74E+06	2.21E+06	2.26E+06	8.92E+05	3.15E+06	1.13E+06	4.23E+05	1.55E+06
Syria	3.15E+05	1.39E+05	2.06E+05	1.34E+05	7.97E+04	2.14E+05	3.09E+05	1.23E+04	3.22E+05
Tajikistan	7.22E+04	1.03E+05	1.15E+05	4.67E+04	1.96E+04	6.64E+04	1.41E+04	7.28E+03	2.14E+04
Tanzania	0.00E+00	4.33E+04	1.05E+05	5.26E+04	6.50E+04	1.18E+05	5.91E+03	3.65E+03	9.56E+03
Thailand	3.27E+06	5.93E+06	5.08E+06	5.50E+06	6.38E+05	6.14E+06	2.86E+06	1.49E+06	4.34E+06
TFYR Macedonia	6.04E+04	2.62E+05	2.60E+05	3.06E+05	2.85E+04	3.35E+05	1.02E+05	2.98E+04	1.32E+05

Continued

Region	Exploitation, production and consumption associated energy use						Energy use embodied in imports			Energy use embodied in exports		
	EED	EEP	EEC	EEI_p	EEI_c	EEI	EEX_p	EEX_c	EEX
Togo	1.08E+05	7.52E+04	5.85E+04	1.60E+04	7.18E+03	2.31E+04	4.91E+04	2.39E+04	7.29E+04
Trinidad and Tobago	1.67E+06	3.91E+04	5.94E+04	6.50E+04	3.28E+04	9.78E+04	1.71E+06	1.25E+04	1.73E+06
Tunisia	3.02E+05	2.82E+05	3.54E+05	2.38E+05	1.22E+05	3.60E+05	2.61E+05	5.02E+04	3.11E+05
Turkey	1.35E+06	8.16E+06	8.55E+06	8.64E+06	1.10E+06	9.74E+06	1.78E+06	7.18E+05	2.50E+06
Turkmenistan	3.20E+06	9.33E+05	2.87E+05	2.13E+05	8.34E+04	2.96E+05	2.48E+06	7.29E+05	3.21E+06
Uganda	0.00E+00	3.76E+04	6.50E+04	3.85E+04	2.82E+04	6.67E+04	1.34E+03	9.09E+02	2.25E+03
Ukraine	3.56E+06	3.74E+06	4.33E+06	3.10E+06	1.07E+06	4.18E+06	2.92E+06	4.81E+05	3.40E+06
UAE	8.44E+06	1.75E+06	2.18E+06	2.01E+06	6.96E+05	2.70E+06	8.73E+06	2.65E+05	8.99E+06
United Kingdom	4.61E+06	1.02E+07	1.26E+07	1.12E+07	4.27E+06	1.55E+07	6.01E+06	1.85E+06	7.86E+06
United States	7.88E+07	1.08E+08	1.15E+08	5.77E+07	1.36E+07	7.13E+07	2.84E+07	6.06E+06	3.44E+07
Uruguay	9.14E+04	2.12E+05	2.54E+05	1.58E+05	6.65E+04	2.25E+05	3.54E+04	2.45E+04	5.98E+04
Uzbekistan	2.27E+06	1.62E+06	1.33E+06	6.42E+04	4.28E+04	1.07E+05	7.02E+05	3.38E+05	1.04E+06
Vanuatu	0.00E+00	3.32E+03	4.65E+03	4.27E+03	1.74E+03	6.01E+03	9.96E+02	4.17E+02	1.41E+03
Venezuela	8.04E+06	1.46E+06	1.56E+06	5.67E+05	1.82E+05	7.49E+05	6.88E+06	8.56E+04	6.96E+06
Viet Nam	2.90E+06	1.98E+06	1.99E+06	8.19E+05	2.62E+05	1.08E+06	1.55E+06	2.52E+05	1.80E+06
Yemen	7.63E+05	7.68E+04	1.15E+05	6.06E+04	4.45E+04	1.05E+05	7.49E+05	6.58E+03	7.56E+05
Zambia	3.68E+05	2.96E+05	2.74E+05	5.96E+04	2.56E+04	8.52E+04	1.29E+05	4.75E+04	1.76E+05
Zimbabwe	4.14E+05	1.80E+04	3.08E+04	4.17E+04	3.07E+04	7.24E+04	6.82E+04	1.79E+04	8.62E+04

Appendix F   139 Sectors Included in the Input-output Table for China

Code	Contents	Sector grouping
1	Farming	Agricultural product
2	Forestry	Agricultural product
3	Animal production	Agricultural product
4	Fishery	Agricultural product
5	Support services to farming, forestry, animal production and fishery	Agricultural product
6	Mining and washing of coal	Resource product
7	Extraction of crude petroleum and natural gas	Resource product
8	Mining of ferrous metal ores	Resource product
9	Mining of non-ferrous metal ores	Resource product
10	Mining and quarrying of nonmetallic mineral	Resource product
11	Mining support activities and other mining and quarrying	Resource product
12	Manufacture of grain mill products	Light manufacturing
13	Manufacture of prepared animal feeds	Light manufacturing
14	Manufacture of crude and refined oils from vegetable	Light manufacturing
15	Manufacture of sugar	Light manufacturing
16	Slaughtering and processing of meat	Light manufacturing
17	Processing of aquatic products	Light manufacturing
18	Processing of other foods	Light manufacturing
19	Manufacture of convenience food products	Light manufacturing
20	Manufacture of milk and dairy products	Light manufacturing
21	Manufacture of flavoring and ferment products	Light manufacturing
22	Manufacture of other food products n. e. c.	Light manufacturing
23	Manufacture of alcohol and alcoholic beverages	Light manufacturing
24	Manufacture of soft drinks and refined tea products	Light manufacturing
25	Manufacture of tobacco products	Light manufacturing
26	Spinning, weaving and finishing of cotton and chemical fibers	Light manufacturing
27	Spinning, weaving and finishing of wool	Light manufacturing

Continued

Code	Contents	Sector grouping
28	Spinning, weaving and finishing of bast and silk fibers	Light manufacturing
29	Manufacture of knitted and crocheted fabrics and articles, except apparel	Light manufacturing
30	Manufacture of made-up textile articles, except apparel	Light manufacturing
31	Manufacture of textile wearing apparel	Light manufacturing
32	Manufacture of leather, fur, feather and its products	Light manufacturing
33	Manufacture of footwear	Light manufacturing
34	Processing of timbers and manufacture of products of woods, bamboo, rattan, palm and straw	Light manufacturing
35	Manufacture of furniture	Light manufacturing
36	Manufacture of paper and paper products	Light manufacturing
37	Printing and reproduction of recording media	Light manufacturing
38	Manufacture of stationeries, musical instruments, products of arts and crafts, sports goods, games and toys	Light manufacturing
39	Manufacture of refined petroleum products, processing of nuclear fuel	Heavy manufacturing
40	Manufacture of coke products	Heavy manufacturing
41	Manufacture of basic chemicals	Heavy manufacturing
42	Manufacture of fertilizers	Heavy manufacturing
43	Manufacture of pesticides	Heavy manufacturing
44	Manufacture of paints, printing inks, pigments and similar products	Heavy manufacturing
45	Manufacture of synthetic materials	Heavy manufacturing
46	Manufacture of special chemical products	Heavy manufacturing
47	Manufacture of daily-use chemical products	Light manufacturing
48	Manufacture of pharmaceutical products	Light manufacturing
49	Manufacture of chemical fibers	Light manufacturing
50	Manufacture of rubber products	Light manufacturing
51	Manufacture of plastic products	Light manufacturing
52	Manufacture of cement, lime and plaster	Heavy manufacturing
53	Manufacture of products of plaster and cement and similar products	Heavy manufacturing
54	Manufacture of brick, stone and other building materials	Heavy manufacturing
55	Manufacture of glass and glass products	Light manufacturing
56	Manufacture of ceramic and porcelain products	Light manufacturing

Continued

Code	Contents	Sector grouping
57	Manufacture of refractory products	Heavy manufacturing
58	Manufacture of products of graphite and other nonmetallic minerals	Heavy manufacturing
59	Manufacture and casting of basic iron and steel	Heavy manufacturing
60	Processing of steel rolling processing	Heavy manufacturing
61	Manufacture of ferroalloy	Heavy manufacturing
62	Manufacture and casting of non-ferrous metals and related alloys	Heavy manufacturing
63	Processing of non-ferrous metals rolling	Heavy manufacturing
64	Manufacture of fabricated metal products, except machinery and equipment	Heavy manufacturing
65	Manufacture of boiler and prime mover	Heavy manufacturing
66	Manufacture of metal working machinery	Heavy manufacturing
67	Manufacture of lifting and handling equipment	Heavy manufacturing
68	Manufacture of pump, valve, compressor and similar machinery	Heavy manufacturing
69	Manufacture of movie, office machinery and equipment, of projector and camera	Light manufacturing
70	Manufacture of other general-purpose machinery	Heavy manufacturing
71	Manufacture of machinery for mining, metallurgy and construction	Heavy manufacturing
72	Manufacture of machinery for chemical industry timber and nonmetal processing	Heavy manufacturing
73	Manufacture of machinery for agriculture forestry, animal production and fishery	Heavy manufacturing
74	Manufacture of other special-purpose machinery	Heavy manufacturing
75	Manufacture of motor vehicles, except parts and accessories for motor vehicles	Heavy manufacturing
76	Manufacture of parts and accessories for motor vehicles	Heavy manufacturing
77	Manufacture of railway transport equipment	Heavy manufacturing
78	Manufacture of boats and ships and floating devices	Heavy manufacturing
79	Manufacture of other transport equipment	Heavy manufacturing
80	Manufacture of generators and electric motors	Heavy manufacturing
81	Manufacture of equipment for power transmission and distribution and control	Heavy manufacturing

Continued

Code	Contents	Sector grouping
82	Manufacture of wire, cable, optical cable and electrical goods	Heavy manufacturing
83	Manufacture of batteries	Light manufacturing
84	Manufacture of household appliances	Light manufacturing
85	Manufacture of other electrical machinery and equipment	Light manufacturing
86	Manufacture of computer	Light manufacturing
87	Manufacture of communication equipment	Light manufacturing
88	Manufacture of broadcasting, television equipment, of radar and related equipment	Light manufacturing
89	Manufacture of audiovisual apparatus	Light manufacturing
90	Manufacture of electronic components and parts	Light manufacturing
91	Manufacture of other electronic equipment	Light manufacturing
92	Manufacture of measuring instruments and meters	Light manufacturing
93	Other manufacture	Light manufacturing
94	Comprehensive utilization of waste resources	Light manufacturing
95	Repair of fabricated metal products, machinery and equipment	Heavy manufacturing
96	Production and supply of electricity and steam	Resource product
97	Production and distribution of gas	Resource product
98	Production and distribution of water	Resource product
99	Construction of buildings	Construction
100	Civil engineering	Construction
101	Construction installation activities	Construction
102	Construction completion and finishing, other construction activities	Construction
103	Wholesale and retail trade	Service
104	Transport via railway	Transport
105	Transport via road	Transport
106	Water transport	Transport
107	Air transport	Transport
108	Transport via pipeline	Transport
109	Cargo handling, transport agency	Transport
110	Storage	Transport

Continued

Code	Contents	Sector grouping
111	Post	Service
112	Accommodation	Service
113	Food and beverage services	Service
114	Telecommunication and other information transmission services	Service
115	Software and information technology services	Service
116	Monetary intermediation and other financial services	Service
117	Capital market services	Service
118	Insurance	Service
119	Real estate	Service
120	Renting and leasing	Service
121	Business services	Service
122	Research and experimental development	Service
123	Professional technique services	Service
124	Technique promotion and application services	Service
125	Management of water conservancy	Service
126	Ecological protection and environmental control	Service
127	Management of public facilities	Service
128	Services to households	Service
129	Repair of motor vehicles, electronic products and household goods and other services	Service
130	Education	Service
131	Health care	Service
132	Social work activities	Service
133	Journalism and publishing	Service
134	Radio, televisions, movies and audio-video recording activities	Service
135	Cultural, art and entertainment activities	Service
136	Sports activities	Service
137	Amusement and recreation activities	Service
138	Social security	Service
139	Public management and social organization	Service

Appendix G   Sectoral Embodied Energy Intensities in Foreign Regions of 2012 (Unit: TJ/10, 000RMB; the Previous Unit J/USD Is Changed into J/RMB Based on Exchange Rate in 2012.)

139 sectors in Chinese economy	26 sectors in global economy	Details	Embodied energy intensity
1	1	Agriculture	3. 41E-02
2	1	Agriculture	3. 41E-02
3	1-Biomass	Embodied intensity of the sector of Agriculture minus the direct intensity of biomass	1. 50E-02
4	2	Fishing	1. 01E-02
5	1&2	Average embodied intensity of the two sectors of Agriculture and Fishing weighted by sectoral total outputs	3. 26E-02
6	3-Crude oil-Natural gas-Nuclear	Embodied intensity of the sector of Mining and quarrying minus the direct intensity of crude oil, natural gas and nuclear energy.	8. 05E-02
7	3-Coal-Nuclear	Embodied intensity of the sector of Mining and quarrying minus the direct intensity of coal and nuclear energy.	2. 04E-01
8	3-Coal-Crude oil-Natural gas-Nuclear	Embodied intensity of the sector of Mining and quarrying minus the direct intensity of coal, crude oil, natural gas and nuclear energy.	2. 23E-02
9	3-Coal-Crude oil-Natural gas	Embodied intensity of the sector of Mining and quarrying minus the direct intensity of coal, crude oil, natural gas.	4. 01E-02
10	3-Coal-Crude oil-Natural gas-Nuclear	Embodied intensity of the sector of Mining and quarrying minus the direct intensity of coal, crude oil, natural gas and nuclear energy.	2. 23E-02
11	3-Coal-Crude oil-Natural gas-Nuclear	Embodied intensity of the sector of Mining and quarrying minus the direct intensity of coal, crude oil, natural gas and nuclear energy.	2. 23E-02

Continued

139 sectors in Chinese economy	26 sectors in global economy	Details	Embodied energy intensity
12	4	Food & beverages	1. 50E-02
13	4	Food & beverages	1. 50E-02
14	4	Food & beverages	1. 50E-02
15	4	Food & beverages	1. 50E-02
16	4	Food & beverages	1. 50E-02
17	4	Food & beverages	1. 50E-02
18	4	Food & beverages	1. 50E-02
19	4	Food & beverages	1. 50E-02
20	4	Food & beverages	1. 50E-02
21	4	Food & beverages	1. 50E-02
22	4	Food & beverages	1. 50E-02
23	4	Food & beverages	1. 50E-02
24	4	Food & beverages	1. 50E-02
25	4	Food & beverages	1. 50E-02
26	5	Textiles and wearing apparel	1. 47E-02
27	5	Textiles and wearing apparel	1. 47E-02
28	5	Textiles and wearing apparel	1. 47E-02
29	5	Textiles and wearing apparel	1. 47E-02
30	5	Textiles and wearing apparel	1. 47E-02
31	5	Textiles and wearing apparel	1. 47E-02
32	5	Textiles and wearing apparel	1. 47E-02
33	5	Textiles and wearing apparel	1. 47E-02
34	6	Wood and paper	1. 28E-02
35	6	Wood and paper	1. 28E-02
36	6	Wood and paper	1. 28E-02
37	6	Wood and paper	1. 28E-02

Continued

139 sectors in Chinese economy	26 sectors in global economy	Details	Embodied energy intensity
38	6	Wood and paper	1. 28E-02
39	7	Petroleum, chemical and non-metallic mineral products	5. 65E-02
40	7	Petroleum, chemical and non-metallic mineral products	5. 65E-02
41	7	Petroleum, chemical and non-metallic mineral products	5. 65E-02
42	7	Petroleum, chemical and non-metallic mineral products	5. 65E-02
43	7	Petroleum, chemical and non-metallic mineral products	5. 65E-02
44	7	Petroleum, chemical and non-metallic mineral products	5. 65E-02
45	7	Petroleum, chemical and non-metallic mineral products	5. 65E-02
46	7	Petroleum, chemical and non-metallic mineral products	5. 65E-02
47	7	Petroleum, chemical and non-metallic mineral products	5. 65E-02
48	7	Petroleum, chemical and non-metallic mineral products	5. 65E-02
49	7	Petroleum, chemical and non-metallic mineral products	5. 65E-02
50	7	Petroleum, chemical and non-metallic mineral products	5. 65E-02
51	7	Petroleum, chemical and non-metallic mineral products	5. 65E-02
52	7	Petroleum, chemical and non-metallic mineral products	5. 65E-02
53	7	Petroleum, chemical and non-metallic mineral products	5. 65E-02
54	7	Petroleum, chemical and non-metallic mineral products	5. 65E-02
55	7	Petroleum, chemical and non-metallic mineral products	5. 65E-02
56	7	Petroleum, chemical and non-metallic mineral products	5. 65E-02
57	7	Petroleum, chemical and non-metallic mineral products	5. 65E-02
58	7	Petroleum, chemical and non-metallic mineral products	5. 65E-02
59	8	Metal products	2. 36E-02
60	8	Metal products	2. 36E-02
61	8	Metal products	2. 36E-02
62	8	Metal products	2. 36E-02
63	8	Metal products	2. 36E-02

Continued

139 sectors in Chinese economy	26 sectors in global economy	Details	Embodied energy intensity
64	8	Metal products	2. 36E-02
65	9	Electrical and machinery	1. 10E-02
66	9	Electrical and machinery	1. 10E-02
67	9	Electrical and machinery	1. 10E-02
68	9	Electrical and machinery	1. 10E-02
69	9	Electrical and machinery	1. 10E-02
70	9	Electrical and machinery	1. 10E-02
71	9	Electrical and machinery	1. 10E-02
72	9	Electrical and machinery	1. 10E-02
73	9	Electrical and machinery	1. 10E-02
74	9	Electrical and machinery	1. 10E-02
75	10	Transport equipment	1. 24E-02
76	10	Transport equipment	1. 24E-02
77	10	Transport equipment	1. 24E-02
78	10	Transport equipment	1. 24E-02
79	10	Transport equipment	1. 24E-02
80	11	Other manufacturing	1. 46E-02
81	11	Other manufacturing	1. 46E-02
82	11	Other manufacturing	1. 46E-02
83	11	Other manufacturing	1. 46E-02
84	11	Other manufacturing	1. 46E-02
85	11	Other manufacturing	1. 46E-02
86	11	Other manufacturing	1. 46E-02
87	11	Other manufacturing	1. 46E-02
88	11	Other manufacturing	1. 46E-02
89	11	Other manufacturing	1. 46E-02

Continued

139 sectors in Chinese economy	26 sectors in global economy	Details	Embodied energy intensity
90	11	Other manufacturing	1. 46E-02
91	11	Other manufacturing	1. 46E-02
92	11	Other manufacturing	1. 46E-02
93	11	Other manufacturing	1. 46E-02
94	12	Recycling	1. 37E-02
95	15	Maintenance and repair	5. 52E-03
96	13	Electricity, gas and water	6. 26E-02
97	13	Electricity, gas and water	5. 46E-02
98	13-hydroenergy -others	Embodied intensity of the sector of Electricity, gas and water minus the direct intensity of hydroenergy and others.	5. 46E-02
99	14	Construction	1. 41E-02
100	14	Construction	1. 41E-02
101	14	Construction	1. 41E-02
102	14	Construction	1. 41E-02
103	16&17	Average embodied intensity of the two sectors of Wholesale Trade and Retail Trade weighted by sectoral total outputs	4. 13E-03
104	19	Transport	9. 33E-03
105	19	Transport	9. 33E-03
106	19	Transport	9. 33E-03
107	19	Transport	9. 33E-03
108	19	Transport	9. 33E-03
109	19	Transport	9. 33E-03
110	19	Transport	9. 33E-03
111	20	Post and telecommunications	4. 04E-03
112	18	Hotels and restaurants	7. 57E-03

Continued

139 sectors in Chinese economy	26 sectors in global economy	Details	Embodied energy intensity
113	18	Hotels and restaurants	7. 57E-03
114	20	Post and telecommunications	4. 04E-03
115	21	Financial intermediation and business activities	2. 90E-03
116	21	Financial intermediation and business activities	2. 90E-03
117	21	Financial intermediation and business activities	2. 90E-03
118	21	Financial intermediation and business activities	2. 90E-03
119	21	Financial intermediation and business activities	2. 90E-03
120	21	Financial intermediation and business activities	2. 90E-03
121	21	Financial intermediation and business activities	2. 90E-03
122	23	Education, health and other services	5. 10E-03
123	23	Education, health and other services	5. 10E-03
124	23	Education, health and other services	5. 10E-03
125	22	Public administration	6. 62E-03
126	22	Public administration	6. 62E-03
127	22	Public administration	6. 62E-03
128	24	Private households	2. 73E-03
129	24	Private households	2. 73E-03
130	23	Education, health and other services	5. 10E-03
131	23	Education, health and other services	5. 10E-03
132	23	Education, health and other services	5. 10E-03
133	23	Education, health and other services	5. 10E-03
134	23	Education, health and other services	5. 10E-03
135	23	Education, health and other services	5. 10E-03
136	23	Education, health and other services	5. 10E-03
137	23	Education, health and other services	5. 10E-03
138	22	Public administration	6. 62E-03
139	22	Public administration	6. 62E-03

Appendix H　Data Definitions and Sources

Variable	Definition/Source
Pollution intensity	Emissions divided by gross value added (tons per million yuan). Source: Environment Protection chapter and Industry chapter, *China Statistical Yearbook* 1998-2004.
Energy consumption	Total energy consumption per unit of value added, including consumption of coal, coke, crude oil, gasoline, kerosene, diesel oil, fuel oil, natural gas and electricity. Source: Energy chapter, *China Statistical Yearbook* 1998-2004.
Energy	Energy consumption divided by gross value added (10,000 tons of standard coal equivalent per 100 million yuan). Source: see individual sources for energy consumption and gross value added.
Gross value added	Gross value added by industry. 100 million yuan (1990 price). Source: Industry chapter, *China Statistical Yearbook* 1998-2004.
PCI	Physical capital intensity: Non-wage value added per worker ((VA-total wage)/number of staff). Source: wage and number of staff data from *China Labour Statistical Yearbook*, Comprehensiveness chapter 1998-2004.
HCI	Human capital intensity: average wage by industry. Source: Comprehensiveness chapter, *China Labour Statistical Yearbook* 1998-2004.
SIZE	Value added per firm. million yuan (1990 price). Source: as gross value added.
TFP	Total factor productivity. Source: data required to calculate TFP is from Industry chapter, *China Statistical Yearbook* 1998-2004.
TFPoutput	Gross output per worker. Source: as above.
CAP	Capital expenditure: investment in capital construction as a share of total physical capital stock. Source: Investment in Fixed Assets chapter, *China Statistical Yearbook* 1998-2004.
RD	Research and development expenditure: investment in innovation per unit of value added, including innovation investment in new construction projects, expansion projects and reconstruction projects within an industry (thousand yuan of investment per million yuan of value added). Source: as above.
REGpros	Regional pollution prosecution: administrative penalty case on pollution divided by region's GDP (1990 price). Source: Environment Statistics chapter, *China Environment Yearbook* 1998-2004.
REGunem	Regional unemployment rate. Source: Employment and Unemployment chapter, *China Labour Statistical Yearbook* 1998-2004.

Continued

Variable	Definition/Source
REGpd	Regional population density: total population divided by region's area. Source: Population chapter, *China statistical Yearbook* 1998-2004; area data from http://www.usacn.com.
REGagepop	Share of population under the age of 15: population under 15 divided region's total population. Source: Comprehensiveness chapter, *China Labour Statistical Yearbook* 1998-2004.
REGedu	Regional level of education: population having acquired college or higher level of education divided by total population. Source: as above.
K	Physical capital stock: original value of fixed assets. Source: Industry chapter, *China Statistical Yearbook* 1998-2004.
L	Total labour force: total number of staff. Source: see above.

Appendix I   Footnotes of Table 3. 2. 1

No.	Item value	Unit	Source
	Renewable inputs of natural resources (*Ires-r*)		
1	Solar radiation Area = 5. 32E+03 Average insolation = 5. 90E+09 Albedo = 20% Energy = (area) x (average insolation) x (1-albedo) = 2. 51E+13 Cosmic exergy transformity = 1. 02E-05 Cosmic exergy = (energy) x (cosmic exergy transformity)= 2. 56E+08	m^2 $J/m^2/yr$ J/yr Jc/J Jc/yr	Market survey a a b c
2	Wind (kinetic) Area = 5. 32E+03 Density of air = 1. 23 Average annual wind velocity = 2. 40 Annual working time = 3. 15E+07 Drag coefficient = 1. 00E-03 Energy = (area) x (density of air) x (average annual wind velocity)^3 x (annual working time) x (drag coefficient) = 2. 85E+09 Cosmic exergy transformity = 3. 21E-02 Cosmic exergy = (energy) x (cosmic exergy transformity)= 9. 15E+07	m^2 kg/m^3 m/s s/yr J/yr Jc/J Jc/yr	Market survey d d a e b c
3	Rain (chemical) Area = 5. 32E+03 Evapotranspiration = 3. 86E-01 Rain density = 1. 00E+03 Gibbs free energy = 4. 94E+03 Energy = (area) x (evapotranspiration) x (rain density) x (Gibbs free energy) = 1. 01E+10 Cosmic exergy transformity = 6. 26E-01 Cosmic exergy = (energy) x (cosmic exergy transformity)= 6. 32E+09	m^2 m/yr kg/m^3 J/kg J/yr Jc/J Jc/yr	Market survey f d g g c
4	Rain (geopotential) Area = 5. 32E+03 Rainfall = 1. 30 Runoff rate = 20% Average elevation = 2. 70E+01 Rain density = 1. 00E+03 Gravity = 9. 80 Energy = (area) x (rainfall) x (runoff rate) x (average elevation) x (rain density) x (gravity) = 3. 66E+08 Cosmic exergy transformity = 3. 62E-01 Cosmic exergy = (energy) x (cosmic exergy transformity)= 1. 32E+08	m^2 m/yr m kg/m^3 m/s^2 J/yr Jc/J Jc/yr	Market survey f d f d g g c

Continued

No.	Item value	Unit	Source
5	Geothermal Area = 5. 32E+03 Heat flow = 7. 00E-02 Annual working time = 3. 15E+07 Energy = (area) x (heat flow) x (annual working time) = 1. 17E+10 Cosmic exergy transformity = 7. 82E-03 Cosmic exergy = (energy) x (cosmic exergy transformity)= 9. 15E+07	m^2 W/m^2 s/yr J/yr Jc/J Jc/yr	Market survey f a g c
	Nonrenewable inputs of natural resources (*Ires-n*)		
6	Topsoil loss Area = 5. 32E+03 Total soil loss per year in China = 1. 37E+12 National territory area = 9. 60E+10 Average organic content = 1. 50% Mass = (area) x (total soil loss per year in China)/(national territory area) x (average organic content) = 1. 14E+03 Cosmic exergy transformity = 4. 33E+07 Cosmic exergy = (mass) x (cosmic exergy transformity)= 4. 94E+10	m^2 kg/yr m^2 kg/yr Jc/kg Jc/yr	Market survey b d b b h
	Renewable and nonrenewable inputs purchased from economic market (*Ieco*)		
7	Labor and services Renewable proportion = 6. 20% Consumption = 4. 00E+03 Cosmic exergy transformity = 5. 45E+07 Cosmic exergy = (consumption) x (cosmic exergy transformity) = 2. 48E+11	 CNY/yr Jc/CNY Jc/yr	i Market survey i
	Pigsty		
8	Cement Renewable proportion = 0. 79% Consumption = 1. 05E+01 Cosmic exergy transformity = 1. 56E+08 Cosmic exergy = (consumption) x (cosmic exergy transformity) = 1. 64E+09	 CNY/yr Jc/CNY Jc/yr	i Market survey i
9	Lime Renewable proportion = 0. 79% Consumption = 1. 50E+01 Cosmic exergy transformity = 1. 56E+08 Cosmic exergy = (consumption) x (cosmic exergy transformity) = 2. 34E+09	 CNY/yr Jc/CNY Jc/yr	i Market survey i

Continued

No.	Item value	Unit	Source
10	Bricks Renewable proportion = 0. 73% Consumption = 1. 60E+01 Cosmic exergy transformity = 1. 72E+08 Cosmic exergy = （consumption）x（cosmic exergy transformity）= 2. 76E+09	CNY/yr Jc/CNY Jc/yr	i Market survey i
11	Steel Renewable proportion = 0. 47% Consumption = 2. 25E+01 Cosmic exergy transformity = 2. 13E+08 Cosmic exergy = （consumption）x（cosmic exergy transformity）= 4. 79E+09	CNY/yr Jc/CNY Jc/yr	i Market survey i
12	Feed Renewable proportion = 46. 63% Consumption = 5. 32E+03 Cosmic exergy transformity = 8. 36E+07 Cosmic exergy = （consumption）x（cosmic exergy transformity）= 4. 35E+11	CNY/yr Jc/CNY Jc/yr	i Market survey i
13	Drugs Renewable proportion = 4. 65% Consumption = 2. 40E+02 Cosmic exergy transformity = 8. 16E+07 Cosmic exergy = （consumption）x（cosmic exergy transformity）= 1. 96E+10	CNY/yr Jc/CNY Jc/yr	i Market survey i
14	Disinfectant Renewable proportion = 1. 17% Consumption = 2. 00E+01 Cosmic exergy transformity = 1. 16E+08 Cosmic exergy = （consumption）x（cosmic exergy transformity）= 2. 33E+09	CNY/yr Jc/CNY Jc/yr	i Market survey i
15	Water Renewable proportion = 1. 49% Consumption = 5. 66E+01 Cosmic exergy transformity = 6. 72E+07 Cosmic exergy = （consumption）x（cosmic exergy transformity）= 3. 80E+09	CNY/yr Jc/CNY Jc/yr	i Market survey i

Continued

No.	Item value	Unit	Source
16	Electricity Renewable proportion = 1. 17% Consumption = 3. 20E+02 Cosmic exergy transformity = 1. 97E+08 Cosmic exergy = (consumption) x (cosmic exergy transformity) = 6. 31E+10	 CNY/yr Jc/CNY Jc/yr	i Market survey i
	Biogas pool		
17	Cement Renewable proportion = 0. 79% Consumption = 1. 35E+01 Cosmic exergy transformity = 1. 56E+08 Cosmic exergy = (consumption) x (cosmic exergy transformity) = 2. 11E+09	 CNY/yr Jc/CNY Jc/yr	i Market survey i
18	Sand and pebble Renewable proportion = 0. 35% Consumption = 1. 30E+01 Cosmic exergy transformity = 3. 28E+08 Cosmic exergy = (consumption) x (cosmic exergy transformity) = 4. 27E+09	 CNY/yr Jc/CNY Jc/yr	i Market survey i
19	Plastic pipe Renewable proportion = 1. 23% Consumption = 4. 50E+00 Cosmic exergy transformity = 1. 04E+08 Cosmic exergy = (consumption) x (cosmic exergy transformity) = 4. 69E+08	 CNY/yr Jc/CNY Jc/yr	i Market survey i
20	Steel mold Renewable proportion = 1. 01% Consumption = 6. 00E+01 Cosmic exergy transformity = 1. 44E+08 Cosmic exergy = (consumption) x (cosmic exergy transformity) = 8. 67E+09	 CNY/yr Jc/CNY Jc/yr	i Market survey i
21	Cooker Renewable proportion = 1. 20% Consumption = 1. 55E+01 Cosmic exergy transformity = 1. 02E+08 Cosmic exergy = (consumption) x (cosmic exergy transformity) = 1. 58E+09	 CNY/yr Jc/CNY Jc/yr	i Market survey i

Continued

No.	Item value	Unit	Source
	Fishpond		
22	Lime Renewable proportion = 0.79% Consumption = 2.88E+01 Cosmic exergy transformity = 1.56E+08 Cosmic exergy = (consumption) x (cosmic exergy transformity) = 4.50E+09	 CNY/yr Jc/CNY Jc/yr	i Market survey i
23	Bleach Renewable proportion = 0.70% Consumption = 3.20E+01 Cosmic exergy transformity = 1.78E+08 Cosmic exergy = (consumption) x (cosmic exergy transformity) = 5.70E+09	 CNY/yr Jc/CNY Jc/yr	i Market survey i
24	Aerator Renewable proportion = 0.88% Consumption = 1.00E+02 Cosmic exergy transformity = 1.23E+08 Cosmic exergy = (consumption) x (cosmic exergy transformity) = 1.23E+10	 CNY/yr Jc/CNY Jc/yr	i Market survey i
25	Feed Renewable proportion = 67.50% Consumption = 7.20E+03 Cosmic exergy transformity = 1.12E+08 Cosmic exergy = (consumption) x (cosmic exergy transformity) = 8.04E+11	 CNY/yr Jc/CNY Jc/yr	i Market survey i
26	Nitrogen fertilizer Renewable proportion = 0.62% Consumption = 4.00E+02 Cosmic exergy transformity = 1.98E+08 Cosmic exergy = (consumption) x (cosmic exergy transformity) = 7.93E+10	 CNY/yr Jc/CNY Jc/yr	i Market survey i
27	Phosphate fertilizer Renewable proportion = 0.62% Consumption = 2.75E+02 Cosmic exergy transformity = 1.98E+08 Cosmic exergy = (consumption) x (cosmic exergy transformity) = 5.45E+10	 CNY/yr Jc/CNY Jc/yr	i Market survey i

Continued

No.	Item value	Unit	Source
Yield (Y)			
28	Pig Production = 8.00E+03 Cosmic exergy transformity = 1.95E+08 Cosmic exergy = (production) x (cosmic exergy transformity) = 1.56E+12	CNY/yr Jc/CNY Jc/yr	Market survey i
29	Biogas Production = 4.00E+02 Coal equivalent = 5.72E+02 Cosmic exergy transformity (coal) = 1.95E+08 Cosmic exergy = (coal equivalent) x (cosmic exergy transformity) = 5.32E+11	m^3 CNY/yr Jc/CNY Jc/yr	Market survey Market survey i
30	Fish Production = 5.40E+04 Cosmic exergy transformity = 1.12E+08 Cosmic exergy = (production) x (cosmic exergy transformity) = 6.03E+12	CNY/yr Jc/CNY Jc/yr	Market survey i
31	GHG(direct) Production = 3.04E+03 Cosmic exergy transformity = 5.42E+07 Cosmic exergy = (production) x (cosmic exergy transformity) = 1.65E+11	kg/yr Jc/kg Jc/yr	Appendix K j
32	GHG(indirect) Production = 4.72E+03 Cosmic exergy transformity = 5.42E+07 Cosmic exergy = (production) x (cosmic exergy transformity) = 2.56E+11	kg/yr Jc/kg Jc/yr	Appendix L j

[a] Refer to *Odum, H.T., 1996. Environmental Accounting: Emergy and Environmental Decision Making. John Wiley and Sons, New York.*

[b] Refer to *Jiang, M.M., Chen, B., Zhou, J.B., Tao, F.R., Li, Z., Yang, Z.F., Chen, G.Q., 2007. Emergy Account for Biomass Resource Exploitation by Agriculture in China. Energy Policy, 35, 4704-4719.*

[c] Refer to *Chen, G.Q., 2006. Scarcity of Exergy and Ecological Evaluation Based on Embodied Exergy. Communications in Nonlinear Science and Numerical Simulation, 11, 531-552.*

[d] Refer to *CDC (Climatic Data Center), 2006. National Meteorological Information Center. Available*

211

at http://www.nmic.gov.cn/web/index.

^e Refer to *Kraus, H., 1973. Energy Exchange at Air-ice Interface. In: the Role of Snow and Ice in Hydrology. Proceedings of Banff Symposium,* 107, 126-164.

^f Refer to *Jingzhou, 2002. Jingzhou yearbook. Publishing House of Local Records, Beijing, China.*

^g Refer to *Chen, B., Chen, Z. M., Zhou, Y., Zhou, J. B., Chen, G. Q., 2009a. Emergy as Embodied Energy Based Assessment for Local Sustainability of a Constructed Wetland in Beijing. Communications in Nonlinear Science and Numerical Simulation,* 14, 622-635.

^h Refer to *Jiang, M. M., 2007. Embodied Cosmic Analysis for Urban Ecosystem. Peking University, Ph. D. Thesis.*

ⁱ Refer to *Chen, G. Q., Chen, Z. M., 2010. Carbon Emissions and Resources Use by Chinese Economy 2007: A 135-sector Inventory and Input-output Embodiment. Communications in Nonlinear Science and Numerical Simulation,* 15, 3647-3732.

^j Refer to *Chen, Z. M., Chen, B., Chen, G. Q., 2011. Cosmic Exergy Based Ecological Assessment for a Wetland in Beijing. Ecological Modelling,* 222, 322-329.

Appendix J   Footnotes of Table 3. 2. 2

No.	Item value	Unit	Source
	Renewable inputs of natural resources (*Ires-r*)		
1	Solar radiation Area = 5. 32E+03 Average insolation = 5. 90E+09 Albedo = 20% Energy = (area) x (average insolation) x (1-albedo) = 2. 51E+13 Cosmic exergy transformity = 1. 02E-05 Cosmic exergy = (energy) x (cosmic exergy transformity)= 2. 56E+08	m^2 $J/m^2/yr$ J/yr Jc/J Jc/yr	Market survey a a b c
2	Wind (kinetic) Area = 5. 32E+03 Density of air = 1. 23 Average annual wind velocity = 2. 40 Annual working time = 3. 15E+07 Drag coefficient = 1. 00E-03 Energy = (area) x (density of air) x (average annual wind velocity)^3 x (annual working time) x (drag coefficient) = 2. 85E+09 Cosmic exergy transformity = 3. 21E-02 Cosmic exergy = (energy) x (cosmic exergy transformity)= 9. 15E+07	m^2 kg/m^3 m/s s/yr J/yr Jc/J Jc/yr	Market survey d d a e b c
3	Rain (chemical) Area = 5. 32E+03 Evapotranspiration = 3. 86E-01 Rain density = 1. 00E+03 Gibbs free energy = 4. 94E+03 Energy = (area) x (evapotranspiration) x (rain density) x (Gibbs free energy) = 1. 01E+10 Cosmic exergy transformity = 6. 26E-01 Cosmic exergy = (energy) x (cosmic exergy transformity)= 6. 32E+09	m^2 m/yr kg/m^3 J/kg J/yr Jc/J Jc/yr	Market survey f d g g c
4	Rain (geopotential) Area = 5. 32E+03 Rainfall = 1. 30 Runoff rate = 20% Average elevation = 2. 70E+01 Rain density = 1. 00E+03 Gravity = 9. 80 Energy = (area) x (rainfall) x (runoff rate) x (average elevation) x (rain density) x (gravity) = 3. 66E+08 Cosmic exergy transformity = 3. 62E-01 Cosmic exergy = (energy) x (cosmic exergy transformity)= 1. 32E+08	m^2 m/yr m kg/m^3 m/s^2 J/yr Jc/J Jc/yr	Market survey f d f d g g c

Continued

No.	Item value	Unit	Source
5	Geothermal Area = 5. 32E+03 Heat flow = 7. 00E-02 Annual working time = 3. 15E+07 Energy = (area) x (heat flow) x (annual working time) = 1. 17E+10 Cosmic exergy transformity = 7. 82E-03 Cosmic exergy = (energy) x (cosmic exergy transformity)= 9. 15E+07	m^2 W/m^2 s/yr J/yr Jc/J Jc/yr	Market survey f a g c
	Nonrenewable inputs of natural resources (_Ires-n_)		
6	Topsoil loss Area = 5. 32E+03 Total soil loss per year in China = 1. 37E+12 National territory area = 9. 60E+10 Average organic content = 1. 50% Mass = (area) x (total soil loss per year in China)/(national territory area) x (average organic content) = 1. 14E+03 Cosmic exergy transformity = 4. 33E+07 Cosmic exergy = (mass) x (cosmic exergy transformity)= 4. 94E+10	m^2 kg/yr m^2 kg/yr Jc/kg Jc/yr	Market survey b d b b h
	Renewable and nonrenewable inputs purchased from economic market (_Ieco_)		
7	Labor and services Renewable proportion = 6. 20% Consumption = 4. 00E+03 Cosmic exergy transformity = 5. 45E+07 Cosmic exergy = (consumption) x (cosmic exergy transformity) = 2. 48E+11	 CNY/yr Jc/CNY Jc/yr	i Market survey i
	Pigsty		
8	Cement Renewable proportion = 0. 79% Consumption = 1. 05E+01 Cosmic exergy transformity = 1. 56E+08 Cosmic exergy = (consumption) x (cosmic exergy transformity) = 1. 64E+09	 CNY/yr Jc/CNY Jc/yr	i Market survey i
9	Lime Renewable proportion = 0. 79% Consumption = 1. 50E+01 Cosmic exergy transformity = 1. 56E+08 Cosmic exergy = (consumption) x (cosmic exergy transformity) = 2. 34E+09	 CNY/yr Jc/CNY Jc/yr	i Market survey i

Continued

No.	Item value	Unit	Source
10	Bricks Renewable proportion = 0.73% Consumption = 1.60E+01 Cosmic exergy transformity = 1.72E+08 Cosmic exergy = (consumption) x (cosmic exergy transformity) = 2.76E+09	CNY/yr Jc/CNY Jc/yr	i Market survey i
11	Steel Renewable proportion = 0.47% Consumption = 2.25E+01 Cosmic exergy transformity = 2.13E+08 Cosmic exergy = (consumption) x (cosmic exergy transformity) = 4.79E+09	CNY/yr Jc/CNY Jc/yr	i Market survey i
12	Feed Renewable proportion = 46.63% Consumption = 5.32E+03 Cosmic exergy transformity = 8.36E+07 Cosmic exergy = (consumption) x (cosmic exergy transformity) = 4.35E+11	CNY/yr Jc/CNY Jc/yr	i Market survey i
13	Drugs Renewable proportion = 4.65% Consumption = 2.40E+02 Cosmic exergy transformity = 8.16E+07 Cosmic exergy = (consumption) x (cosmic exergy transformity) = 1.96E+10	CNY/yr Jc/CNY Jc/yr	i Market survey i
14	Disinfectant Renewable proportion = 1.17% Consumption = 2.00E+01 Cosmic exergy transformity = 1.16E+08 Cosmic exergy = (consumption) x (cosmic exergy transformity) = 2.33E+09	CNY/yr Jc/CNY Jc/yr	i Market survey i
15	Water Renewable proportion = 1.49% Consumption = 5.66E+01 Cosmic exergy transformity = 6.72E+07 Cosmic exergy = (consumption) x (cosmic exergy transformity) = 3.80E+09	CNY/yr Jc/CNY Jc/yr	i Market survey i
16	Electricity Renewable proportion = 1.17% Consumption = 3.20E+02 Cosmic exergy transformity = 1.97E+08 Cosmic exergy = (consumption) x (cosmic exergy transformity) = 6.31E+10	CNY/yr Jc/CNY Jc/yr	i Market survey i

Continued

No.	Item value	Unit	Source
Farmer			
17	Coal Renewable proportion = 0. 18% Coal equivalent = 5. 72E+02 Cosmic exergy transformity (coal) = 1. 95E+08 Cosmic exergy = (coal equivalent) x (cosmic exergy transformity) = 5. 32E+11	CNY/yr Jc/CNY Jc/yr	i Market survey i
Fishpond			
18	Lime Renewable proportion = 0. 79% Consumption = 2. 88E+01 Cosmic exergy transformity = 1. 56E+08 Cosmic exergy = (consumption) x (cosmic exergy transformity) = 4. 50E+09	CNY/yr Jc/CNY Jc/yr	i Market survey i
19	Bleach Renewable proportion = 0. 70% Consumption = 3. 20E+01 Cosmic exergy transformity = 1. 78E+08 Cosmic exergy = (consumption) x (cosmic exergy transformity) = 5. 70E+09	CNY/yr Jc/CNY Jc/yr	i Market survey i
20	Aerator Renewable proportion = 0. 88% Consumption = 1. 00E+02 Cosmic exergy transformity = 1. 23E+08 Cosmic exergy = (consumption) x (cosmic exergy transformity) = 1. 23E+10	CNY/yr Jc/CNY Jc/yr	i Market survey i
21	Feed Renewable proportion = 67. 50% Consumption = 7. 20E+03 Cosmic exergy transformity = 1. 12E+08 Cosmic exergy = (consumption) x (cosmic exergy transformity) = 8. 04E+11	CNY/yr Jc/CNY Jc/yr	i Market survey i
22	Nitrogen fertilizer Renewable proportion = 0. 62% Consumption = 4. 00E+03 Cosmic exergy transformity = 1. 98E+08 Cosmic exergy = (consumption) x (cosmic exergy transformity) = 7. 93E+11	CNY/yr Jc/CNY Jc/yr	i Market survey i

Continued

No.	Item value	Unit	Source
23	Phosphate fertilizer Renewable proportion = 0.62% Consumption = 2.75E+03 Cosmic exergy transformity = 1.98E+08 Cosmic exergy = (consumption) x (cosmic exergy transformity) = 5.45E+11	 CNY/yr Jc/CNY Jc/yr	i Market survey i
Yield (Y)			
24	Pig Production = 8.00E+03 Cosmic exergy transformity = 1.95E+08 Cosmic exergy = (production) x (cosmic exergy transformity)= 1.56E+12	CNY/yr Jc/CNY Jc/yr	Market survey i
25	Fish Production = 5.40E+04 Cosmic exergy transformity = 1.12E+08 Cosmic exergy = (production) x (cosmic exergy transformity)= 6.03E+12	CNY/yr Jc/CNY Jc/yr	Market survey i
26	GHG(direct) Production = 1.85E+03 Cosmic exergy transformity = 5.42E+07 Cosmic exergy = (production) x (cosmic exergy transformity)= 1.00E+11	kg/yr Jc/kg Jc/yr	Appendix K j
27	GHG(indirect) Production = 1.41E+04 Cosmic exergy transformity = 5.42E+07 Cosmic exergy = (production) x (cosmic exergy transformity)= 7.63E+11	kg/yr Jc/kg Jc/yr	Appendix M j
28	Pig manure Production = 3.20E+03 Cosmic exergy transformity = 3.72E+05 Cosmic exergy = (production) x (cosmic exergy transformity)= 1.19E+09	kg/yr Jc/kg Jc/yr	Market survey j

[a] Refer to *Odum, H.T., 1996. Environmental Accounting: Emergy and Environmental Decision Making. John Wiley and Sons, New York.*

[b] Refer to *Jiang, M.M., Chen, B., Zhou, J.B., Tao, F.R., Li, Z., Yang, Z.F., Chen, G.Q., 2007. Emergy Account for Biomass Resource Exploitation by Agriculture in China. Energy Policy, 35, 4704-4719.*

[c] Refer to *Chen, G.Q., 2006. Scarcity of Exergy and Ecological Evaluation Based on Embodied Exergy. Communications in Nonlinear Science and Numerical Simulation, 11, 531-552.*

217

[d] Refer to *CDC (Climatic Data Center)*, 2006. *National Meteorological Information Center. Available at http://www.nmic.gov.cn/web/index.*

[e] Refer to *Kraus, H.*, 1973. *Energy Exchange at Air-ice Interface. In: the Role of Snow and Ice in Hydrology. Proceedings of Banff Symposium*, 107, 126-164.

[f] Refer to *Jingzhou*, 2002. *Jingzhou Yearbook. Publishing House of Local Records, Beijing, China.*

[g] Refer to *Chen, B., Chen, Z. M., Zhou, Y., Zhou, J. B., Chen, G. Q.*, 2009a. *Emergy as Embodied Energy Based Assessment for Local Sustainability of a Constructed Wetland in Beijing. Communications in Nonlinear Science and Numerical Simulation*, 14, 622-635.

[h] Refer to *Jiang, M. M.*, 2007. *Embodied Cosmic Analysis for Urban Ecosystem. Peking University, Ph. D. Thesis.*

[i] Refer to *Chen, G. Q., Chen, Z. M.*, 2010. *Carbon Emissions and Resources Use by Chinese Economy 2007: A 135-sector Inventory and Input-output Embodiment. Communications in Nonlinear Science and Numerical Simulation*, 15, 3647-3732.

[j] Refer to *Chen, Z. M., Chen, B., Chen, G. Q.*, 2011. *Cosmic Exergy Based Ecological Assessment for a Wetland in Beijing. Ecological Modelling*, 222, 322-329.

Appendix K Direct GHG Emissions of the Integrated Biogas Engineering

	CO_2 (kg/yr)	CH_4 (kg/yr)	N_2O (kg/yr)	GHG [a] (kg CO_2-eq/yr)
Pigsty		1.20E+01 [b]		2.52E+02
Biogas	8.31E+02 [c]		1.14E+00 [d]	1.18E+03
Fishpond	6.47E+02 [e]	4.54E+01 [e]		1.60E+03
Total				3.04E+03

[a] Based on the global warming potential (GWP) as 1: 21: 310 for CO_2: CH_4: N_2O according to 2006 *IPCC guidelines for national greenhouse gas inventories. Available at http://www.ipcc-nggip.iges.or.jp/ public/2006gl/index.html http://www.ipcc-nggip.iges.or.jp/public/2006gl/index.html.*

[b] Refer to 2006 *IPCC guidelines for national greenhouse gas inventories.*

[c] Biogas composition is considered as 70% CH_4 and 30% CO_2.

[d] Refer to *Ma, Z. H., Nan, G. L., 2008. Evaluation of Greenhouse Gas Emission Reductions from Implementation of Anaerobic-aerobic Waste Treatment Systems on Swine Farm. China Biogas, 26, 3-8 [In Chinese].*

[e] Refer to *Xing, Y. P., Xie, P., Yang, H., Ni, L. Y., Wang, Y. S., Rong, K. W., 2005. Methane and Carbon Dioxide Fluxes from a Shallow Hypereutrophic Subtropical Lake in China. Atmospheric Environment, 39, 5532-5540.*

Appendix L   Indirect GHG Emissions of the Integrated Biogas Engineering

Item	Raw data (CNY/yr)	CO_2 Intensity [a] (kg/CNY)	CO_2 Mass (kg/yr)	CH_4 Intensity [a] (kg/CNY)	CH_4 Mass (kg/yr)	N_2O Intensity [a] (kg/CNY)	N_2O Mass (kg/yr)	GHG (kg CO_2-eq/yr)
Labor and services	4.55E+03	1.20E-01	5.45E+02	1.41E-03	6.41E+00	8.55E-05	3.89E-01	8.00E+02
Cement	1.05E+01	1.45E+00	1.52E+01	4.85E-03	5.09E-02	2.23E-05	2.34E-04	1.64E+01
Lime	1.50E+01	1.45E+00	2.18E+01	4.85E-03	7.28E-02	2.23E-05	3.35E-04	2.34E+01
Bricks	1.60E+01	7.92E-01	1.27E+01	4.91E-03	7.86E-02	2.29E-05	3.66E-04	1.44E+01
Steel	2.25E+01	6.07E-01	1.37E+01	3.89E-03	8.75E-02	1.75E-05	3.94E-04	1.56E+01
Feed	5.20E+03	1.42E-01	7.38E+02	2.65E-03	1.38E+01	3.07E-04	1.60E+00	1.52E+03
Drugs	2.40E+02	2.00E-01	4.80E+01	2.28E-03	5.47E-01	9.93E-05	2.38E-02	6.69E+01
Disinfectant	2.00E+01	4.30E-01	8.60E+00	2.90E-03	5.80E-02	3.20E-05	6.40E-04	1.00E+01
Water	5.66E+01	3.12E-01	1.77E+01	2.10E-03	1.19E-01	1.19E-05	6.74E-04	2.04E+01
Electricity	3.20E+02	1.09E+00	3.49E+02	7.37E-03	2.36E+00	2.59E-05	8.29E-03	4.01E+02
Cement	1.35E+01	1.45E+00	1.96E+01	4.85E-03	6.55E-02	2.23E-05	3.01E-04	2.10E+01
Sand and pebble	1.30E+01	3.02E-01	3.93E+00	1.93E-03	2.51E-02	1.48E-05	1.92E-04	4.51E+00
Plastic pipe	4.50E+00	3.83E-01	1.72E+00	2.51E-03	1.13E-02	2.02E-05	9.09E-05	1.99E+00
Steel mold	6.00E+01	4.21E-01	2.53E+01	2.75E-03	1.65E-01	1.66E-05	9.96E-04	2.90E+01
Cooker	1.55E+01	2.90E-01	4.50E+00	1.94E-03	3.01E-02	1.64E-05	2.54E-04	5.21E+00
Lime	2.88E+01	1.45E+00	4.18E+01	4.85E-03	1.40E-01	2.23E-05	6.42E-04	4.49E+01
Bleach	3.20E+01	6.95E-01	2.22E+01	4.59E-03	1.47E-01	2.41E-05	7.71E-04	2.56E+01
Aerator	1.00E+02	3.58E-01	3.58E+01	2.35E-03	2.35E-01	1.42E-05	1.42E-03	4.12E+01
Feed	7.20E+03	9.99E-02	7.19E+02	1.04E-03	7.49E+00	6.62E-05	4.77E-01	1.02E+03
Nitrogen fertilizer	4.00E+02	8.11E-01	3.24E+02	5.42E-03	2.17E+00	2.58E-05	1.03E-02	3.73E+02
Phosphate fertilizer	2.75E+02	8.11E-01	2.23E+02	5.42E-03	1.49E+00	2.58E-05	7.10E-03	2.57E+02
Total			3.19E+03		3.55E+01		2.52E+00	4.72E+03

[a] Refer to Chen, G. Q., Chen, Z. M., 2010. Carbon Emissions and Resources Use by Chinese Economy 2007: A 135-sector Inventory and Input-output Embodiment. Communications in Nonlinear Science and Numerical Simulation, 15, 3647-3732.

Appendix M   Indirect GHG Emissions of the Conventional Production System

Item	Raw data (CNY/yr)	CO_2 Intensity [a] (kg/CNY)	CO_2 Mass (kg/yr)	CH_4 Intensity [a] (kg/CNY)	CH_4 Mass (kg/yr)	N_2O Intensity [a] (kg/CNY)	N_2O Mass (kg/yr)	GHG (kg CO_2-eq/yr)
Labor and services	4.00E+03	1.20E-01	4.80E+02	1.41E-03	5.64E+00	8.55E-05	3.42E-01	7.04E+02
Cement	1.05E+01	1.45E+00	1.52E+01	4.85E-03	5.09E-02	2.23E-05	2.34E-04	1.64E+01
Lime	1.50E+01	1.45E+00	2.18E+01	4.85E-03	7.28E-02	2.23E-05	3.35E-04	2.34E+01
Bricks	1.60E+01	7.92E-01	1.27E+01	4.91E-03	7.86E-02	2.29E-05	3.66E-04	1.44E+01
Steel	2.25E+01	6.07E-01	1.37E+01	3.89E-03	8.75E-02	1.75E-05	3.94E-04	1.56E+01
Feed	5.20E+03	1.42E-01	7.38E+02	2.65E-03	1.38E+01	3.07E-04	1.60E+00	1.52E+03
Drugs	2.40E+02	2.00E-01	4.80E+01	2.28E-03	5.47E-01	9.93E-05	2.38E-02	6.69E+01
Disinfectant	2.00E+01	4.30E-01	8.60E+00	2.90E-03	5.80E-02	3.20E-05	6.40E-04	1.00E+01
Water	5.66E+01	3.12E-01	1.77E+01	2.10E-03	1.19E-01	1.19E-05	6.74E-04	2.04E+01
Electricity	3.20E+02	1.09E+00	3.49E+02	7.37E-03	2.36E+00	2.59E-05	8.29E-03	4.01E+02
Coal	5.72E+02	5.87E+00	3.36E+03	4.00E-02	2.29E+01	1.10E-04	6.29E-02	3.86E+03
Lime	2.88E+01	1.45E+00	4.18E+01	4.85E-03	1.40E-01	2.23E-05	6.42E-04	4.49E+01
Bleach	3.20E+01	6.95E-01	2.22E+01	4.59E-03	1.47E-01	2.41E-05	7.71E-04	2.56E+01
Aerator	1.00E+02	3.58E-01	3.58E+01	2.35E-03	2.35E-01	1.42E-05	1.42E-03	4.12E+01
Feed	7.20E+03	9.99E-02	7.19E+02	1.04E-03	7.49E+00	6.62E-05	4.77E-01	1.02E+03
Nitrogen fertilizer	4.00E+03	8.11E-01	3.24E+03	5.42E-03	2.17E+01	2.58E-05	1.03E-01	3.73E+03
Phosphate fertilizer	2.75E+03	8.11E-01	2.23E+03	5.42E-03	1.49E+01	2.58E-05	7.10E-02	2.57E+03
Total			1.14E+04		9.03E+01		2.69E+00	1.41E+04

[a] Refer to Chen, G. Q., Chen, Z. M., 2010. *Carbon Emissions and Resources Use by Chinese Economy 2007: A 135-sector Inventory and Input-output Embodiment. Communications in Nonlinear Science and Numerical Simulation*, 15, 3647-3732.

Appendix N

We use the expected damage function (EDF) to estimate the marginal damage cost of hurricanes due to one unit loss of mangrove area from 1800-2010. We constructed a binary variable, *hurricane*, denoting a hurricane event over the 211 years, as the dependent variable in our model. We also constructed two binary variables, $T1$, denoting a hurricane event over 1800-1938, and $T2$, denoting a hurricane event over 1972-2010, as explanatory variables. According to data sources of hurricane event, we constructed an additional explanatory variable, *EM-DAT*, which denotes data gathered from EM-DAT. We also had two continuous variables, *mangrove*, as a measure of mangrove area in terms of hectare, and *popden*, as a measure of population density. A Poisson regression model was used to estimate the probabilities of a hurricane (Table A1). Based on this model, we estimated the probability of damaging hurricane using the coefficient for mangrove interacted with T2, the time period that covered our GNNP estimate. We estimated the marginal effect along with the standard error using the delta method, -0.0005818 [p-value = 0.089, 95% confidence interval is $(-0.0012518, 0.0000882)$]. This indicates that a one hectare loss of mangrove area increases the probability of hurricane event by 0.0005818. Our calculations also suggested the average damage cost of hurricane over 1899-2010 was \$52 million per year. Thus, we can simply estimate the expected marginal damage cost due to one hectare loss of mangrove area as, Expected marginal damage cost = \$52,014,245x(-0.000581) $= -\$30,262$ per hectare Upper bound marginal damage cost = \$52,014,245x(-0.0012518) $= -\$65,111$ per hectare.

Table A1　Poisson Regression Results

Poisson Model	
Variable	
Mangrove	.00478 (2.69)***
Popden	.0115 (2.65)***
EM-DAT	−1.753 (−4.64)***
T1	32.680 (2.60)***

Continued

Poisson Model	
Variable	
T2	45. 989 (2. 94) ***
T1 * mangrove	-. 00418 (-2. 45) **
T2 * mangrove	-. 00667 (-2. 97) ***
Constant	-42. 657 (-3. 05) ***
Observations	211
Margins dy/dx: mangrove over T2	-. 0. 005818 (-1. 70) *
Log pseudolikelihood	-97. 58
Wald chi^2(7)	69. 00
Prob > chi^2	0. 0000
Pseudo R^2	0. 0979

Note: z statistics in parentheses. * significant at 10% level; ** significant at 5% level; *** significant at 1% level.